DATE DUE

MAY 07			
DEC 17			

READING AFTER FREUD

Reading After Freud

ESSAYS ON GOETHE, HÖLDERLIN, HABERMAS, NIETZSCHE, BRECHT, CELAN, AND FREUD

Rainer Nägele

COLUMBIA UNIVERSITY PRESS

NEW YORK   1987

The Andrew W. Mellon Foundation, through a special grant, has assisted the Press in publishing this volume.

Library of Congress Cataloging-in-Publication Data

Nägele, Rainer.
  Reading after Freud.

  Bibliography: p.
  Includes index.
  1. German literature—History and criticism.
2. Psychoanalysis and literature.   3. Freud, Sigmund,
1856–1939—Influence.   I. Title.
PT129.N34   1987   830'.9353   86–20730
ISBN 0–231–06286–9

Columbia University Press
New York   Guildford, Surrey
Copyright © 1987 Columbia University Press

Printed in the United States of America
This book is Smyth-sewn.

Book design by J. S. Roberts

CONTENTS

ACKNOWLEDGMENTS

Essay I was first published in German: "Das Imaginäre und das Symbolische: Von der Anakreontik zum Schleiersymbol," in *Goethezeit: Studien zur Erkenntnis und Rezeption Goethes und seiner Zeitgenossen*. Festschrift für Stuart Atkins (Bern/München: Francke Verlag, 1981), pp. 45–68.

Essay II was originally published as "The Discourse of the Other: Hölderlin's 'Voice of the People' and the Dialectic of Enlightenment," in *Glyph* (1979), 5:1–33. It has been thoroughly revised for this book.

Essay III first appeared under the title "Freud, Habermas, and the Dialectic of Enlightenment: On Real and Ideal Discourses," in *New German Critique* (1981), 22:41–62. It has been thoroughly revised for this book.

Essay IV was first published in German: "Nietzsches Hexentrank: Ressentiment, Identität, und Verneinung," in *Der Wunderblock* (1985), 13:28–45.

Essay V was first published in German: "Brechts Theater der Grausamkeit: Lehrstücke und Stückwerke," in Walter Hinderer, ed., *Brechts Dramen: Neue Interpretationen* (Stuttgart: Reclam, 1984), pp. 300–320.

READING AFTER FREUD

INTRODUCTION

"Wir bringen aber die Zeiten untereinander" (Hölderlin)

Reading *after* Freud: in a very obvious sense there is no way that we cannot read after Freud, if we read at all. Our position in time and history seems to place us ineluctably after Freud. But, after all, it places us after an almost infinite number of names.

To say that we are reading after Freud implies a determination of our reading in a much more specific sense than a merely temporal one, although that very determination entangles us in such a way in the order of time that the "merely temporal" can no longer be described as a simple sequence of before and after. The sequence of essays in this book leads to that knotting of time that Freud calls *Nachträglichkeit*—deferred action or belatedness. In this temporality the "after" becomes constitutive of the "before."

To raise the question of time in terms of the prepositional "after" evokes the "now" of contemporary discourses that privilege the "after" to such a degree that the very concept of our time now finds its most prominent mark in a Latin "after": *post*. The archetypal contemporary critic lives in a postindustrial society, reads postmodern literature, is surrounded by postmodern architecture and furniture, and turns his/her reading into poststructuralist criticism.

Like the long nose in a caricature, the *post* sticking out from this archetypal scene points at a neuralgic spot in our contemporary experience of time and history. We might be tempted to simply discard the ever-new generations of *posts* as a symptom of intellectual laziness and as a crutch in the absence of more specific terms for a confusing multiplicity and accumulation of *isms*. But while intellectual laziness is certainly not lacking in the countless critical noises for and against "postmodernism" and "poststructuralism," laziness usually grasps whatever is nearest at hand. It might grasp without grasping what it grasps. Poe's *Purloined Letter* should warn us not to discard that which is at hand too quickly, lest we follow the example of the stupid police.

One of the recurring motifs in the following readings after Freud is the attention to the surface and a certain mistrust of an all-too-eager desire to go into the depth and the various forms of a *Sehnen dem Abgrund zu* (desire toward the abyss) against which Hölderlin warns in *Stimme des Volks* (Voice of the People). As it turns out, staying on the surface, grasping the superficial, does not make things easier. Goethe's poetic veil, the manifest mystery of the text, Hölderlin's gesetzlicher Kalkül" (rigorous calculability), the calculated permutations of tone sequences, Brecht's radical theatricality of the body and the gesture, the staging of the language surface in "concrete" poetry, and the vertiginous turns of Celan's *Atemwende*, of his *Wände* (walls) and *Einwände* (counterturns, objections, but also in-walls), testify not only to a poetic insistence on the surface by some of the major poets and writers of the last two centuries,[1] but also to the power released by that surface where its traces are mapped with a certain intensity.

Such a reading of literary texts that have been read (with the possible exception of Brecht) in the opposite direction, as signals from the depth and interiority of a specifically modern subjectivity, can itself be read as the effect of a deferred action, a belated rereading that reads what could not be read at the time of writing. As such, our reading participates in a shift of attention that is frequently attributed to poststructuralism. Yet we could with equal justification point back (or, given the inversions of temporal knottings, forward) to Walter Benjamin, whose reading of the past in the form of redemptive criticism is thoroughly shaped by the laws of *Nachträglichkeit*.

The question of the *post* is not limited to a school. Its proliferation shifts the function from a merely descriptive "after" to the marking of a specific immanent function of time.

This shift precedes the *post*. Before postmodernism there was modernism, a term that already had moved from a descriptive designation of whatever is new at a given time to the naming of a specific historical period. Newness itself assumes a particular position. Its increasing positive status as an aesthetic category under the laws of the bourgeois marketplace, which literature had to enter in the eighteenth century,[2] turns into an almost absolute privilege in modernism. Yet this position of newness is highly ambivalent: if, at first glance, it seems to be the mimetic reproduction of the commodity in the social order, it is no less apparent that the artistic production of modernism is shaped by feverish attempts to escape the status of commodity in the marketplace.[3] The frantic search for an ever-new newness that cancels the preceding one is as much an attempt to escape the commodification of any form by giving it up before it has become a trademark as it is the reproduction of the law of commodities. Romantic irony has taken a new shape and turn.

In a peculiar way, time and temporality have been transformed from an accidental exteriority to a substantial and constitutive immanence in the works of modernism. Or, to be more precise: the constitutive immanent temporality has become explicit. Aesthetics and poetics of modernism are dominated by the question of time.

Peter Szondi was one of the most perceptive critics engaged in tracing this shift. He developed a hermeneutical model that emphasizes time and history in the work of art instead of the work of art in time and history. This being of time and history in the work of art is not a content but an organizing principle. In his lectures on the fin-de-siècle lyrical drama, he pleads for a historical criticism as immanent criticism, because "each work of art is at home in the three dimensions of time, or better: they participate in the work of art, forming that inner tension that is its historicity."[4] The shift from the abstract temporality of the three dimensions of time to specific historicity is produced by an "inner tension" in the relationship of temporal dimensions in the work.

In this conception time is not a smooth, continuous sequence from past to present to future, but a conflictual configuration of fragmentary moments. Szondi joins Benjamin and Adorno in a radical critique of the homogeneous time of historicism. He suggests a rethinking of hermeneutics in terms of the relationship of work and temporality, pointing toward a new historical theory of form.[5]

Szondi's explicit references to Benjamin, Adorno, and the early Lukács must be extended to the name of Siegfried Kracauer, whose memory, unfortunately, has nearly been reduced to his film history *From Caligari to Hitler*. Despite its perceptiveness, this book gains its full resonance only in the context of Kracauer's other works. His essays, collected in *Das Ornament der Masse*, are all reflections on the historical and cultural organization of time and space.[6] The desire of historicism is the homogeneous totality of time and space, in which everything is present, as in a photograph. This picture is contrasted with the memory image, composed of fragmentary moments and organized by a significant structure.

It is in such a relationship of time and significance that a reading after Freud can be more than a "psychoanalytical approach." Whatever their specific designation, approaches are invariably moves from the outside, impositions of the vocabulary of one discipline onto another. Invariably they lead nowhere. What psychoanalytical approaches generally leave out is precisely that which is immanent to the work of art as well as to the analytic process: the order of time in relation to the order of signification.

If modernism is the valorization of time as the master signifier that gives it its name, postmodernism, while marking the supposed end and negation of modernism, still asserts and repeats in the act of negation the constitution of time as the signifying master. In whatever combination the *post* appears, its function is a denegation. If the *post* has any substance at all, it is only as a result of working through the elements of a specific past occupied by the *post*. As the phenomenon of *Nachträglichkeit*, the opportunity of the *post* is the possibility of redeeming those elements of the past that in their own time could not enter into the economy of signification and were therefore excluded, repressed, or marginalized.

Reading *after* Freud cannot be a simple affirmation of Freud, as if "Freud" were a known entity to be either negated or affirmed. Reading after Freud first means reading Freud, interpreting his texts; it also means reading Freud after Lacan, which in turn involves a reading of Lacan after Freud.

The knots and networks of such readings, inescapable if we read at all, indicate another intonation of my title: *Reading* after Freud. Contrary to a widespread ideological rhetoric that pits "literature" against "theory" and sees particularly in poststructuralism a new theory that has taken over literature, the major texts that have shaped the poststructuralist critical scene question the status of theory as a privileged metalanguage, aloof and independent of the figurations of literary language. The impact of Lacan, Derrida, and Paul de Man affects first of all the act of a reading, including the reading of theories.

If, according to Freud, the effect of *Nachträglichkeit* takes place in specific situations of a crisis that demand a reordering, reorganization, and reassessment of our lived experiences, the poststructuralist emphasis on reading can be understood precisely as a symptom of *Nachträglichkeit*. It might be that we are among the last readers. The demise of the book, the end of the Gutenberg era of printed communication, the threat of a new illiteracy, belong by now to the standard elements of contemporary cultural critics. I have no desire to join their ranks and rhetoric. To do so would be an act of not reading.

It is one thing to register the symptoms of a crisis that obviously affects deeply traditional modes of reading under the impact of the electronic revolution in communication and information, but it is quite another to read these symptoms. To read them would confront us with the question of how to change our reading habits in order to decipher the alphabets, grammars, and graphemes of these new kinds of "texts."

Such questions are shunned by the rhetoric of a moralistic "back to the basics" and "good books." To the degree that such a rhetoric advocates reading as a stable process of acquiring an increasing stock of cultural goods and heritage, it is the advocate of non-reading. Reading in an emphatic sense is not compatible with the acquisition of cultural capital, because every such reading radically destabilizes the fragile economy of our configurations of meaning.

Whatever our readings of the crisis of reading might be, they will force us to reassess both the praxis and theory of reading. The title of one of Paul de Man's later books, *Allegories of Reading*, accurately describes what constitutes the common ground of contemporary criticism.[7] To the degree that we are interested in reading, we are producing ever-new allegories of our reading.

In this sense, my reading after Freud is also an attempt to develop such an allegory in a sequence of specific readings. To call it an allegory involves implications that can best be unfolded by contrasting allegory with some related terms.

The more familiar and expected term in the genre of literary criticism would be a *theory* of reading. In contrasting allegory with theory, some obvious differences become immediately visible: first, a difference in the register of discourse. Allegory belongs to the realm of literature and art, theory to scholarship and science. A theoretical discourse makes different truth claims from an allegorical presentation. Theories are supposedly either true or false; at least they have to make a claim for probability that is subject to verification or falsification.

Allegories have truth claims too, some of them quite dogmatic. Yet their claims are differently situated. The dogmatism associated with some allegories does not come from the allegory as such, but from the system of an otherwise encoded truth that it represents or illustrates. More often than not, the allegorical representation will subvert and displace the stability of that truth. The truth of the allegory qua allegory is not identical with the truth it might claim to represent. Yet its truth is not immanent. The very word and structure of allegory indicate that whatever is said is not "it," but something else.

Because of this immanent displacement in the structure of allegory, allegories do not compete with each other on a basis of exclusion, as theories must do at least potentially. I might recognize other theories as equally probable hypotheses, but in that "tolerance" remains the expectation that one day the process of verification and falsification will eliminate all but one. Theories are implicitly monotheistic, allegories are polytheistic. That does not make them peaceful, harmonious entities. Allegories are battlefields of conflicts and oppositional forces; the battle is their paradigm, from the *Psychomachia* to the *Hamlet machine*.[8]

A theory of reading is a virtual claim to a mastery of reading; an allegory of reading is itself an act of reading that cannot come to an end. Nor is there a steady "development" from one reading to the next, from one allegory to another. Each one stakes out its own scene, and each one works with fragments of other readings and the violent interventions of the real. Allegories are of such stuff as dreams are made of.

Within the aesthetics of the last two centuries, allegory has been pitted against another powerful term: the symbol. While the explicit opposition of symbol versus allegory found its strongest formulation through Goethe and then Coleridge, the set of oppositions associated with each of these terms thoroughly permeates European and American aesthetic thought and literary criticism: organic totality against mechanical construction, autonomy against heteronomy, interiority against exteriority.

The oppositional forces, while explicitly privileging the symbol, stage an allegorical battle, a kind of *psychomachia* for and in the soul of the modern bourgeois and his subjectivity. Goethe, who invested the privilege of the symbol with the forceful authority of his name, not only paid occasional tribute to the courtly demands of baroque allegorical representation, but also laid the groundwork for a modern transformation of allegory in his late works, the second part of *Faust* and *Wilhelm Meisters Wanderjahre*.

Walter Benjamin's seismographic sensitivity registered, articulated, and accompanied, as an allegorical reading, the radical inversion of allegorical and symbolic modes in modernism.[9] Lukács, a critic of modernism generally in opposition to Benjamin, is yet in complete agreement with Benjamin in his diagnosis of modernism as a revalorization of allegory.[10]

This is not the place to enter into a detailed analysis of the transformations and implications of allegory in modernism. I would like merely to draw attention to a specific trait: one of the oppositional pairs that set allegory off from the symbol is exteriority versus interiority, connected with a topological model of surface and depth. In this model, allegory is generally devalorized as shallow surface, a mechanical, external force that imposes signification from the outside, while the symbol signifies through the power of an immanent force. The "classic" texts of modernism radically subvert this model and its valorizations, not simply by an inversion of the values, from "depth" to "surface," but by a retracing of the surface that demands another kind of topology. This topology will emerge in more detail in the essay on Celan and Freud, with Kafka's shadow—in the background, I was tempted to write—but "background," in this topology, is no longer a place.

The following fragments of various retracings of the surface are readings after *Freud* to the degree that Freud's psychoanalysis is not a *Tiefenpsychologie* (depth psychology). It takes leave, forever, from psychology: *Zum letzenmal Psychologie!*

Such an understanding of Freud and psychoanalysis goes against the grain of what is generally called the "psychoanalytical approach" to literature. In order to characterize and problematize this approach, I will briefly discuss Kurt Robert Eissler's psychoanalytical study of Goethe.[11] One might object that this is not a good choice, since Eissler's book is mainly a study of Goethe's life rather than his literary productions. Yet it is precisely this emphasis that locates the crucial problem of psychologizing criticism. Just as Eissler's analysis of Goethe's personality and development can proceed only through Goethe's texts, literary studies in the name of psychoanalysis rely almost invariably on the individual author as the source and creator of the text. If they are ambitious, they usually aim at a theory of genius and creativity. The preface of a recent German translation presents Eissler's study as a model of the intersection of psychoanalysis and literary criticism.[12] It is this model I would like to examine.

The blurb of the German edition quotes two literary critics. The first is Peter von Matt, a psychoanalytically oriented critic. He deplores the rejection of psychoanalysis in the history of German literary criticism, where it has often been regarded with utter suspicion. The second critic, Jost Hermand, keeps his distance from psychoanalysis: "Even the anti-Freudian will discover that Eissler is a real biographer who discovers in Goethe's private life many fascinating details that have been overlooked until now." The constellation of these quotations documents the ambivalence in the introduction of psychoanalysis into literary criticism. Many of the generally enthusiastic reviews repeated the same gesture: one may think of psychoanalysis whatever one likes, the book reads well, tells interesting stories, and reveals perhaps some indiscreet details of Goethe's private life.

One cannot object to such an interest. The pleasure of well-told stories is a beautiful pleasure. But let us be honest, then, and not moralize against those who wish to draw a borderline between literary criticism and psychoanalysis. The moralizing gesture indicates a furtive repression that is more resistant than open opposition. Jost Hermand's straightforward distancing from psychoanalysis at least clarifies positions: Eissler as a "real biographer" finds himself on the opposite side of Freud, who, in his letter of May 31, 1936, to Arnold Zweig, stated unequivocally the incompatibility of biography with psychoanalysis: "He who becomes a biographer is obliged to lying, dissimulation, hypocrisy, and whitewashing, and he even has to conceal his lack of understanding; because the biographical truth cannot be had, and if one had it, it would be of no use."[13]

There is no reconciliation between Freud's psychoanalysis and any kind of psychologically inclined biography.

Of course, Eissler's book operates on more than one textual level and thus is able to address various interests. The question is, how do they relate to that genre that is the determinant one according to the subtitle: "A Psychoanalytic Study"?

Three particular literary models shape Eissler's text. All three have a specific relationship either to Goethe's own writing or to the literature of his time: literary biography, *Bildungsroman*, and the detective novel.

Eissler as a "real biographer" participates in a literary historical tradition that finds its manifest or latent model in Goethe's autobiography. This model is determined by a tendency to genetically derive the understanding of literary and other works from the life experience of the writing subject. Hermeneutical models ranging from a naive biographical positivism to Dilthey's antipositivistic hermeneutical reflection on "Erlebnis und Dichtung" (experience and literature) emerge from such a basic assumption. A psychoanalytical study seems to fit well in this frame. The analytic ear for those over- or undertones connecting the present speech with past experience might well be apt to hear latent resonances. Thus Eissler is often able to evoke convincing new configurations in Goethe's texts and to draw attention to the repetitive insistence of certain motifs. Yet, for a reason still to be explored, they remain strangely mute and seem to withdraw into ever-deeper silence the more Eissler makes them perfectly clear.

Literary biography is closely connected with that specific German genre called *Bildungsroman*. The *Bildungsroman* organizes biographical material in teleological form. It generally tells the story of a particular segment of life, the transition to maturity and thus the story of the social organization of the initially polymorphous subject. It is a genre that emerges from the age of Enlightenment, and it also concerns another connotation of the German word for enlightenment, *Aufklärung*, as sexual education. Sexual education is not simply the introduction of the child into the knowledge of his or her sexuality, it is also the transformation of sexuality into the culturally and socially accepted forms. It is a kind of circumcision of sexuality. The German word for legal maturity is *Mündigkeit*, which comes from *Mund* (mouth) and indicates the state of the subject as a speaking subject, no longer *infans*. *Mündigkeit* also means taking leave from the oral phase, circumcising the lips in order to form them for speech and language. Saint Augustine already formulated this circumcision of the lips: "Circumcide ab omni temeritate omnique mendacio interiora et exteriora, labia mea. Sint castae deliciae meae scripturae tuae." (Circumcise from all temerity and all lie both my interior and exterior lips. Let your scripture be my chaste bliss.)[14]

The circumcision of the lips in order to open them for the rapture of the signifier does not take place without the intervention of an authority. Goethe's *Wilhelm Meister* gives it the shape of a *Turmgesellschaft*, a kind of masonic, secret tower-society that provides, not accidentally, the ghost of Hamlet's father. In the everyday life of the middle class such things are done with less ceremony. Ernst Jandl's memory stands for many: "Open your mouth! father and mother would say, not when I was supposed to eat, but in order to teach me to speak in an articulate way."[15]

While the life segment that Eissler chooses for his study—the crucial years of Goethe's development toward classicism from the early Weimar period to the end of the Italian voyage—fits comfortably in the frame of the *Bildungsroman*, there is also a tension between the psychoanalytic study and the literary genre. Ultimately, it seems that the two exclude each other. Toward the end of Eissler's story, Goethe's *Wilhelm Meister*, the paradigm of the *Bildungsroman*, appears as a second repression in which Wilhelm's childhood story is largely erased. Eissler's study would then not be a *Bildungsroman*, but rather that story excluded by the *Bildungsroman*. Yet this separation cannot completely succeed. In Eissler's own words, in *Wilhelm Meister* the repression finds its "actual as well as symbolic representation" (p. 1164). Eissler's story can only tell what Goethe's text already represents. That is of course true for any analytic situation. The deceptions start with the belief of many analysts that their stories are not representations, but the "actual" thing itself. Unlike Freud, most analysts do not often think about representation.

My insistence on the discussion of literary genres is not merely dictated by the interest of the literary critic. The psychoanalyst cannot discard this field as foreign to him. He has entered it in writing. And we are no less in his field by entering into Freud's writing. The strange topology of this field might, however, have the effect of the proverbial whale and polar bear: we cannot even meet for a quarrel.

When Eissler points at the erasure of Wilhelm's childhood story in *Wilhelm Meisters Lehrjahre*, one might ask whether this story is not told elsewhere: in Mignon's story, for example, or in the story of Wilhelm's son. In a certain sense the novel even tells its own childhood story, its genesis in the pietistic story of the beautiful soul. The closer such genetic stories come to the true story, the more they are bracketed and removed from the figure whose story they tell. Perhaps it is not only Eissler who tells the untold story of the *Bildungsroman*, but also the *Bildungsroman* that tells the untold story of Eissler's psychoanalytic study.

There is an immanent complicity between the *Bildungsroman* and psychoanalysis, not only in regard to their genetical interest, but also in their relation to the function of authority. The *Bildungsroman* and psychoanalysis both tell stories of the constitution of authority. In telling such stories they analyze them and thus threaten and reinforce authority.

There can be no question of excluding authority—such exclusions are never more than denegations—but we may ask how its function enters into the game. In Eissler's study, the analytic position is clearly that of the tower-society in Goethe's novel. Eissler's few allusions to the genesis of his study inscribe authority in a double way. The first motivation describes an exemplary scene of authoritarian pedagogy: military training. "While serving in the armed forces, I found myself trying to convince certain military personnel responsible for the training of recruits that the unconscious of the trainers bore significantly on the success or failure of their dealings with those being trained" (p. xviii). A magnificent fantasy of *Bildung* is at the beginning. In this pedagogical process, the psychoanalyst squarely posits himself on the side of the military trainers. He wants to improve their force, and if the powers above will not help, he will invoke the Acheronian powers of the unconscious.

Wherever authority is constituted, it will also be questioned according to the law of ambivalence. Thus, Eissler's book, which arose from an identification with authority, has a second origin:

> It grew out of the fascination that gripped me—as I suppose it must grip everyone—when I immersed myself in the contemplation of the vicissitudes of Goethe's life. Of course, that contemplation led to reflection, and occasion thus arose for theoretical reasoning. . . . In connection with Goethe's pheasant dream . . . I thought for a while that, if my analysis was correct, I had perhaps demonstrated an instance of a new aspect of dream function, but I find, after all, on closer examination, that it falls within the range delimited by Freud in his book on dreams. (p. xxvi)

It begins with a fascination that has something of the generality and force of a law: it must grip everyone. At the same time, this fascination is not grounded in the sublime character of the work, evoked earlier in the text, but in "the vicissitudes of Goethe's life." This shift from work to life implies an ambivalent gesture. On the one hand it does what pious Goethe admirers have always feared from psychoanalysis:

the human-all-too-human aspects of the author's life subvert the sublime work. But if this can be read as an aggressive act against the authority of the author, it is no less a restitution of that authority in the name of the "great man." Freud writes about this notion of the great man in *Moses and Monotheism*. It is not enough that someone "is a great poet, painter, mathematician, or physicist. When we declare Goethe, Leonardo da Vinci, Beethoven, for example, without reservation to be great men, there must be something else that moves us besides the admiration for their magnificent creations." This "something else" that moves us to acknowledge the great man has to do with his life, not his work: "And now the insight might dawn upon us that all the traits which we bestowed upon the great man are traits of the father, that in this analogy the essence of the great man consists."[16]

In quoting the "father of psychoanalysis" we conjure up that great man with whom a psychoanalytical study has to come to terms. The book that arose from a fascination with the vicissitudes of Goethe's life and moves directly to Goethe's pheasant dream, with its fantasies of potency and fears of castration, contains in its origin a moment of rebellion against the fatherly authority. For a moment it seems that Eissler has found something that would question Freud's theory of dreams. Yet it is only a moment; then things are again rectified.

To mark this ambivalence is not to be read as an *argumentum ad hominem*. It is not an argument at all, but rather the description of a conflict that enters every scene of writing.

The only question is how it enters that scene and how the conflict is carried out. Eissler does not discuss the role of authority at this point, but many pages later we find the analyst institutionalized in the position of social authority: "Under ideal conditions, in this phase the analyst is seen realistically in the social context as the carrier of a social, therapeutic function that it is his obligation to fulfill" (p. 184). One sentence knots ideal, reality, and obligation into the iron necessity of a social net in the center of which the analyst positions himself. To be sure, it is described here only as a phase, but it is both the beginning phase and the end point of the analysis where the analyst is again viewed by the patient "in realistic proportions." At this time, ideal and obligation have merged into the category of "realistic" and have the force of a second nature in the name of reality. It is a *Bildungsroman* as a tower-society might dream and prescribe it.

The secret of the tower-society is the manifest secret of internalized authority. It is a common trait of the literary fictions from the Enlightenment to Fontane's *Effie Briest* that the paternal authority enters the subject, if not literally as a ghost, at least accompanied by mysterious, uncanny machineries and rituals. It is from this twilight of mystery and paternal machineries that a new genre is born: the detective novel and its hero, the immaculate rationality of the master detective.

The analytic case history and the detective story share many traits. Both work to uncover something that is hidden, to unravel a traumatic event. At the beginning things seem to be in order, often in an almost obtrusive order. That order is disturbed, the cause is not yet known. The detective comes and unravels the knots of circumstances that often reach far back into the prehistory of the story, until at the end the case is solved and order restored. The dead will not come back to life, the corpse can be buried.

The detective is usually accompanied by a good-hearted but somewhat slow-witted friend. This good-hearted friend is not simply stupid, he is stupid in a very specific way. He often becomes impatient because the detective, instead of digging deep and getting straight to the essence of things, gets involved most frivolously with all kinds of marginalia, distractions, and even manifest lies. The good-hearted friend wants to pull the truth out from the depth and throw away all the covers and misleading traces. The detective knows that the hidden secret is not under cover, but that it is the cover. He thus follows the detours or the distractions leading precisely to that from which they distract. In Poe's *Purloined Letter* the detective story and the analytical story find their allegory.

Freud noted with some uneasiness that his case histories read like novellas. He was uneasy because he knew that what he wrote had some contiguity with that of which the poets write. He often quotes them—Goethe in particular—as witnesses. But by invoking their testimony he runs the risk of acknowledging them as progenitors and fathers of psychoanalysis.[17] Because of this threatening proximity he must insist on separation and independence. It is the same on the other side: those poets whose writing substantially touches the work of Freud are often those who distance themselves most from Freud (Robert Musil is exemplary in this respect), while those writers who claim Freud as their relative are not necessarily the most perceptive recorders of the unconscious.

We are moving along a borderline which demands a delimitation all the more precise as it is constantly about to fade away. Each psychoanalytical study that deals with literature (as well as each act of literary criticism that invokes psychoanalysis) has its legitimation only to the degree that it is able to trace the topology of this borderline.

It is a frequent phenomenon not only in "psychoanalytical approaches," but in "approaches" in general, that the more reductive the procedure is, the more pious is the expression of aesthetic appreciation. The more effusively the critic assures us of the incommensurability and sublimity of the work of art, the less inhibited he is to pursue the work of reduction. It is a paradigmatic gesture of the phenomenon that Freud calls "isolating": the one has nothing to do with the other, because they have all too much to do with each other. At the end of his story, Eissler can thus let Goethe's genius fly off, because it has nothing to do with the analytic findings: "That we find in its wake the trace of a psychosis ought not to disturb us, for it left Goethe's genius without a blemish" (p. 1165). Without a blemish the genius rises at the end of a book that, although it does not claim to be a theory of genius, wants to give us some hints about the nature of genius.

In the recent German translation, the English "genius" is translated as *Genie*. This is justified by the context of Eissler's book. There are two words for "genius" in German: the Latin form *Genius* and the French form *Genie* (whatever it is, it seems to be something foreign). Although the Latin form has almost disappeared from general use, it did mark a significant difference from *Genie*.

The shift from *Genius* to *Genie* in German takes place in the second half of the eighteenth century, and it indicates not only the point of a fundamental shift in aesthetic and poetological conceptions but also the point where psychoanalysis radically differs from psychology. The shift in the eighteenth century can be described as an internalization of creativity, as a claim for creativity of the individual subject that in turn is located in the ego. One can also describe it as a grammatical difference: one can *have* a *Genius*, but one can *be* a *Genie*—at least, so it is said. The *Genius* comes from the outside to the subject, or so it is viewed from the perspective of a world where the I is the subject. The actual linguistic usage is more precise and ascribes to the *Genius* its own form of immanence, although not within an I. There are many *Genien*, but no *Genius* of the I. He might appear as *genius loci*, as *Genius* of a language, of music, of a people, etc. He steps forth and emerges from an interior created by two or more subjects; where there are two or more assembled in his name, there he is. They bring him forth, or rather, he is brought forth by that which unites them.

When, throughout his work, Theodor W. Adorno insists on the priority of the immanent logic of aesthetic production over the opinions and intentions of the poet or artist, he reconnects his aesthetic theory with the discourse of the *Genius* which has nearly been buried by the discourse and delirium of the *Genie*.

The cult of the *Genie* reduces language to the dead letter by investing the I with the power of speech. The psychologizing literary and art criticism of the nineteenth century took this up, and it has continued until the present. Perhaps it has lost some of its Promethean gesture and speaks now in more pedestrian ways.

The majority of so-called psychoanalytical approaches continues the psychologizing tradition. It searches for the secret of the *Genie*, for the creativity in the individual; it digs and digs with both text and letter in front of the unseeing eye, like that of the police in Poe's *Purloined Letter*. It is not by chance that Lacan performed one of his exemplary literary readings through this text. Shoshana Felman has formulated concisely the difference between this reading and a "classical" psychoanalytic study of Poe. Since the German Eissler translation and Eissler himself refer explicitly to Marie Bonaparte's Poe study as a model and parallel, Felman's characterization is valid for Eissler's book as well:

> If the purloined letter can be said to be a sign of the unconscious, for Marie Bonaparte the analyst's task is to uncover the letter's *content*, which she believes—as do the police—to be *hidden* somewhere in the

real, in some secret biographical *depth*. For Lacan, on the other hand, the analyst's task is not to read the letter's hidden referential content, but to situate the superficial indication of its textual movement, to analyze the paradoxically invisible symbolic evidence of its displacement, its structural insistence, in a signifying chain.[18]

It is this shift to the level of the text that has attracted literary critics with textual interest to Lacan, although not always to the best interest of Lacan or of literary criticism.

It was, however, Freud himself who firmly placed analysis within the field of language and speech: "Nothing else happens in the analytical treatment but an exchange of words between the analyst and the doctor."[19] "Nothing else" (*nichts anderes*) takes place—this does not exclude the involvement of some Other, but not an Other outside of speech and language, rather the Other as language.

There are two dimensions that specifically determine the field of psychoanalysis: language and the unconscious. For the moment we will consider the degree of their interrelation as an open question, and insist only that together they form the kernel of psychoanalysis.

Yet at the same time this specification immediately blurs the borderlines through which we hoped to delineate the field of analysis. Language is something that is of equal interest to poets, literary critics, and linguists. And the unconscious is, according to Freud, not only the field of the analyst, but also of the poet, who "directs his attention to the unconscious in his own soul, listens to the possibilities of its unfolding, and allows them into artistic expression instead of suppressing them with conscious critique."[20] Thus, the very specificity of art seems to rest on its particular relationship to the unconscious. But Freud emphasizes the difference in the procedure taken by the analyst and the artist: "Our procedure is based on the conscious observation of abnormal psychic phenomena in others. . . . The poet works differently. . . . He experiences in himself what we learn from others."

The difference would then be one of different attitudes and relationships to the unconscious. By analogy one might say the same about the place of language: if psychoanalysts, poets, literary critics, and linguists share an interest in language as their common object, the relationship to this object differs substantially. Just as Freud sets himself off from the poets, his chief witnesses in the field of the unconscious, Lacan sets himself off from his friend and chief witness in linguistics, Jakobson, by differentiating his relationship to language as "linguisterie" in contrast to Jakobson's "linguistique."[21]

Although this delimitation is both necessary and convincing, it still remains a very fragile difference. Freud's differentiation between two modes of observation—observing the unconscious in others or in one's own soul—is problematic, not only in an empirical-historical sense (Freud's development of psychoanalysis is very much based on intensive self-observation), but even more for systematic reasons. That which emerges as the unconscious in Freud's experience and in the psychoanalytic experience renders expressions like "my" or "your" or "his" unconscious questionable. The unconscious appears as a phenomenon that seems to exist, just like the *Genius* of earlier times, only in a strange and not easily graspable "in-between." In this it also resembles language. This in-between allows no fixed delineations. But each discourse draws its own borderlines within this space.

Eissler's one-dimensional attention to the imaginary figure of the *Genie* treats language only as an inconvenient cover to be pulled away as quickly as possible. In his analyses of Goethe's letters the stylistic conventions of the time are hardly taken into consideration, and when occasionally the question of historical style arises, it is only in order to subtract these elements—as if that were possible—and as if we had, then, the pure expression of the subject.

The language of the analyzed subject remains unanalyzed and so does the subject. This method protects the analyst's own language and fixates it as *the* language of psychoanalysis. When Goethe formulates his experience in the image of a fortified city and citadel, Eissler translates it immediately into the language of ego psychology: "Actually, we are fairly well informed about the defense of what Goethe called 'the city,' by which figure of speech he meant the ego and more specifically the periphery. . . . It was the firm defense of the citadel that saved him. By his figure of speech a territory within the ego is meant, perhaps its core, of which little is known yet" (p. 299). One figure of speech is translated into another. This is, of course, a legitimate procedure of interpretation. The fallacy begins with the belief that the translation is the naming of the "actual" thing, that which is actually meant as opposed to the figure of speech. The

interpretation operates on the naive assumption that its language belongs to a register outside of the rhetorical tropes. It is this assumption
that renders many psychoanalytical approaches so sterile. Instead of
developing the terms out of the analyzed text and thus keeping them
in a certain fluctuation, as Freud did, the post-Freudian approaches
often presuppose the terms as fixed entities and subsume whatever fits
under these terms. The result is a series of tautological Aha! recog-
nitions: the reader recognizes with great pleasure what he already
knew. The text becomes a vehicle for confirming the reader's opinions.

   Yet there are moments when Eissler discovers a gold mine. One
is the account of Goethe's mother telling stories to the children
(pp. 74ff.). She would invent her own stories for the children, develop
the plot before their eager ears, see the expression of satisfaction or
annoyance on her son's face, break off the story, and continue the
next evening. In the meantime, she could be sure that little Wolfgang
would have confided his version of the further development of the
story to his grandmother, who would in turn tell her. And thus the
next evening Goethe would hear his own fantasies from the mouth of
his mother. One could hardly find a more ideal situation to analyze
the subject's position in "his" stories. Eissler touches upon it and
passes it by.

   The story that Eissler does not tell has all the marks of the appearance of the Genius in between the speaking subjects. The topological configuration of this in-between not only has a spatial
dimension, but it is characterized as well by the specific logic of a
temporal deferral and Nachträglichkeit. It is here that the work of the
text and the effects of the unconscious meet, in the Werkstatt (work-
shop) of the spirit, as Hölderlin calls it.

   As a psychoanalytical study, Eissler's book has surprisingly little
to say about the unconscious. To be sure, the unconscious is often
invoked, and, like Freud, Eissler considers the artistic work as the
result of a specific relationship to the unconscious. Yet it is left in the
false familiarity of that which is not known. Perhaps it is in the nature
of the unconscious not to be known, but the "not" of this not knowing
is not a general negation. It is a determinate and determining bar that
refracts and shapes our knowing.

Eissler often speaks of the unconscious in the recurring formula of "preconsciously or unconsciously." The "or" of this formula suggests that preconscious and unconscious mingle undecidably, and that they together are opposed to consciousness. Eissler's unconscious is thus a purely descriptive term. Freud's notion of the unconscious is doubly set apart from a mere descriptive concept: in the systematic sense of a topology according to which "consciousness perception" is a *system* composed of the preconscious and consciousness, and a completely different system called the unconscious; and as a dynamic term of an economy that operates with an enigmatic, unknown, and unanalyzable X.

In Eissler's study, the lack of any serious working-through to the systematic effects of the unconscious is most painfully noticeable in regard to texts that are themselves the result of intense work and reworking. Goethe's *Iphigenie* emerges from a long chain of reworkings from the mythical tradition to Euripides, Racine, and Goethe's own revisions and transformations of the text.

Eissler's introductory remarks to the discussion of this play touch explicitly on the interrelation of psychoanalytic and aesthetic interests: "The next literary achievement that may give testimony as to the road Goethe took during those years is his tragedy *Iphigenie auf Tauris*, a play as great from the artistic viewpoint as it is important from the psychological" (p. 292). In a remarkably consistent shift, this first sentence changes the genres in both fields: what Goethe's subtitle calls *Ein Schauspiel* (one could translate it as "play," but it demarcates in German a form clearly distinct from "tragedy") is renamed as "tragedy," and Eissler's own subtitle, "A Psychoanalytical Study," appears now as a "psychological" viewpoint. I must apologize for being so pedantic about questions of genre, but I think that genre and gender are essential not only to aesthetics but to psychoanalysis as well. The fact that Eissler shifts the genres on both textual fields indicates that the confusion is of a fundamental nature.

Eissler is not unaware of the long chain of tradition and work from which Goethe's *Iphigenie* emerges; he even adds a few more links with figures from Goethe's Walpurgisnacht, from Shakespeare, and from Ovid. The entanglements of these chains of tradition and configurations in Eissler's account form a kind of container from which he lifts "the hidden unconscious meaning" (p. 305) and an "unconscious core" (p. 306). Eissler brings it to light in the form of a red mouse that means menstruation.

What is it that Eissler has brought to light? An unconscious meaning or core, he says. But while he thinks that he has brought it to consciousness with the name of menstruation, he is extremely vague about the status of this unconscious core or meaning. It is supposedly "the latent core of Shakespeare's play" (A *Midsummer Night's Dream*), but it also seems to be Goethe's opinion, "perhaps quite unconsciously meant" (p. 310). Again it is evident that Eissler operates with a purely descriptive notion of the unconscious; in Freud's systematic use an expression like "quite unconscious" does not make sense.

But more important here is another question. Eissler deduces his "unconscious core" from a textual chain that reaches back to the Greek myths. But he never even approaches the question of what this means for the *place* of the unconscious and how we are supposed to understand its topology. What is the relationship of what Eissler might call "Goethe's unconscious" to the unconscious core he finds in Shakespeare, Ovid, and the mythical narratives?

If we pursue Freud's own work in regard to such questions, we might perhaps come to the point where metaphors such as unconscious core, hidden meaning, and content turn out to be misleading. Since Eissler never touches on such questions everything becomes blurred; and because the actual work of the text is least important to Eissler, we are precipitated quickly to the depth of "a deep biological root" (p. 317). While Freud occasionally hoped to find a firm scientific basis for psychoanalysis in biology, he was always aware of the fact that psychoanalysis concerns psychic representations, structured by language. In Eissler's book the "sadistic imagery about the biological relationship" merges simply with the "biological root."

The work on and through the myth (*die Arbeit am Mythos*, to use Hans Blumenberg's phrase) has no end, and in each working through, the unconscious constitutes itself in a specific way. In this sense, it would be possible to speak of "Goethe's unconscious" with regard to his *Iphigenie auf Tauris*, for example. But Eissler never really speaks of this *text*. His approach to texts is condensed in a remark about some lines from the *Walpurgisnacht*: "It was observed earlier that the quatrain actually pictures a dream within a dream. A crude paraphrase was suggested that ought now to be replaced by a more exact rewording of how Goethe, had he not been the great poet he was, might have reported that night's experience. He might then have said . . ." (p. 311). Twice the text is displaced: first by a "crude paraphrase," then by "a more exact rewording" of that which Goethe did *not* say, but might have said if he were not Goethe. Who then says it? Who speaks? Apparently Eissler.

This is the point where another analysis could begin: Goethe analyzes Eissler. Eissler treats Goethe as the object of analysis, but from this analysis Goethe emerges as the subject-agent of the analysis. Structurally and thematically Goethe dominates the study as model analyst and model analysand. Goethe's active presence in analysis already marks Freud's work. In a subtle essay, Avital Ronell has pursued some of the Goethe effect in Freud's work.[22] It is worth comparing this essay with Eissler's voluminous study to see the difference of a reading that allows itself to be entangled in the detours of the text.

I have dwelled on Eissler's book because it seems to me paradigmatic of a certain sterility in this kind of psychoanalytic approach: the reader of literature learns nothing about literature and mainly misunderstandings about psychoanalysis; the analyst learns nothing as long as he reads the texts only as confirmations of his concepts.

The following chapters of readings after Freud are fragments of a working-through that has no desire to confirm anything or to convince anyone. If the pleasure of the text that has motivated these readings continues its effect on the reader, then each reading will produce its own manifest secret, what Goethe called *offenbares Geheimnis*.

I

THE WEAVING OF THE VEIL:
GOETHE AND THE
SYMBOLIC ORDER

Goethe's so-called "anacreontic" (after the Greek poet Anacreon) or rococo poetry, written while he was a student in Leipzig from 1765 to 1768, is not very highly regarded. It is not that this poetry suffers from the inexperience and awkwardness of the beginner. On the contrary, these poems display an amazing degree of artistic virtuosity. It is rather the tendency or the very principle of this kind of poetry that has come under general critical disapproval. Anacreontic and rococo are seen as artistic forms that indulge in daintiness, charm, lightness, and wit. Serious literary critics usually add superficiality and emptiness to the series. This kind of poetry lacks "the objective-metaphysical background of the baroque and the subjective metaphysics of the age of idealism. It remained literature, play of wit, forms of gallantries, fit for the rococo society. It lacks depth, but possesses formal virtuosity, pointedness, and lightness."[1] In short: literature instead of metaphysics, form instead of depth. The dichotomy has a long history, particularly in German studies.

Our introduction, however, is no less apt to evoke all-too-familiar expectations: the well-known strategy of scholarly legitimation used to reevaluate and vindicate unjustly underestimated periods, authors, and texts. And thus our ritual could begin: "Goethe's so-called anacreontic . . . poetry . . . is not very highly regarded, but . . ."

There is no "but." I have no desire to change the reader's appreciation or lack of appreciation. My interest is directed toward certain implications of this form of poetry and the implications of the critical judgments about it.

We can start with the position that is generally given to Goethe's earliest poetry in the context of his oeuvre. These playful rococo poems are not simply seen as the beginning of a development. In a certain sense they are seen as preceding the authentic work and its development; they do not yet belong to its coherence and continuity. There is initially a certain artistic virtuosity, a formal skill, but this poetry is not yet the personal expression that breaks through a few years later in Strasbourg and Sesenheim. There is a rupture between the "actual" work, emanating from Goethe's life, and an earlier poetry determined by purely external influences and formal play. To be sure, many of Goethe's later poems arose from and were intended for social and courtly occasions, yet they can be seen as part of the organic whole of a life ranging from the depth of subjective intimacy to the worldliness of the Weimar Geheimrat.

This schema is based on theoretical premises rooted in the eighteenth century and shaping the form of critical discourse until today. In German literary criticism, Goethe's writing has become the embodiment of these premises. Their kernel is a concept of literary texts, according to which texts are the foremost *expression* of a specific, unique, and homogeneous subject. The coherence and continuity of a life, its biography, provide the horizon of meaning. Specific key terms form a network of aesthetic appreciation and judgment: originality, immediacy, naturalness, truth, wholeness. A text's expressive value, its immediacy to and its origin in the wholeness of the producing subject, are the aesthetic criteria for its genuineness and truth. In some way Goethe's autobiography *Dichtung und Wahrheit* has canonized the biographical context as the horizon of meaning and has often been the latent paradigm of literary history and criticism. The methodological problems of this paradigm are most evident when it is applied retroactively to periods such as the Middle Ages and when medieval texts are read as "confessions" and expressions of individual subjects.

Such premises are not limited to straightforward, simple biographism and positivism. In more subtle forms, they have entered the hermeneutics of identificatory understanding, as for example in Wilhelm Dilthey's coupling of "Erlebnis und Dichtung" (experience and poetry). Neither Goethe nor Dilthey would see the connection between life experience and text in the trivial sense that texts "reproduce" or "mirror" specific, positively datable events and experiences. But the coherence and totality of the individual life history, the *Lebenszusammenhang*, form the crucial horizon of meaning and understanding. Jürgen Habermas, whose own theory of communication and language is deeply rooted in this tradition, has summarized Dilthey's hermeneutics as a paradigm of understanding:

> The history of a life [*Lebensgeschichte*] is the elementary unit of the life process of the human species. It is a system that delimits itself. It (re-)presents itself [*stellt sich . . . dar*] as a course of life [*Lebenslauf*, also *curriculum vitae*] delimited by birth and death; and it is furthermore a cohesion [*Zusammenhang*] that can be experienced as such, that connects the particles of the course of life, and it connects them by a "meaning" [*Sinn*]. The life history constitutes itself from life relations [*Lebensbezüge*]. Life relations consist of the I on the one hand, things and people who enter the world of the I on the other hand. A *life relation* fixates both specific meanings of things and people of a subject and specific modes of behavior of the subject toward its surrounding.[2]

In this context, autobiography assumes a paradigmatic importance and meaning. Here the subject, as I, ascertains his or her life history, takes hold of it, and thus constitutes a horizon of meaning for him- or herself.

But there is something odd about autobiography. The subject who would like to take hold of his or her life history finds at least two insurmountable limits: the beginning and the end of the story are

inaccessible to the reflective glance. No subject can reflectively reconstruct his or her birth, even less his or her death. Thus the wholeness of this "elementary unit" of life is not directly accessible to the
living subject, and even in between these two inaccessible limits only
fragments are available. (Goethe, quite knowingly, talks about *Bruch-
stücke einer großen Konfession*—fragments of a large confession—in
regard to his literary work.) As a whole and a continuous coherence
of meaning, the life history can only be construed by the subject
through mediations and as a fiction. Goethe's own awareness of this
problem is indicated not only in the two terms of his autobiography—
Dichtung und Wahrheit—but also in his approach to his birth. It is
first as a story doubly mediated through his friend Bettina who, in
turn, got the story from Goethe's mother (who was herself a talented
storyteller, spellbinding the children with her improvisations). Goethe
adds another dimension, introducing the story of his birth with the
astrological constellation. One cannot simply discard this astrological
frame as ironic or tongue-in-cheek. Irony is never a simple negation
of the manifest text. As a narrative strategy, the astrological tale marks
the story of the birth as a foreign discourse. The beginning of one's
own life is already inscribed in a symbolic order that escapes the
imaginable story of the I.

The hermeneutical tendency to locate the horizon of meaning
almost exclusively in the horizon of life experience loses sight of the
double axis of the constitution of meaning in speech, emphasized by
Schleiermacher.[3] Whenever a subject speaks, two orders participate
in the constitution of meaning: the transsubjective order of language
and the story of the speaking subject (which, as story, already presupposes the order of language).

The intersection of these two orders is nicely illustrated by the
different ordering and editions of Goethe's lyric poetry. For most readers familiar with this poetry, the individual poems are quite clearly
ordered in a biographical, chronological order, paradigmatically embodied in the handy and beautiful *Hamburger Ausgabe*. It is symptomatic, however, that the editor, Trunz, had to make some
compromises between purely chronological and thematic or formal
criteria. In any case, "purely chronological" has to be qualified: the
chronological order is already not simply an external sequence of life,

but an immanent organic "growing," marked by specific phases, known to the student of German literature by the familiar terms of *Sturm und Drang*, *Klassik*, and *Altersdichtung*. If one comes from this familiar schema (used to introduce students to Goethe) to Goethe's own edition and ordering of his poetry, a strange defamiliarization takes place. Goethe's ordering of his poems according to themes and poetic forms without regard for chronological order seems artificial by comparison. And it is artificial in a very precise sense: ordered according to categories of art within a long tradition of poetics. Yet Goethe too has some difficulties with this order. Many of the poems don't quite fit and thus testify to the mutual resistance of two textual principles that cannot easily be synthesized.

If we take this double axis of the text and its meaning seriously, the move from the early foreign influences, external style, and formal artistic virtuosity to the genuine, true, and personal later poetry of Goethe is no longer simple. To be sure, anacreontic poetry explicitly wants to be nothing but style and form, distancing itself from any personal expression. These poems and their poets insist again and again that they are not communicating personal experiences, but presenting us with playful masks.[4] (Yet they protest so much that one might wonder. . . . And anyway, what is the pleasure of these masks, where does it come from, and what does it appeal to?)

The rhetoric of this rococo poetry is clearly opposed to the later confessional poetics of the *Sturm und Drang* generation. But perhaps it only articulates a rupture that marks all speech, no matter how confessional and "true" it seems. It is perhaps from this rupture that the symbolic veil of the text emerges and from which it weaves the imaginary, fragile wholeness of the speaking subject, giving it a precarious body in the *corpus* of the text. A continuity of ruptures connects the light-footed melancholy of rococo verses, in which a desire that has renounced any reality of its object in the play of masks splits the speaking subject into the gay fictive voice and the melancholic persona, with the veil that is left behind by Helena at the end of the third act of *Faust II*.

The fact that anacreontic poetry openly admits the split and even plays with it is an irritation for a poetic and critical tradition that wants to believe in immediacy and unruptured wholeness as aesthetic criteria. The stronger the faith, the more moralistic the tone. Anacreontic poetry approaches sinfulness: not only is it lighthearted and charming, but it is a lie, because it does not make any pretentions to speak from the fullness of the heart. It stages openly what has been suggested about poetry and poets from Plato to Nietzsche: that they lie. Is it possible perhaps that these charming fictions, lacking all seriousness of truth, might be closer to the truth of poetry than the texts that speak from the hearts of serious and honest subjects?

The literary-historical place of the anacreontic, rococo poetry is rather ambivalent. Cysarz locates it in the baroque tradition, while Kindermann interprets it as a late and decadent phenomenon of the Enlightenment.[5] The general tendency is now to see it more or less as part of the Enlightenment. This allows for a clear separation of the triumphant irrationalism of the grandiose *Sturm und Drang* feelings from the "cold" rationalist poetry of the Enlightenment. The rupture is thus between the texts, rather than in them. The rationalist character of anacreontic poetry is marked by a tendency toward a *pointe*, the explosion of a witty punch line. According to this logic, wit is the product of rational calculation rather than organic *Gestalt*. Witty poems are *made*, they do not grow out of the depth of the soul.[6] The commentary of Trunz, the editor of the *Hamburger Ausgabe*, is paradigmatic: "In the superficiality of its content the spirit of the rococo society lives; one feels the vicinity of rationalism in the witty rationality of its form. It is the formal principle of wit: playful, willed, clear, surprising, pointed, analyzable, impersonal."[7] In a similar way, the editors of Goethe's letters comment on his use of *Witz* in a letter of November 24, 1768: "*Witz*; used here in the sense of Gottsched as the faculty of rational insight, the combinatory acumen by which the poet is endowed. . . . Poetry, understood in this sense as rationally manipulated, forms the opposite pole to the pietistic immersion of the soul in God, which is essentially an emotional, mystical process."[8]

On second thought, it might seem curious that wit and jokes are supposed to be so rational. No matter how one understands *Witz*, in the older sense of wit and *esprit* or in the prevalent modern sense as a joke, it is placed in an oblique if not contradictory position in regard to reason and rational discourse. It does not help to appeal to the sense in which Gottsched uses the term, because this sense takes on ambivalent implications upon closer reading. Gottsched locates *Witz* in the same position where the ancients placed the divine *ingenium* of the poet. It is his way of explaining the divine nature of poetry: "This is, in my opinion, the best explanation one can give of the divine in poetry, about which scholars quarrel so much. Generally speaking, it is a happy, gay head; a vivid wit as the learned world would call it: it is what Horace called *ingenium et mens divinior*. This wit is a faculty of the mind which can easily perceive similarities between things and is able to compare them."[9]

One can of course argue that this is Gottsched's attempt to demystify the quality of the divine and to inscribe it into the realm of the rational faculty. Yet, while this probably was Gottsched's intention, the place of inscription does not leave the rational faculty untouched. It is the logic of the linguistic sign that any signifier replacing another will be affected in its value by the position it enters. Gottsched is not unaware of the dubious realm he has entered and eagerly tries to control the "natural gifts" of wit with rigid pedagogy:

> Children who lack instruction remain stuck despite their natural abilities, even if they excel with more vivacious qualities among their equals; yet all their wit is like an unploughed field that brings forth only wild plants; a tree, growing on its own, producing only unshapely branches and twigs. If such people in later years come upon rhyming they turn into buffoons, harlequins, and foolish poetasters who mix together insipid ideas, who consider everything permissible, and only search for the applause of the vulgar masses. They only follow their fantasy and rhyme together quodlibets, songs, romances, harlequin jokes, and other fanciful inventions from the theatrical world, without rules and skill. It is possible, however, to wake up young boys in time and, so to speak, straighten out their wit.[10]

Unawares, wit appears in the realm of fantasy and fancy, where things are slightly crazy, if sense and reason do not intervene in time. It seems that the reasonable world in the realm of wit runs little Alice's risk of falling into the rabbit hole. Alice falls into the hole and thus imitates the wit that, in German, is as much an *Einfall* as it is a calculated construct.

There is no doubt that wit flirts with the intellect, with reason, with the spirit; it wants to be *geistreich* (rich in spirit). But that is

precisely when it plays its game with the spirit and threatens to mul-
tiply into spirits. Indeed, what is generally feared of wit is not its
rationality, but its subversion of reason. Goethe takes a rather distanced look at wit. In his notes to the *West-östliche Divan* he delineates proximity and difference of *Geist* and *Witz*:

> The highest quality of Oriental poetry is what we Germans call *Geist*,
> the predominance of a higher governing principle. . . . *Geist* is mainly
> a matter of old age or of an aging world period. We find in all poetry
> of the Orient a general view of the world, irony, sovereign use of talent.
> . . . These poets see all things present before them, they see relations
> between the most distant ones, and thus they come close to what we
> call *Witz*; but *Witz* has not the same dignity, it is more selfish, com-
> placent, something of which *Geist* remains free; that is why it can and
> must be called ingenious. [11]

In one of his aphorisms, Goethe is even more decidedly negative:
"Analogy must fear two aberrations: one is to give itself over to wit
where it dissolves into nothing, the other to wrap itself in tropes and
similes, which, however, is less harmful."[12] The most threatening
aspect of wit is its method, which is also the method of thinking and
reasoning: finding analogies, relations, connections; and the fact that
this method is at the same time the road into the "nothing." *Witz*
threatens *Geist* in its own form.

Among Goethe's contemporaries Jean Paul was perhaps the
sharpest and wittiest connoisseur of wit. His *Vorschule der Ästhetik*
(1804) gives much space to the phenomenon of wit. He begins with
a categorical difference: everyone can say of himself without vanity
that he is "sensible, reasonable, that he has fantasy, feeling, taste; but
no one must say that he has wit," just as no one should refer to him-
or herself as beautiful.[13] Thus, a relation is introduced between wit
and beauty, which is then extended: both are "*social* qualities and
triumphs (for what would be the gain of a witty hermit or a beautiful
solitary woman?" (p. 169). Both are *effects* not in the control of the
subject. I may want to make a joke, but whether it succeeds will be
decided by the laughter of the company, and here again their laughter
is not a matter of decision. It happens or it does not happen. Forced
laughter is as embarrassing as strained wit. By pointing at this partic-

ularity of wit, its social character, Jean Paul foreshadows Freud's central emphasis on the "third person" in the constellation of the joke.[14]

According to Jean Paul, comparison is both the most general and the most particular mode of wit. The comparing subject occupies a rather curious position in the act of comparing. What emerges in this act is "the miraculous birth from our creator-I, both freely created—because we wanted it and strived for it—and with necessity—because otherwise the creator would have seen the creature before he made it" (p. 171). Intended and strived for, the witty effect is yet the product of a necessity and mechanism that is no more under the control of the witty subject than the procreative act established by Jean Paul as a consistent metaphorical relation. In this case, however, it is not nature's work but the play of signifiers, "the sly and punning velocity of language" (p. 174), that runs its dis-courses while we speak.

The pun is the point where the subversive threat of wit becomes particularly acute. Even Jean Paul is forced to make some curious moves. In the form of wit taken by puns, the borderline between *esprit* and silliness is quite unclear, and the demarcation between admiration and contempt often seems difficult to decide. Apparently something rather dubious is involved. What are we to think when the non-sense of accidental configurations of letters and homophonies produces meaning instead of self-conscious, dignified reason? We will have to admit that our reason is highly dependent on the non-sense of arbitrary signs. But curiously enough, this is precisely where Jean Paul posits a sign of freedom. One of the reasons for our pleasure in puns, he says, is the freedom of spirit (*Geistes-Freiheit*) that shines forth from it (p. 194). Freedom of spirit? At the point where the letter reigns? In Jean Paul's argument, the freedom of the spirit shining forth from the pun is based on the fact that "the glance is turned away from the thing to its sign; and when one of two things conquers and devours us, it is less of a weakness to be conquered by the more powerful one" (*ibid.*). Freedom is reduced to the choice of by which force we would rather be conquered and devoured.

The aporias of this freedom continue: because there is something uncanny in wit and puns, they must be limited. Jean Paul too is concerned about these limits and how to control the irruption of non-sense, the power of the signifier; because the sign of the thing is more powerful than the thing. Yet even while it is more honorable to be conquered by the more powerful agency, the honor demands some rules of victory and submission, through which the dignity and freedom of the subject assert themselves in a curious displacement: "I must find the pun, not make it; or else I show ugly arbitrariness [*Willkür*] instead of freedom" (*ibid.*). It seems as if the arbitrariness of the sign had displaced "freedom" to its opposite. *My* freedom, it would seem, is shown in that which I *make*, in my arbitrariness (*Willkür*: literally, choice of my will), not in what I find and what occurs to me.

It is not Jean Paul's faulty logic that leads to such aporias, but rather his perceptiveness to the knotty implications of the subject's demand for autonomy. The constitution of free subjectivity in the negation of the subject pervades romantic thought. The structure of the joke and of wit touches the paradox of romantic irony in which free subjectivity asserts itself in a series of self-annihilations. The same is true for the tragic constellation as Schelling explains it in the model of Oedipus: the ultimate freedom is asserted at the moment when the subject assumes responsibility even for the deeds imposed by necessity.[15]

The specific differential mark of wit and the joke is their social character. The witty subject is a sociable and socially acknowledged subject; its problematic subjectivity is expanded to a no less problematic intersubjectivity. Wit earns social appreciation, it procures social identity and is part of social culture, at the same time that it threatens them. There is no (good) joke that is not *risqué*, a risk for the witty subject as well as for (good) society. The effect of jokes depends on their touching on social taboos. According to Freud, the joke is a "rogue who speaks with a double tongue and who serves two masters at the same time."[16] Clothed as the social dandy, it veils its threat to the social order. The metaphor of cloth has its own witty accuracy: cloth not only hides and veils the forbidden sexuality of the body, but in veiling it becomes its erotic language.

We have arrived at a metaphor of metaphor with a long tradition, reaching back at least to Cicero. The clothing and disguising of metaphor is that which, according to Gottsched, manifests a poet's wit.[17] Jean Paul too unfolds his phenomenology of wit above all in the model of the metaphor. In order for this clothing to be decent and proper, Gottsched advises that the wit of young boys already be, "so to speak, properly pleated" (*so zu reden, in die Falten rücken*).[18]

The decent pleating of the clothes does not seem to be the major concern of anacreontic poetry, quite the contrary. Its favorite game is unveiling and undressing—although, and that is most frequently its point and joke, in order to veil and disguise at the same time. It is a decidedly voyeuristic poetry. Its predilection for seeing is part of a general obsession in the Enlightenment: the eye was considered the privileged organ to find truth and certainty, and particularly *oversight* (*Übersicht*).[19] To be sure, anacreontic frivolity is not much concerned with grandiose overviews of the world and *Weltanschauungen*. It prefers an overview of smaller spaces; it contracts its glance with pleasure to the boudoir or a small meadow, surrounded by bushes, where a beauty is just about to undress for a refreshing bath. The following poem by Johann Peter Uz (1720–1796) is exemplary:

> Ein Traum
>
> O Traum, der mich entzücket!
> Was hab ich nicht erblicket!
> Ich warf die müden Glieder
> In einem Thale nieder
> Wo einen Teich, der silbern floß,
> Ein schattigtes Gebüsch unschloß.
>
> Da sah ich durch die Sträuche
> Mein Mädchen bey dem Teiche.
> Das hatte sich, zum Baden,
> Der Kleider meist entladen,
> Bis auf ein untreu weiß Gewand,
> Das keinem Lüftgen widerstand.
>
> Der freye Busen lachte,
> Den Jugend reizend machte.
> Mein Blick blieb sehnend stehen
> Bey diesen regen Höhen,
> Wo Zephyr unter Lilien blies
> Und sich die Wollust greifen ließ.
>
> Sie fieng nun an, o Freuden!
> Sich vollends auszukleiden;

Doch, ach! indems geschiehet,
Erwach ich und sie fliehet.
O schlief ich doch von neuem ein!
Nun wird sie wohl im Wasser seyn. [20]

(O dream that raptured me! What did I not see! I rested my tired body in a valley where shady bushes enclosed a pond with silvery water. There I saw through the bushes my girl near the pond. For the bath, she had gotten rid of almost all her cloths, except an unfaithful white robe that did not resist the smallest wind. The free bosom, made charming by youth, smiled. My glance rested with desire on these animated hills, where zephyr blew among the lilies and where bliss could be grasped. She now began, o joy! to undress completely; but, alas! just when it happens I wake up and she escapes. O if I only would fall asleep again! Now she will probably be in the water.)

It is not only the voyeuristic scene in this poem that makes it paradigmatic, but even more its pointed ending: the joke is on the voyeur, in the fact that at the moment of seeing, he sees *not*. The formula of enthusiasm at the beginning says it already: "Was hab ich nicht erblicket!" (What haven't I seen!). The symbol of negation that rhetorically marks the amazement turns into the grammatical function of negation at the end. The joke here is in fact a veiling, doubly ironic because it is achieved by a waking up, by an opening of the eyes.

This kind of poetry is dominated by the desire to be "all eyes," as a poem by Lessing puts it:

Wenn ich, Augenlust zu finden,
Unter schattich kühlen Linden
Schielend auf und nieder gehe,
Und ein schönes Mädchen sehe,
Möcht ich lauter Auge sein. [21]

(When, in order to find pleasure for my eyes, I walk up and down, crosseyed, under shady cool linden trees, and I see a beautiful girl, I would want to be nothing but eye.)

At the same time, however, the object of seeing must be veiled because, as another poem by Lessing says in mocking-playful melancholy, we would otherwise perish from our eyes:

O Reize voll Verderben!
Wir sehen euch und sterben.

O Augen, unser Grab!
O Chloris, darf ich flehen?
Dich Sicher anzusehen,
Laß erst den Flor herab![22]

(O charms, full of corruption! We see you and we die. O eyes, our grave!
O Chloris, can I flee? Let first down your veil so that I may look at you
securely!)

Through the figures of fan and face, a late poem by Goethe condenses
the situation into an allegory of language:

Das Wort ist ein Fächer! Zwischen den Stäben
Blicken ein Paar schöne Augen hervor.
Der Fächer ist nur ein lieblicher Flor,
Er verdeckt mir zwar das Gesicht,
Aber das Mädchen verbirgt er nicht,
Weil das Schönste, was sie besitzt,
Das Auge mir ins Auge blitzt.[23]

(The word is a fan! A pair of beautiful eyes looks out through the bars. The
fan is a lovely mist, it veils the face, but it does not hide the girl, because
the most beautiful thing she possesses, her eye flashes into my eye.)

What remains visible here is the eye of the other, the seeing of seeing:
instead of meeting an object, desire meets the desire of the other.
     This shift is crucial for Goethe's unfolding of the symbolic veil.
The shift already occurs with dreamlike certainty in an early poem,
written in the album of a friend in 1767. In fact it is an almost
verbatim adaptation of a typical anacreontic poem by Gleim, with
only one small change of a verse. Gleim wrote: "Ein Mädchen hab
ich, gut zu küssen" (I have a girl, good for kissing); Goethe writes:
"Ein Mädgen, willig mich zu küssen" (A girl, willing to kiss me).[24]
The shift changes Gleim's reified object, juxtaposed with a bottle of
wine, into a subject of desire.
     Between the eyes of desire a gaze intervenes: the eye of the law
and interdiction, often embodied in the eye of the watchful mother.
Typically, the lovers try to evade this eye, to blind it. Occasionally
they seem to succeed:

Aeltern, habet hundert Augen,
Mädgen, wenn sie List gebrauchen,
Machen hundert Augen blind. [25]

(Parents, you may have a hundred eyes, girls, when they use cunning, blind
a hundred eyes.)

Yet the blinding of the eye of authority is a most ambivalent wish;
were it fulfilled, the blinding would hit the eye of desire as well.
Seeing, the lovers would no longer see, as the young Goethe virtuously
advises a steadfast girl:

Dank es dem harten Streite,
Daß du zur Sonn' unschuldig blikst,
Bey'm Anblick jener heil'gen nicht erschrikst,
Mich nicht verachtend von dir schikst.
Freund, dieses ist der Tugend Lohn;
O wärst du gestern thränend nicht entflohn,
Du sähest mich heute
Und ewig nie mit Freude. [26]

(Be thankful to the hard struggle that you now look up to the sun innocently
and are not terrified looking at the sacred one and that you are not sending
me away with contempt. Friend, this is virtue's reward; if you had not escaped
tearfully yesterday, you would not see me today nor in eternity with joy.)

The watchful eye of the law is intermingled with the eye of desire.
Thus, to blind it would mean to blind oneself. He who sees sees no
more. Only the veil or the joke saves desire.

On the borderline of anacreontic poetry, the following two poems
by Goethe clearly mark a shift: *Die Nacht* (in a later version: *Die
schöne Nacht*) and *An den Mond* (later *An Luna*). [27]

Die Nacht
Gern verlass' ich diese Hütte,
Meiner Schönen Aufenthalt,
Und durchstreich mit leisem Tritte
Diesen ausgestorbnen Wald.
Luna bricht die Nacht der Eichen,
Zephirs melden ihren Lauf,
Und die Birken streun mit Neigen
Ihr den süßten Weihrauch auf.

Schauer, der das Herze fühlen,
Der die Seele schmelzen macht,
Wandelt im Gebüsch im Kühlen.
Welche schöne, süße Nacht!
Freude! Wollust! Kaum zu fassen!
Und doch wollt' ich, Himmel, dir
Tausend deiner Nächte lassen,
Gäb' mein Mädchen eine mir.

(The Night: With pleasure I leave this cottage, the abode of my beloved, and I roam with soft step through this deserted forest. Luna breaks the night of the oaks, zephyrs announce her course, and the birch trees, bending down, disperse sweet incense for her. Shudder, that causes the heart to feel and the soul to melt, ambulates in the bushes in the coolness. What beautiful, sweet night! Joy! rapture! Hardly to grasp! And yet, heaven, I would leave to you thousands of such nights if my girl would give me only one.)

An den Mond

Schwester von dem ersten Licht,
Bild der Zärtlichkeit in Trauer,
Nebel schwimmt mit Silberschauer
Um dein reizendes Gesicht.
Deines leisen Fußes Lauf
Weckt aus tagverschloßnen Höhlen
Traurig abgeschiedne Seelen,
Mich, und nächt'ge Vögel auf.
Forschend übersieht dein Blick
Eine großgemeßne Weite.
Hebe mich an deine Seite,
Gib der Schwärmerei dies Glück!
Und in wollustvoller Ruh
Säh' der weitverschlagne Ritter
Durch das gläserne Gegitter
Seines Mädchens Nächten zu.
Dämmrung, wo die Wollust thront,
Schwimmt um ihre runden Glieder.
Trunken sinkt mein Blick hernieder—
Was verhüllt man wohl dem Mond!
Doch was das für Wünsche sind!
Voll Begierde zu genießen,

So da droben hängen müssen—
Ei, da schieltest du dich blind!

(To the Moon: Sister of the first light, image of tenderness in sadness, fog swims with silvery shower around your charming face. The course of your soft foot awakens from the caves, closed to the day, sad departed souls, me and nightly birds. Inquiringly your glance overlooks a wide-measured distance. Lift me up to your side, grant this happiness to my enthusiasm! And in blissfull calmness, the knight, drifted so far away, would watch the nights of his girl. Twilight swims around her round limbs where rapture thrones. Intoxicated, my glance sinks down. What would one hide before the moon! But what kind of wishes are this! To enjoy full of desire, to have to hang up there—you would ogle yourself blind!)

The poem *Die Nacht* starts with an abrupt change of scenery: the speaker emerges from the cozy cottage of his beloved into a deserted forest. The most curious thing about this change of scenery is the speaker's attitude: "*Gern* verlass' ich diese Hütte." Why would someone be happy to leave the abode of his beloved in order to go out into a deserted forest? Might it be that the coziness of the cottage is the real uncanny place with which the speaker cannot cope? The interior of the cottage remains hidden, the erotic center does not enter the poem directly. It remains a secret place; but it produces an uncanny outside. Only in this outside realm can its spell be broken: "Luna bricht die Nacht der Eichen." The breaking of the spell works with ritualistic formulas and anacreontic requisites: *Luna* and *Zephyr* are the magical words, and the sweet "incense" (*Weihrauch*) of the birch trees gives the ritual its sacred aura.

The second stanza repeats the displacement of an interior into the outside. *Schauer* (a shudder), if not used in the meteorological sense (showers), usually describes an inner feeling that transmits a fine trembling to the skin. Goethe's poem reverses the movement: the *Schauer* is promenading out in the bushes and transmits its effects from there to the interior of heart and soul. Now, however, in this displacement, the beauty from which the speaker seemed to flee ("Gern verlass' ich diese Hütte, / Meiner *Schönen* Aufenthalt") can be enjoyed in different form: "Welche *schöne*, süße Nacht!" The embodied beauty has been replaced by the disembodied beautiful night. Now even *Wollust* (rapture, with strong sexual connotations) is thinkable, imaginable, although hardly tangible ("Kaum zu fassen"). As in Uz's poem, the rhetorical function of negation assumes grammatical literalness. There is something for the heart, but nothing for the hand. The only thing left at the end is desire. Now it can speak directly, but only from a safe distance and in the form of a joke: someone gladly leaves his beloved in order to fantasize from a distance about a night with her.

The first lines of the poem to the moon again evoke indirectness. The distanced reflection of another light shines from the moon, merely the "sister of the first light," more absence than presence, and thus the image of a "tenderness in sadness" ("Bild der Zärtlichkeit in Trauer"). Even this distant reflection is half-veiled. But the position of distance and reflection promises enlightenment, overview (*Übersicht*: "Forschend übersieht dein Blick / Eine großgemeßne Weite"). The searching eye of the Enlightenment and its desire for a universal worldview merges completely with the voyeuristic desire to peep into the bedroom of the beloved. Again desire has distanced itself from the place of an object of desire in order to indulge all the more in a safe and quiet rapture: "in wollustvoller Ruh." At the very moment, however, when the glance penetrates to the scene of pleasureful revelation, the text abruptly breaks off. A dash crosses out whatever could be seen and replaces it with a rhetorical question: what does one hide from the moon? Nothing—but everything in the text. If the glance should insist on the lunar and lunatic view, and if it could see, it would— predictably—be blinded ("schieltest du dich blind"). He who saw sees no more.

In a later version that Goethe integrated into his collected poems in 1815, the third stanza of the poem has significantly changed:

Des Beschauens holdes Glück
Mildert solcher Ferne Qualen,
Und ich sammle deine Strahlen,
Und ich schärfe meinen Blick.
Hell und heller wird es schon
Um die unverhüllten Glieder,
Und nun zieht sie mich hernieder,
Wie dich einst Endymion.

(The blissful happiness of contemplation soothes the pains of such distance. And I gather your rays, and I sharpen my glance. Clear and clearer it grows already around her unveiled limbs, and now I am pulled down to her as you were once, Endymion.)

Here, the seeing seems to succeed, and more: it attains the fulfillment of desire. There is no more blinding. On the contrary: "Hell und heller wird es schon." Where does this light come from? It is a mythological simile that, on the imaginary level, stills the pain of distance through the blissful happiness of a quiet glance ("Des Beschauens holdes Glück") and evokes fulfillment on the symbolic level in the mythological displacement.

We have here condensed the main direction of some of Goethe's major symbolic moves. Two motifs are particularly important in this constellation: the reflective mirroring (*Abglanz*) and the veil. Invariably there is a lack or an inhibition of a desire or movement at the beginning. The interrelation of inhibition and reflection emerges most clearly in the river poems. While the youthful poetry of the seventies (e.g., *Mahomets Gesang*, 1772–73) celebrates in the river the great *Genie* who violently forces his course through all hindrances and unfolds his/its creative, name-giving power after and through the act of violence, in the later poems the inhibition itself becomes the place of a reflective fulfillment and the place of the text. Already in the poem *Gesang der Geister über den Wassern* (1779) such a shift has occurred:

> Im flachen Bette
> Schleicht er das Wiesental hin,
> Und in dem glatten See
> Weiden ihr Antlitz
> Alle Gestirne.[28]

(In the flat bed he ambles along through the valley, and in the smooth lake all stars enjoy their reflected faces.)

The most famous paradigm of this reflective transformation is the sonnet *Mächtiges Überraschen* (1807). The forceful rushing of the river down the mountain is suddenly interrupted by a "demonic" landslide. And now the transformation takes place:

Die Welle sprüht und staunt zurück und weichet
Und schwillt bergan, sich immer selbst zu trinken:
Gehemmt ist nun zum Vater hin das Streben.
Sie schwankt und ruht, zum See zurückgedeichet;
Gestirne spiegelnd sich, beschaun das Blinken
Des Wellenschlags am Fels, ein neues Leben.[29]

(The wave sprays and rears in amazement and yields and rises up the mountain, swallowing up itself again and again: blocked is now the striving towards
the father. It staggers and comes to rest, dammed to a lake; stars, reflecting
themselves, contemplate the twinkle of the sprayed waves on the rock, a new
life.)

The "new life" and the text in which it represents itself are the result
of a double reflective move: a narcissistic self-devouring ("Und schwillt
bergan, sich immer selbst zu trinken") forms the basis for another
reflection: the constellations of the stars in the mirror of the lake. We
can see more clearly the connection with the astrological constellation
at the beginning of the autobiography, where the *autos*, the self, is as
much the scene of another inscription as it is the writing subject.

The subject is thus split, barred by the signifier, as Lacan describes it.[30] The mode of this barring can take many forms, shaped by
individual and historical experiences and conditions. The socialization
processes that integrate the subject into the social order so that it may
speak from there may also silence it, and they always leave their
wounds and scars. In the eighteenth and early nineteenth centuries
such wounds may have been felt with a particular intensity: the intensity of those who found themselves in the gaping contradictions
between the rhetoric of emancipation and real oppression. Those who
kept the wounds open, like Lenz, perished. Others saved themselves
in precarious and fragile compromises. Goethe points to the scar of a
deadly wound. The place of reflection is also a place of death; and
even the reflection still has the lure of death. On January 19, 1778,
after he helped dig the grave for a girl who had drowned herself, he
wrote to Charlotte von Stein:

He worked into the night; at the end I alone until the hour of her
death, it was just one of these evenings. Orion stood beautifully up in
the sky when we rode gaily over from Tiefurth. I have enough mem-

ories and thoughts for my pleasure, and cannot go out anymore. Good night angel, take care and don't go down there. There is something dangerously enticing in this inviting melancholy as in the water itself, and as in the reflection of the stars in the sky that shines from both and lures us.[31]

Two desires meet. One is deadly, the other distributes itself into the reflecting lights of the water and lets the warning echo speak from the text.

In the same years of the first decade in Weimar, when the motif of reflection and mirroring takes shape, the symbol of the veil also unfolds its structure and finds condensed articulation in the allegorical poem *Zueignung* in two often-quoted lines: "Aus Morgenduft gewebt und Sonnenklarheit, / Der Dichtung Schleier aus der Hand der Wahrheit" (Woven from morning mist and clearness of the sun, the veil of poetry from the hand of truth). The poem shows the marks of the familiar constellation. It begins with the opening of the eyes. The poet wakes up and leaves the cottage in order to see. But the scene darkens and fog covers the world. Through the fog, however, the sun, the central organ of the naked truth, is unveiled, and the poet stands— blinded. He who saw sees no more, unless he can save himself with another veil. This is what he does in the poem. When the poet opens his eyes again, he no longer sees the sun, but in its place an allegory of a beautiful woman, both the object and interdiction of desire: the desire of the boy (l. 40) and the calming of the passion (ll. 43–44). In this process the glance is transformed. The poet no longer sees an object, but he sees another seeing in which he *reads himself*: "Ich konnte mich in ihrem Auge lesen" (l. 75). The I that had lost blow by blow its imaginary identity and self-confidence in the preceding stanzas now finds itself again as a text that can be read. And that is what the poet receives from the hand of truth: a text(ile), a veil.

The two motifs of the veil and the mirror reflection recur and are interwoven in *Faust* in various modes. The chorus of the elfs at the beginning of the second part intonates the theme:

Große Lichter, kleine Funken
Glitzern nah und glänzen fern;
Glitzern hier im See sich spiegelnd,

Glänzen droben klarer Nacht,
Tiefsten Ruhens Glück besiegelnd
Herrscht des Mondes volle Pracht. (ll. 4644–49)

(Big lights, little sparks glitter near and shine afar; glitter here, reflecting in the lake, shine above to the clear night, sealing the happiness of deepest rest, the moon's full splendor dominates.)

When Faust wakes up from this deep sleep which betrays the luring traces of death in the very seal of happiness, his first monologue culminates in the most significant turn from the direct sun to its *Abglanz* in the rainbow of the waterfall. It is noteworthy that at the same moment, when Faust says "I" for the first time in this monologue, he is blinded by the direct light of the sun. At the place where the I speaks it is blind. I am not where I speak.

In the Helena theme the genesis of the veil is traced back to its early voyeuristic moments. The procreation of Helena is represented in a voyeuristic scene that uses all the requisites of anacreontic *delectatio morosa*. Homunculus functions as the voyeur, or rather as the interpreter of Faust's voyeuristic dream. The scenery is familiar—an open place with water, surrounded by bushes, women undressing for a bath: "Klar Gewässer / im dichten Haine! Fraun, die sich entkleiden, / Die allerbliesten!" (ll. 6903–05). Among them is Leda, Helena's future mother, approached by the swan. At the moment, however, when the text approaches the voyeuristic primal scene, the coupling of the parents, it breaks off with a dash and the scene is veiled:

Er scheint sich zu gewöhnen.—
Auf einmal aber steigt ein Dunst empor
Und deckt mit dichtgewebtem Flor
Die lieblichste von allen Szenen. (ll. 6917–20)

(He seems to get accustomed.—But suddenly a mist rises up and covers with densely woven texture the loveliest of all scenes.)

Later, in the classical Walpurgis night, Faust repeats the scene. Looking through the bushes, he hopes to see his dream come true: "Der Blick dringt scharf nach jener Hülle, / Das reiche Laub der grünen Fülle / Verbirgt die hohe Königin" (ll. 7292–94). Again the swans are approaching, among them the one destined for Leda: "Welle selbst, auf Wogen wellend, / Dringt er zu dem heiligen Ort . . ." (ll. 7305–06). Three dots mark that which cannot be seen, the place where the text turns away and the scene is veiled.

There is a veiling at the beginning, and there is a veil and a piece of clothing at the end: the remainders of Helena who has returned to the underworld after Euphorion's death. Two bodies have disappeared, two garments remain. In these two garments another difference is indicated. While Helena's veil and garment literally lift Faust up and carry him away to new adventures, to new textiles and textualities, Euphorion's garment and coat are lifted up by Phorkyas/ Mephisto as material for new poets.

A fundamental difference is indicated between the sublimating, uplifting garment of the true and genuine text, and the garment taken up as the purely epigonal text: clothes are both fulfilled and fulfilling form and empty shell. Yet the traces of the texts we have followed also indicate how difficult it is to establish the difference once and for all. Those texts that proclaim self-confidently to speak from the fullness of the heart are most likely the scene of blindness and delusion. The delusion dissolves only at the point where the subject is ready to dissolve and to read itself in the Other. The qualitative and temporal distance between the late *Faust* verses and the early anacreontic poetry is not simply one of foreign influence and Goethe's authentic expression. While there certainly is a horizon of experience that shapes poetic language, its resonances and echoes are created by the intervention and resistance of a language shaped by foreign discourses. What we have read as a continuity is the continuity of a splitting intervention that continues its articulation wherever modern subjectivity reflects upon itself. There is a historical continuity that connects Helena's veil with the monological voice of Beckett's *Unnamable*:

> Where now? Who now? When now? Unquestioning. I, say I. Unbelieving. Questions, hypotheses, call them that. Keep going, going on, call that going, call that on. Can it be that one day, off it goes on, that one day I simply stayed in, in where, instead of going out, in the old way, out to spend day and night as far away as possible, it wasn't far. Perhaps that is how it began. You think you are simply resting, the better to act when the time comes, or for no reason, and you soon find

yourself powerless ever to do anything again. No matter how it happened. It, say it, not knowing what. Perhaps I simply assented at last to an old thing. But I did nothing. I seem to speak, it is not I, about me, it is not about me. These few general remarks to begin with. What am I to do, what shall I do, what should I do, in my situation, how proceed? By aporia pure and simple? Or by affirmations and negations invalidated as uttered, or sooner or later? Generally speaking. There must be other shifts. Otherwise it would be quite hopeless. But it is quite hopeless. I should mention before going any further, any further on, that I say aporia without knowing what it means. Can one be ephectic otherwise than unawares? I don't know. With the yesses and noes it is different, they will come back to me as I go along and how, like a bird, to shit on them all without exception. The fact would seem to be, if in my situation one may speak of facts, not only that I shall have to speak of things of which I cannot speak, but also, which is even more interesting, but also that I, which is if possible even more interesting that I shall have to, I forget, no matter. And at the same time I am obliged to speak. I shall never be silent. Never.[32]

II

THE DISCOURSE OF THE OTHER: HÖLDERLIN'S VOICE AND THE VOICE OF THE PEOPLE

Stimme des Volks
Du seiest Gottes Stimme, so glaubt' ich sonst
In heil'ger Jugend; ja, und ich sag' es noch!
 Um unsre Weisheit unbekümmert
  Rauschen die Ströme doch auch und dennoch,

Wer liebt sie nicht? und immer bewegen sie
Das Herz mir, hör' ich ferne die Schwindenden,
 Die Ahnungsvollen meine Bahn nicht,
  Aber gewisser ins Meer hin eilen,

Denn selbstvergessen, allzubereit den Wunsch
Der Götter zu erfüllen, ergreift zu gern
 Was sterblich ist, wenn offnen Aug's auf
  Eigenen Pfaden es einmal wandelt,

Ins All zurück die kürzeste Bahn; so stürzt
  Der Strom hinab, er suchet die Ruh, es reißt,
    Es ziehet wider Willen ihn, von
      Klippe zu Klippe den Steuerlosen

Das wunderbare Sehnen dem Abgrund zu;
  Das Ungebundne reizet und Völker auch
    Ergreift die Todeslust und kühne
      Städte, nachdem sie versucht das Beste,

Von Jahr zu Jahr forttreibend das Werk, sie hat
  Ein heilig Ende troffen; die Erde grünt
    Und stille vor den Sternen liegt, den
      Betenden gleich, in den Sand geworfen

Freiwillig überwunden die lange Kunst
  Vor jenen Unnachahmbaren da; er selbst,
    Der Mensch, mit eigner Hand zerbrach, die
      Hohen zu ehren, sein Werk der Künstler.

Doch minder nicht sind jene den Menschen hold,
  Sie lieben wieder, so wie geliebt sie sind,
    Und hemmen öfters, daß er lang im
      Lichte sich freue, die Bahn des Menschen.

Und, nicht des Adlers Jungen allein, sie wirft
  Der Vater aus dem Neste, damit sie nicht
    Zu lang' ihm bleiben, uns auch treibt mit
      Richtigem Stachel hinaus der Herrscher.

Wohl jenen, die zur Ruhe gegangn sind,
  Und vor der Zeit gefallen, auch die, auch die
    Geopfert, gleich den Erstlingen der
      Erndte, sie haben ein Theil gefunden.

Am Xanthos lag, in griechischer Zeit, die Stadt,
  Jetzt aber, gleich den größeren die dort ruhn
    Ist durch ein Schiksaal sie dem heilgen
      Lichte des Tages hinweggekommen.

Sie kamen aber nicht in der offnen Schlacht
  Durch eigne Hand um. Fürchterlich ist davon,
    Was sort geschehn, die wunderbare
      Sage von Osten zu uns gelanget.

Es reizte sie die Güte von Brutus. Denn
  Als Feuer ausgegangen, so bot er sich

Zu helfen ihnen, ob er gleich, als Feldherr,
    Stand in Belagerung vor den Thoren.
Doch von den Mauern warfen die Diener sie
    Die er gesandt. Lebendiger ward darauf
        Das Feuer und sie freuten sich und ihnen
            Streket' entgegen die Hände Brutus
Und alle waren außer sich selbst. Geschrei
    Entstand und Jauchzen. Drauf in die Flammen warf
        Sich Mann und Weib, von Knaben stürzt' auch
            Der von dem Dach, in der Väter Schwerdt der.
Nicht räthlich ist es, Helden zu trozen. Längst
    Wars aber vorbereitet. Die Väter auch
        Da sie ergriffen waren, einst, und
            Heftig die persischen Feinde drängten,
Entzündeten, ergreiffend des Stromes Rohr,
    Daß sie das Freie fänden, die Stadt. Und Haus
        Und Tempel nahm, zum heilgen Aether
            Fliegend und Menschen hinweg die Flamme.
So hatten es die Kinder gehört, und wohl
    Sind gut die Sagen, denn ein Gedächtniß sind
        Dem Höchsten sie, doch auch bedarf es
            Eines, die heiligen auszulegen.[1]

                    Voice of the People
That you were God's voice: I believed it once,
    In my sacred youth—yes and I say it still!
        Heedless of our wisdom though
            The rivers too thunder on and yet,
Who does not love them? and my heart
    Is always touched by them—hearing the dwindling
        Ones, the ones full of premonition, take a different
            Course and hurry more surely into the sea afar.
For in self-forgetfulness, too ready to fulfill
    The god's wish, what's mortal too quickly seizes,
        When with an open eye it once travels
            Upon its own paths,
The shortest course back into the cosmos; so
    The river plunges downward seeking rest,

But it grabs, it pulls him against his will
   From ledge to ledge—rudderless the river,
Drawn down by an uncanny yearning toward the abyss.
   What is unbound provokes and the people too
      Are seized by desire for death, while defiant
         Cities, after striving toward the best,

Driving on the work, year in, year out, are
   Struck down by a sacred finish; the earth greens
      And there before the stars, like people in
         Prayer, flung into the dust before those

Inimitable ones, lies the long art, overthrown
   In free-will; he himself, the human being,
      Dashed his own work and so gave
         Homage to the lofty ones.

But they do not love mankind less for this;
   They love again, in equal measure, as they are loved,
      And often they restrict the course of man
         So that he might linger to rejoice in the light.

And not only the eagle's brood are thrown from the nest
   By the father so that they'll not stay
      With him too long; we too are driven out
         With a timely thorn by the lord.

Happy are they, they who have gone to their rest,
   Who fell before their time: they too, they too
      Were sacrificed like the earliest harvest—
         They have found a portion.

In Greek times the city lay on the Xanthos,
   But now, as with the greater ones who rest there,
      It has moved through a fate
         From the holy light of day.

But they died—not in open battle—
   By their own hand. From the East to us
      Has come the uncanny tale of what happened
         There and horrifying it was.

The generosity of Brutus provoked them.
   For when the fire had broken out, he offered
      To help them, though he himself, as general,
         Laid siege before the gates.

Yet the servants threw those he had sent
　　From the walls. And then the fire grew livelier;
　　　　They rejoiced and Brutus stretched
　　　　　　Out his hands to them

And they were beside themselves. There was
　　Shouting and jubilation. It was then that man and woman
　　　　Threw themselves into the flames, while some children
　　　　　　Leapt from rooftops, others to their fathers' blades.

Defiance of heroes is inadvisable. But it had long
　　Been prepared for. Their fathers too, when they
　　　　Were once seized in the past and sorely pressed
　　　　　　By the Persian foe,

Set fire to the reeds in the river—seizing them
　　So that they might break free in the open city.
　　　　And the flame took both house and temple—dwellers too—
　　　　　　Soared up with them to sacred aether.

That was the way the children heard it,
　　And no doubt the sagas have worth, for they
　　　　Are a memorial to the highest, but still
　　　　　　It takes someone to interpret the holy sayings.

Translated by Robert G. Eisenhauer

Goethe's symbolic veil, the text of his poetry, is the result of an I reading itself in the eye of another I, although the voice that says "I" might come from the mouth of an allegorical persona. Hölderlin's poetry stages a different scene for the poetic voice(s). The I is confronted with the voice of an Other that does not say "I," not even allegorically. One form taken by that voice is the *Voice of the People*.

The first version of this poem appeared in Neuffer's *Taschenbuch 1800* and was probably written in 1798 or early 1799. The later version with the Xantos episode, quoted here, was probably written in 1800 and appeared in the poetic almanac *Flora* in 1802.[2]

At the end of the first decade of the French Revolution, a text that identifies, albeit with some hesitancy, the voice of the people with the voice of God assumes political resonances. Strangely enough, however, even in the intense debates about Hölderlin and the French Revolution provoked by Pierre Bertaux[3] and by the politicization of literary criticism in the wake of the student movement of the late sixties, this text plays no role in the discussions. On the other hand, those who do discuss the poem hardly touch on its virulent political and historical implications. What could be closer to a fundamental interpretation of the French Revolution than the question of its supposed subject and agent: the people and its/their voice? The problem of the status of this subject is already indicated by its indecision between the singular and the plural possessive.

The question of the voice of the people implies at the same time the question of the interpretative discourse that listens and tries to understand that voice, and even to speak in its name. That is precisely the point reached by Hölderlin's text after many workings and reworkings:

> und wohl
> Sind gut die Sagen, denn ein Gedächtniß sind
> Dem Höchsten sie, doch auch bedarf es
> Eines, die heiligen auszulegen. (ll. 69–72)

(As if to seal the signature of the one who interprets, part of Hölderlin's left hand is visibly imprinted on the manuscript at the bottom, partly covering the last stanza.)[4]

A similar movement and process can be observed in other poems of Hölderlin. Among the two-stanza odes Hölderlin sent to Neuffer in the summer of 1799, in addition to *Stimme des Volks*, was the poem *An die Deutschen* (*To the Germans*). It also problematizes the agency, or in this case the lack of agency, of a people: of the Germans described as *thatenarm und gedankenvoll* (poor or lacking in action and full of thoughts). More than in *Stimme des Volks*, the solution remains open. In 1800 this poem is also subjected to an intense reworking, so much so that the ode *To the Germans* becomes a poem called *Rousseau*. This apparently radical change and break from the earlier theme parallels the textual process of *Stimme des Volks*; the historical reflection is brought to the point where another problem emerges: the status of the speaking subject and its legitimation to speak about or even in the name of history and the people. The text becomes self-reflective for political reasons. One might even say that it is only here that it becomes truly and seriously political beyond political rhetoric.

In Hölderlin's later poetry, this textual movement leads to an interrelation of text and history. History is a text written into the mute wilderness of the world, and the poetic text a hermeneutical act, deciphering and interpreting the script of history. There is, however, a problem with such an intertextuality: the hermeneutical-poetic discourse and the discourse of history do not belong to the same register, they are radically different, and in addition, they are conflictual in themselves. More precisely: the difference between them is also within them to the degree that each participates in the other.

The difference between these textual registers is occasionally formulated in terms of rational versus irrational. The reflective, rational voice of the individual subject is opposed to the irrational utterances of the masses and their unpredictable, crazy shifts. The events of the French Revolution were apt to confirm such oppositions in the eyes of the bourgeois intellectuals, some of whom were in sympathy with the revolution as long as it remained within the boundaries of an orderly debate among civilized, reasonable subjects. Hölderlin's poem was written at a time when such notions had long found their bloody refutation, and the poem is haunted by that.

The short first version is already full of tension. In the very emphasis of the recognition and acknowledgment of the voice of the people as God's voice the resistance to such an identification can be heard. The "ja, und ich sag' es noch" (yes, and I still say so) is the assertion of an I that has had some doubts. The following verses articulate the problem: the discourse of the voice of the people pursues very different courses from the paths followed by the thoughts of the I. But that difference is also one within the speaking subject: between the present assertion and an earlier faith and premonition in "heil'ger Jugend" (sacred youth). It is not so much a difference in content as a difference in the register of thought. The earlier form is *ahndet*, a mode of thought that is not yet articulated language but that forms the ground of language, and of poetic language in particular, as Hölderlin discovered in his poetological essay on the poetic spirit. The present thought takes the form of an articulated and assertive *sagen* (to say it), yet in saying it to displace it, because the metaphorical and semantic threads indicate the voice of the people might be closer to the register of sacred youth and its *Ahnung*.

The present assertion needs to be grounded in that other sphere, indicated in the poem through an argument *per analogiam*, in which the reason that reasons for its doubtful assertion has to take recourse in the slippery field of metaphor. The rivers that run their course unconcerned with the discourses of our wisdom have to support the choice of reason. The introduction of a natural phenomenon not only points in the direction of nature, it places the poem squarely within the political rhetoric of the time.

The origin of the proverbial *vox populi, vox dei* that is at the base of Hölderlin's poem is uncertain. But whatever its origin, it has been more frequently negated than asserted. In a letter to Charlemagne, Alcuin polemicized against what must already have been known as a proverb at that time: "Nec audiendi, qui solent dicere: Vox populi, vox *Dei*. Cum tumultuositas vulgi semper insaniae proxima sit."[5] (And one should not listen to those who say: the voice of the people is the voice of God. For the noisiness of the masses is always very close to madness.) The utterances of the people are reduced to an inarticulate "tumultuositas," excluded from reason, belonging to madness. The insane unpredictability of public opinion and voice has been a rhetorical topos since antiquity. With the emphatic invocation of the people during the French Revolution, the rhetoric gains new resonance. The sphere of nature becomes a privileged metaphorical playground. The revolutionary masses are described in terms of volcanic eruptions, fires out of control, floods that have broken the dams, and wild beasts unchained. As the position of nature itself is ambivalent in the eighteenth century, the threatening Other and liberating utopia, so the rhetorical function of these metaphors works on both sides of the political lines. The same "wild beast" or elemental force of nature can be the terrifying phantasm of anxiety for the enemies of the revolution who see in the action of the masses only the madness of a primal world, as well as the expression of purifying nature that sweeps and burns away the evils of society in the eyes of the sympathizers. Thunderstorms are among the favorite images. Klopstock celebrates the French Revolution as a purifying storm:

Wie die schwüle Stille den Sturm
Der vor sich her sie wirbelt, die Donnerwolken, bis Glut sie
Werden und zerschmetterndes Eis.
Nach dem Wetter atmen sie, die Lüfte, die Bäche
Rieseln, vom Laube träufelt es sacht,
Frische labet, Gerüch' umduften, die bläuliche Heitre
Lächelt, das Himmelsgemälde mit ihr.[6]

(As the sultry stillness [announces] the storm that whirls before itself the
thunderclouds until they turn into glowing fire and smashing ice. After the
thunderstorm they breathe, the airs, the brooks ripple, softly it trickles from
the leaves, freshness invigorates, scents gather around, the azure serenity
smiles, the sky's painting with it.)

Hölderlin, who refers to Klopstock's poetry as an exception in an
otherwise still childlike culture, takes up the same image of the purified air after the thunderstorm in his Pindaric ode *Wie wenn am
Feiertage*. In this poem the invocation of the historical storms again
leads to a reflection upon the task and the danger of the poetic voice.

Carl Philipp Conz celebrates the new constitution in France in
terms of thunder and floods:

Da weilet heute mein entzückter Geist
Von hohem Mitgefühle angezogen,
Vom Ruf, der donnernd dort die Luft zerreißt,
Gleich der empörten Katarakte Wogen.[7]

(There my enraptured spirit lingers today, attracted by sublime sympathy, by
the call that tears through the air with thunder like the enraged waves of
cataracts.)

The order seems inverted: the despots are rebels against nature, the
revolutionaries restore the order of nature. The young Hölderlin in
Tübingen pits the impotent discourse of tyrants against the forces of
nature: "Kann Tyrannenspruch die Meere bannen? / Hemmt Tyrannenspruch der Sterne Lauf?" (*F.A.* 2:166).

The rhetorical gesture of these metaphors can easily be turned
in the opposite political direction, as the rewriting of a poem by Lavater illustrates. The first version enthusiastically greets the revolution
because it has done away with the tyrannical beasts of prey: "Daß kein
Minister-Tigerzahn / Mehr Mark des Landes frißt."[8] In the later ver-

sion, Lavater simply exchanges the agents and leaves the metaphors untouched: the "Feiheitsrufer-Tigerzahn" now ravishes the land. In Schiller's *Lied von der Glocke* anxiety creates surreal images of castrating, bloodthirsty women (*Weiber*) who turn into hyenas with the teeth of panthers tearing the twitching hearts of their enemies to pieces. The sexual anxieties of the bourgeois patriarch mingle with the anxiety of the orderly citizen looking with horror at the revolutionary *Weiber* as furies who know no other happiness than lust.[9]

While most of these examples are of merely symptomatic value, they are nevertheless echoes of a dimension that speaks in the poetic force of Blake's apocalyptic pathos. History and nature appear as a single conflictual power. The agents of history, although human subjects, seem transcended by their actions. When the worried king enters the chamber of council, it is also an event of elemental forces of nature:

> Troubled, leaning on Necker, descends the King to his chamber of
>   council; shady mountains
> In fear utter voices of thunder; the woods of France embosom the
>   sound;
> Clouds of wisdom prophetic reply, and roll over the palace roof
>   heavy.[10]

Blake and Hölderlin reveal some of that force that echoes still in the most worn-out rhetorical clichés.

Hölderlin himself had to work through an already well-established mass of rhetorical formulas and images. The long rhymed poems of the student in Tübingen still participate in the idealized and abstractly harmonious notions of the revolution. But another element is already present: "chaos" becomes a necessary element of the process.[11] Although it is still integrated into the postulate of an ultimately harmonious historical process, it opens the path to the painful receptivity for that which the subject cannot control and simply integrate. One form taken by the otherness of the events is the elevation of the *Zeitgeist* to the status of a god: "Gott der Zeit."

The political implications of this recognition of the *Zeitgeist* as one of the gods become clear when we recall the connotations of the term *Zeitgeist* in the conservative political rhetoric up to this day.

Hölderlin's conservative contemporaries already denounced it as the basest of all spirits. A poem by Gleim on the *Geist der Zeit* exemplifies the horror of *Zeitgeist*:

> Er ist der häßlichste von allen Erdengeistern;
> Er nennt sich Patriot,
> Und seine Freunde sind von allen Henkermeistern
> Die Blutbegierigsten! Er schlägt mit Keulen tod![12]

(He is the ugliest of all the earthly spirits; he calls himself a patriot, and his friends are of all the henchmen the most bloodthirsty ones! He kills with clubs.)

Gleim also wrote a poetic response to Klopstock's celebration of the Etats généraux, in which he expressed his opinion of the "voice of the people":

> Nicht mehr als etwa nur zwölfhundert
> Despoten wollt ihr? Ha! mich wundert
> Daß ihr, der Despotie so hold!
> Nicht mehr noch ihrer haben wollt?
>
> . . . .
>
> Den *Einen* macht' er's euch zu toll,
> Den, dächt' ich, zwänge man noch wohl
> Auch ist des *Einen* Wuth nicht erblich:
> Zwölfhundert aber sind nicht sterblich.
> Der Weise, dächt' ich, sollt' ich meinen,
> Der hielt es immer mit dem *Einen*.[13]

(No more than around twelve hundred despots do you want? Ha! I wonder that you, so fond of despotism, don't want any more of them? [. . .] *One*, if he gets too crazy, one could, I would think, still handle, also, the craziness of *one* is not hereditary: but twelve *hundred* are not mortal. The sage, I would think, I should believe, would still hold on to the *one*.)

Gleim's emphatic opposition of the *one* against the madness and rage of the many, the insistent repetition of the I that thinks and opines ("dächt' ich," "sollt' ich meinen") against the folly of those who trust the unpredictable and uncontrollable many, finds a more subtle parallel in the tension between Hölderlin's I and the voice of the people.

The difference, however, in Hölderlin's reworking of the problem of the *Zeitgeist* and the voice of the people is precisely that it is a working-through that does not allow for a simple denunciation of the opposition. It is rather an *Auseinandersetzung* that involves an immersion in the Other as much as a separation and differentiation from the Other. It is a hesitating recognition of the Other that is also aware of the difference of its own voice and thought.

While the short version of the poem laconically states the stakes, the later versions elaborate the process of working through. There is no doubt that the voice of the people is the voice of a threatening Other for the voice of the I. As such it is negative, even deadly. The different versions of Hölderlin's poem try to come to terms with this negativity. Hegel makes the same demand of the spirit, who gains its power not by turning away from the negative (as when we say: "This is false" or "This is nothing") but by remaining before it and facing it.[14]

The expanding versions of *Stimme des Volks* are the labor of this lingering before the negative, the forceful effort not to turn away, until at the end the one, *der Eine*, can be invoked, in contrast to Gleim, who posits a simple opposition between the one and the many.

The difficulty of Hölderlin's text is related to this ever-expanding lingering as well as to an underlying conflict between desire and will. The difficulty of reading is doubled by the difficulty of describing it. Verbal description depends on a certain order of sequence. But sequence is a problem in a text that is dominated by a logic of lingering and repetition. Perhaps we can investigate the problem of sequence via one of those words that function as connecting members. Let us begin with a conjunction, since a conjunction inaugurates the expansion of the original two stanzas:

> Denn selbstvergessen, allzubereit den Wunsch
> Der Götter zu erfüllen, ergreifft zu gern
> Was sterblich ist und einmal offnen
> Auges auf eigenem Pfade wandelt,
> Ins All zurück die kürzeste Bahn, so stürzt
> Der Strom hinab. (F.A. 5:593, ll. 9–14)

"Denn" (for, because) seems to indicate a clear logical function: it establishes a causal connection for the poetological analogy of the course of the rivers. Yet the connection is a problematic one, because the analogy connects the rivers with something that is mortal and something that moves along its own path with open eyes ("offnen / Auges auf eigenem Pfade"). This quality does not fit the stream. It implies an individual ("eigenem") consciousness. In the Rhine poem rivers are referred to as the blindest of the sons of the gods. The analogy between that which moves with open eyes along its own path and the rivers that fall from cliff to cliff is an uneasy one. It seems possible only when that which moves with open eyes along its own path negates that very quality and follows, "selbstvergessen" (forgetting itself), a mysterious desire toward the abyss ("wunderbare Sehnen dem Abgrund zu," l. 17). The analogy also contains an opposition.

The same dialectic unfolds the relationship between men and gods. The desire for the abyss is the desire of the gods ("Wunsch / Der Götter"), articulated through human beings. To fulfill that desire would mean self-destruction. But since the gods need humans to articulate their desire, they must prevent its fulfillment.

A similar paradox appears between the voice of the I and the voice of the people, acknowledged by the I "den Himmlischen / Zulieb" (for the sake of the heavenly ones):

> Drum weil sie fromm ist, ehr' ich den Himmlischen
> Zulieb des Volkes Stimme, die ruhige,
> Doch um der Götter und der Menschen
> Willen, sie ruhe zu gern nicht immer! (ll. 49–52)

The voice of the people appears on the same scene as the gods. The voice of the I therefore honors it as it honors the gods, and in their name. Yet the I also expresses a distance and a warning to the people, and this too in the name of the gods, or more precisely in the name of gods and men: "um der Götter und der Menschen / Willen." It is in the name of a relationship that guarantees the being of both. Because they are both grounded excentrially outside of themselves, desire must change its direction. The rhythmic emphasis on the word "Willen," grammatically weakened to a prepositional function, directs attention to its substantive derivation from *Willen* (will) while at the same time positioning the substance prepositionally in terms of relationship. The text points to a double prepositional relation and its difference: "Zu liebe" (for the sake of, for the love of) and "um . . .

willen" (because of, for the sake of the will of). Love and will, desire and will, which Kant subjected to a rigorous analysis of differentiation and separation to the point where the one must have nothing to do with the other (what Freud describes as the work of *Isolieren*), enter the scene of a new *Auseinandersetzung*, of differentiation and entanglement.

But the major restlessness of the text concentrates on another term: that of rest (*Ruhe*). It is the restlessness of a desire that wants to come to rest as quickly as possible in the abyss of everlasting peace. Hölderlin saw two historical forms of this desire: the French and their revolution which drove the guillotine into ever more feverish activity, and the Germans who seemed to have settled peacefully for rest already: "Thatenarm und gedankenvoll." This latter form seems to trouble Hölderlin more than the guillotine. The poetic voice raises a somber warning: "Doch um der Götter und der Menschen / Willen, sie ruhe zu gern nicht immer."

The warning implies the authority of the poetic voice. In the last revision of the poem, the voice of the people is subjected to a wary questioning:

> So hatten es die Kinder gehört, und wohl
> Sind gut die Sagen, denn ein Gedächtniß sind
> Dem Höchsten sie, doch auch bedarf es
> Eines, die heiligen auszulegen. (ll. 69–72)

As in the earlier versions, there is still a mixture of acceptance, acknowledgment, and distancing. But the subject is no longer a knowing I, but the agency of a "one" speaking in the name of what "it" says. The voice of the people appears as *Sagen* (legends; literally, sayings) that have no namable subject. They indicate a text that comes from somewhere else.

How does the poem come to the "somewhere else" of this other scene? Apparently through a mere anecdotal extension or detour, illustrating "Das wunderbare Sehnen dem Abgrund zu" and "die Todeslust" (the yearning for, or the pleasure of, death). The anecdote introduces a new principle: repetition that marks historical action as the return of something older ("Längst . . . vorbereitet") as well as discourse itself. The agents are decentered, quite literally outside themselves: "Und alle waren außer sich selbst" (l. 57). This decentering brings about changes in subtle details. While those who have gone to rest and have been sacrificed prematurely gained *"ihr* Teil" (their share) in the earlier version, the later version speaks of *"ein* Theil" (a share) they have found (l. 40).

Desire for death ("Todeslust"), decentering the subject, and the principle of repetition emerge as the dominant threads of the poem. To name the constellation in such a way recalls in an almost embarrassingly obtrusive manner Freud's *Beyond the Pleasure Principle.*[15] Freud's text not only introduces the new concepts of the repetition compulsion and the death drive, it also forces a revision of Freud's toppology with crucial consequences, for the placing of the subject in psychoanalysis is essentially a reading of *Beyond the Pleasure Principle.*[16]

Such parallels are inherently problematic for the interpreter. They invite easy analogies instead of immanent reading and argument. All too often, such analogies are temptations for a translation of one text into the categories of another text. And yet we cannot read without such interventions of other texts; we translate whenever we "understand" or interpret. There is no innocent, original reading. That is precisely the point of the last stanza of Hölderlin's poem: the appeal to the interpreter to translate the *Sagen.*

To read Hölderlin's *Stimme des Volks* after Freud's *Beyond the Pleasure Principle* is not a matter of asserting similar concepts, such as "death drive" or "repetition compulsion." If Freud is right about their role in the agency of the subject, they will speak in countless other texts as well. I would prefer to emphasize the verb "to read": to read Hölderlin after Freud, and to read Freud after Hölderlin. This reading opens up parallels on another level of the texts. It reveals striking similarities in their strategies and procedures, all the more surprising since the two texts not only are historically far apart, but also belong to different genres.

Hölderlin wrote an ode, while Freud wrote a "scientific" text leading into "speculation." Yet, within this difference, a striking similarity appears: both texts stretch the limits of their respective genre to the point of transgression. Hölderlin uses the devices of the ode, which by tradition is open to narrative and reflective elements within the lyrical realm; but he uses these elements so much that they threaten to dissolve the genre. In a similar way, Freud underplays the rules of the scientific text with its own elements. Those parts of the text that borrow most strongly from the terminology of the natural sciences are also the ones that stand under Freud's own warning that what follows "is speculation" (G.W. 13:23; S.E. 18:24). Yet perhaps this warning is only a distraction, a strategy, not uncommon within scientific and scholarly discourse, to cover less obvious deviations.

In both texts, narrative passages play a central role in a subtle but radical displacement. The position of the narrative passages, however, differs in the two texts: while Hölderlin places his narrative toward the end, Freud opens his text after a brief introduction with a story. The difference in the narrative position can be read in terms of the textual genres involved: Hölderlin's narrative would then be a poetic illustration, a stabilization of the lyrical mood in the narrative scene. Freud's story would be the empirical case from which the scientific analysis evolves. Yet it does not take long to recognize that Hölderlin's story cannot be reduced to an illustration, because it introduces a new dimension that destabilizes the preceding text and opens it up to a new question. On the other hand, Freud's anecdote of the child's play is, in scientific terms, too singular to carry inductive weight. Its singularity appears like the singular event of the traumatic shock that redirects the whole thrust of the text.

In fact, both narratives seem to articulate an initial shattering of firm assumptions. Both texts begin with a skeptical re-vision of former beliefs and opinions. Hölderlin looks back on what he once heard and accepted in "sacred youth." Freud begins his essay with a condensed summary of one of the major principles of psychoanalysis: "In psychoanalysis we assume unhesitatingly that the course of the psychic processes is automatically regulated by the pleasure principle, i.e., we believe that it is stimulated each time by an unpleasurable tension" (G.W. 13:3; S.E. 18:7). The pleasure principle, unhesitatingly (*unbedenklich*) assumed by psychoanalytic theory, is not rejected by the hesitation of this reflective text, but the introduction of new principles begins to shift it into a different position. Yet these new principles in Freud's theory also point back to much earlier speculations of Freud, not unlike Hölderlin's poem that resumes the confrontation with notions from a sacred youth. Freud's *Beyond the Pleasure Principle* also resumes and revises some concepts from his speculations on the psychic apparatus in the 1890s. Repetition, a theme of both texts, seems to be the principle of their genesis as well.

Both texts, then, are marked by an attempt to reformulate a discourse that has been destabilized and decentered within itself. The formulation is at the same time an attempt at a new grounding. The terms of the reformulation operate by analogy in both texts.

Hölderlin attempts to grasp the phenomenon of repetition and to interpret it (and thus to control it) when he shifts from a passive to an active mode:

> die Väter auch
> Da sie *ergriffen* waren einst, und
> Heftig die persischen Feinde drängten,
> Entzündeten, *ergreiffend* des Stromes Rohr,
> Daß sie das Freie fänden, die Stadt. (ll. 62–66; my emphasis)

The transformation of the passive mode into the active mode occurs toward the end of Hölderlin's poem. Freud begins his tentative interpretation of the child's repetition with the following explanation: "Through impartial observation one gets the impression that there is another motive for the child to turn the experience of absence into a game. It was passive, hit [*betroffen*] by the experience, and assumes now an active role, by repeating it playfully, although it was unpleasurable" (*G.W.* 13:14; *S.E.* 18:16).

Yet there is also a substantial difference between the two interpretations, at least in their immediate effect. The child in Freud's anecdote supposedly frees himself through the repetition in the active role; he becomes independent and survives the traumatic absence. Hölderlin's paradigm is also seen as an act of liberation ("Daß sie ins Freie fänden"), but the liberation is at the same time an act of self-destruction. Those who move from being seized (*ergriffen*) to become active agents who *seize* (*ergreiffend*) seize only their own destruction. They seem to perform what Lacan has perceptively described as the phantasm of existential freedom:

> L'existentialisme se juge aux justifications qu'il donne des impasses subjectives qui en résultent en effet: une liberté qui ne s'affirme jamais

si authentique que dans les murs d'une prison, une exigence d'engagement ou s'exprime l'impuissance de la pure conscience à surmon-
ter aucune situation, une idéalisation voyeuriste-sadique du rapport
sexuel, une personnalité qui ne si réalise que dans le suicide, une
conscience de l'autre qui ne se satisfait que par le meurtre hegelien. [17]

This might be one of the reasons why Hölderlin could become the
mouthpiece of all kinds of existentialism. That is possible, however,
only where the *Sage* of the poem is removed from the textual process
that ends in the demand for an interpretation and an interpreter.

This demand introduces a new category: repetition appears as
discourse (*Sagen, auslegen*) and as memory (*Gedächtniß*) rather than
as action. In this sphere, Hölderlin's demand joins Freud's demand
to remember instead of to repeat (*G.W.* 13:16; *S.E.* 18:18). At the
end, the desire of the gods would be fulfilled in the discourse of the
Sagen. Yet they are not the end either, since they too are in need of
interpretation. As interpreters we continue to be the instruments of
the gods, whose immortality needs our tongues and pens and even
our word processors.

Our parallel reading of Hölderlin and Freud cannot and must
not reduce them to an identity. It is their distance from each other
that allows a reading of each through the other and a reflection that
has its focus outside both of them in the *Auslegung.*

Hölderlin questions the voice of the people as the voice of God.
But he does not negate it, nor does he declare it false. He questions
the course and discourse of his specific historical time as well as his
own discourse that loses its own conviction as the voice of reason and
wisdom in the confrontation with the voice of the Other. This does
not allow us to turn Hölderlin's poetry into the voice of the irrational
against the Enlightenment, since his poetry is deeply marked by the
discourse and thought of the Enlightenment. It is not by chance that
at the climax of a poem, key words of the Enlightenment often appear,
as for example in the fifth stanza of *Stutgard*:

Und allmächtig empor ziehet ein ahnendes Volk,
Bis die Jünglinge sich der Väter droben erinnern,
Mündig und hell vor euch steht der besonnene Mensch. (ll. 88–90)

(And almightily rises up a people with divination, until the youths remember their fathers up there, mature and enlightened stands before you prudent humanity.)

Mündig, hell, besonnen, condense the idea of Enlightenment. Yet this appeal to the key terms of Enlightenment does not exclude a critique of a form of enlightenment that invokes the maturity of the sovereign speaking subject without acknowledgment of the ground from which the subject speaks, and with no ears for the voice of the Other. (*Mündig,* to be of age, mature, comes from *Mund,* mouth; it designates the status of an *infans* that has grown up to use his/her mouth and to speak for him/herself.) Jakob Michael Reinhold Lenz, Goethe's friend until he was abruptly banned from the court of Weimar under mysterious circumstances, had already embodied the deafness of such an "enlightened" voice in the figure of the *Geheime Rat* in the play *Der Hofmeister* (1772). The very reasonable speeches of this secret council are confronted with the discourse of a subject named Läuffer (runner). It is not so much that one discourse refutes the other, since they run past each other, but the *Geheime Rat* does not hear the other, while Läuffer hears him and what he hears becomes reason: *Vernunft* (a word that comes from *vernehmen,* to hear) violently and literally cuts off what has bothered Läuffer's speech and acts.

Hölderlin's poem is a poetic act of reason that listens and hears: a *Vernehmen* of the voice of the people that implies yet another connotation of *vernehmen:* to interrogate. In this interrogation, the interrogator is not in the position of power that would make him deaf, but rather his voice takes shape as the voice of reason in its entanglement with the voice of the Other. The interrogator as the voice of reason is always vulnerable and aware of his or its own fragility and contingency. In the recourse to the voice of the Other, the promise of another discourse is indicated:

> Viel hat von Morgen an,
> Seit ein Gespräch wir sind und hören voneinander
> Erfahren der Mensch; bald sind wir aber Gesang. (*Friedensfeier,*
>   ll. 91–93)

(Much has experienced Man from morning on, since we have been a discourse and have heard of each other; but soon we will be song.)

III

PUBLIC VOICE
AND PRIVATE VOICE:
FREUD, HABERMAS,
AND THE DIALECTIC OF
ENLIGHTENMENT

"Ach" (Alkmene in Kleist's *Amphytrion*)

The voice of the people is the voice of God. We heard it in not so sacred a youth. And we still hear it, albeit in a more secularized, scientific vocabulary. It is now called communication.

"Yes, and I still say it." Hölderlin's hesitant reaffirmation of the voice of the people as the voice of God does not transform the speaking I into a collective voice "we." On the contrary, at the beginning and at the end there is an emphatic distancing between I and that other voice. That voice and its *Sagen* are "good," but there is also the need for *one* to interpret the sacred ones. Hölderlin's voice does not join the voice of the people in a consensus. Just as the rivers run their own course, without heeding our reason and wisdom, the voice of the people in Hölderlin's poem has its own direction and a sense that is not the sense of the I. There is no consensus possible between them.

Such a difference and otherness has no place in theories of communication that consider consensus as the fundamental principle. "Communication" has become a sacred term particularly in Germany. Some text linguists declare texts that are non-communicative to be non-texts. This is a valuable model. It says what is at the center of communication theory: exclusion in the name of universal inclusion. What cannot be incorporated will be spit out into non-existence.

Whoever does not communicate is suspicious. In the democratic postwar society in West Germany, exclusion no longer takes place in the name of the *Vaterland*, but rather in the name of communication. We are now dealing with pathological cases of individuals with private-language deformations (*privatsprachlich deformierte Individuen*). We hope to be able to help them, of course.

Habermas's theory of communication is a complex and sophisticated articulation of the relationship between communication and consensus. It has been and still is widely discussed.[1] It would be foolish to attempt in a short chapter to enter into a full discussion of *the theory*. Indeed, my own procedure here questions the very thrust of such a discussion and moves instead toward a specific reading of Habermas's reading. It is odd that while most critics and followers of Habermas agree that language, speech, and communication are at the center of his thinking and writing, they are solely treated as objects of the theory. The theory itself and its performance as reading, speaking, writing, even perhaps communicating, seem to be of no interest. The praxis of discourse is bracketed. This bracketing takes place wherever the intention of the theory is used to defend Habermas against his critics; it is the most common defense of Habermas. Even critics who see one of the distinguishing marks of Critical Theory in "the possibility of a theoretical and critical language which goes beyond the mere understanding of subjective meanings to investigate objective meanings which obtain behind the backs of the subjects involved" refrain from reading the theory itself in this way.[2]

To read in such a way implies the risk of falling into the hypo- critical gesture of "unmasking" the speaking subject by pointing trium- phantly at what goes on behind its back. The gesture might lose some of its hypocritical implications if it is performed with the resonance of that which goes on behind my back. In reading a text by someone else, and not just by anyone else but someone who has no doubt participated in shaping my own thought, I also read to a certain point my own reading. Only to a certain point, however, because whatever is written and said reaches further than I can read.

My reading of Habermas reading Freud is based on my own interest in Freud as well as in the position and role that Habermas attributes to Freud and psychoanalysis in the great scheme of com- municative order, particularly at the time when he wrote *Erkenntnis und Interesse*.[3] "Reflection" is the key term of the book as well as of Habermas's understanding of psychoanalysis. Explicitly, Habermas sees the reconstruction of the history of reflection as his project against positivism: "The fact that we deny reflection *is* positivism," he declares programmatically in the introduction (*E*, 9). In this attempt at recon- struction, the chapter on Freud becomes a paradigm of reflection (*als ein Beispiel*; *E*, 10), or even as the only graspable paradigm (*als das einzige greifbare Beispiel*; *E*, 262) where self-reflection finds a meth- odological articulation.

To locate this placement and perhaps displacement of psycho- analysis and to clarify its implications, let us turn to Habermas's first important book on the *Structural Change of the Public Sphere*, where the major terms and their relationship to each other are already es- tablished.[4]

The analysis in *Structural Change of the Public Sphere* offers a wealth of historical material concerning the changes in the relation- ship between the public and private spheres in the eighteenth century, and their further development in the nineteenth century toward mod- ern consumer society and cultural industry. At the same time, it is an attempt at a model of an interdisciplinary methodology that brings together and integrates sociology, economy, legal studies, political science, and intellectual history (S.W., 7). The book's major claim is the emergence of a new form of a liberal public sphere in the eighteenth century based on the ideals of consensus formation and the questioning of authority in the name of rational legitimation through public debate between free, equal subjects.

The book had an unusual and lasting impact in Germany on the theoretical debates within sociology, political science, intellectual history, and literary criticism. Its influence was also noticeable in the theory and praxis of university and school reforms during the seventies.

There was no lack of critical reaction either. Hohendahl's well-informed review of the Habermas critics differentiates between two major critical thrusts: the empirical critique is directed at particular details and leads in some cases to the reproach that the Habermasian model of a liberal bourgeois public sphere ultimately has a very small historical base for support.[5] While some of this criticism has its own blind positivistic spots, it cannot be simply brushed away with the argument that it concentrates solely on "peripheral weaknesses."[6] The decision to declare certain resistant phenomena as peripheral is already an ideological act of marginalization in the very tradition of the Enlightenment that was criticized by Adorno and Horkheimer. And in this particular case, it means the marginalization of the overwhelming dominant bourgeois *praxis* against its dominant rhetoric.

A closer inspection of Habermas's historical material is called for. Despite the immense quantities of quotations and material from various spheres, they belong almost exclusively to one particular type of documentation: statements about discourse intentions and studies about the forms of intercourse and discourse within the bourgeois public sphere. For example, there are lots of quotations from primary and secondary sources about the development of the English Parliament, or about literary criticism and its intentions, but no analysis of a single actual discourse in either of these realms. When materials of another kind appear, e.g., descriptions of the real economic and social relations, they are almost invariably at odds with the statements of intention and the bourgeois self-expressions.

Habermas is aware of this inherent tension and tries to come to terms with it in a chapter called "Idea and Ideology." But the chapter never comes to a critical differentiation between "idea" and "ideology," but moves undecidedly between the two in the form of a constant "on the one hand"—"on the other hand." Oskar Negt and Alexander Kluge, two of the most perceptive readers and critics of Habermas, have formulated this procedure as follows: "The shifting between an idealizing and critical observation of the public sphere does not lead to a dialectical, but to an ambivalent result."[7] Ambivalence is the phenomenon of a compromise formation in a conflict that is not allowed to open up to a full and radical *Auseinandersetzung*. If we read it after Freud, it is a symptom of bourgeois compromise formations; he reenacts the symptom.

The structure of this central idea-ideology chapter is noteworthy. It is a teleological movement from the negative prehistory of the concept of "public opinion" to its classical and positive articulation in Kant (the secular form of the people's voice as the voice of God), to its critique by Hegel and Marx, and from there into the modern history of its disintegration. As much as Habermas seems to participate in Hegel's and Marx's critique of bourgeois ideology, his real model of identification is Kant. But it is a slightly expurgated Kant, even in passages where Habermas quotes him as a key witness. In a passage from the *Critique of Practical Reason*, Kant testifies to a society involved in reasoning and discussion: "If one pays attention to the course of conversations in mixed society which contains not only scholars and intellectuals [*Vernünftler*] but also business people and women, he finds that not only stories and wit find a place in the entertainment, but also reasoning."[8]

"If one pays attention to . . ." (*Wenn man . . . acht hat*): it is a phrase that occurs at various particular moments in Kant's texts, most emphatically in the *Critique of Practical Reason*. Kant's reasoning discourse pays tribute to an Other and listens to it: *Vernunft* as *Vernehmen* (to listen to, to interrogate). It is, however, a particular kind of listening: *acht haben* (to pay attention) presupposes *Achtung* (respect, awe). The phenomenology of *Achtung* as the impossible link between pure, practical reason and our phenomenal being is the Sadian kernel of Kant's moral imperative, the result of a process in which humiliation (*Demütigung*), contempt (*Verachtung*), pain, and displeasure are all experienced as a form of bliss. The ear (like all ears) that is constituted in and through *Achtung* is attuned only to specific tones. It is above all the organ needed to hear that utterance which is, in its very essence, a voice: the voice of conscience. This voice is not identical with consciousness, but it is reason insofar as reason speaks.

The reasoning discourse that pays attention hears itself speaking above all. Thus, *wenn man acht hat*, one can hear among these mixed discourses the voice of reason participating in the conversation. But Kant's ear hears the voice of reason among other registers of discourse such as telling stories (*Erzählen*) and joking (*Scherzen*), and it almost seems as if reasoning finds its place among these other registers as a latecomer. In any case, it finds its place, but it does not take over. It is part of a conversational chorus.

In commenting on this passage of Kant, Habermas casually silences the other voices and hears only the reasoning which seems to have occupied all the places. Although we can no longer hear the voices speaking to Kant, we can still *read* the texts of the Enlightenment. We can also read its obsession with jokes, wit, comedy, tears, ghosts and ghostbusters, *Schwärmer* and *Geisterseher*, criminals, clowns, and *Hanswürste*.

Habermas's work has opened up a project worthy of pursuit, but it has been pursued with a wider range of receptivity to the various and often heterogeneous voices of discourse by his students and critics Oskar Negt and Alexander Kluge. Their book *Öffentlichkeit und Erfahrung* (Public Sphere and Experience) already indicates in its title their difference from Habermas's project. Since the subtitle introduces the "proletarian public sphere," the book has often been read simply as an attempt to substitute the proletarian for the bourgeois public sphere. Yet already the subtitle projects not a substitution of the one for the other, but a constellation of terms: organization of experience in the bourgeois *and* proletarian public sphere. As the book demonstrates, the "and" is not a harmonious copula, and the heterogeneity demands a procedure radically different from Habermas. There is another kind of attention at work here: "Historical ruptures—crises, war, capitulation, revolution, counterrevolution—designate concretely the constellation of social forces in which a proletarian public sphere forms itself. Because it does not exist as a dominant public sphere, it has to be reconstructed from these ruptures, from marginal phenomena, from rudimentary traces."⁹ While Habermas tries to reconstruct his model from the self-expressed ideal of the bourgeoisie and from the coherence of its rationalizations, Negt and Kluge analyze the ruptures and incoherences.

The difference of method is most evident in the kinds of stories that are told. Habermas's stories are almost exclusively synoptic summaries of developments: stories are immediately subsumed to history. The stories told by Negt and Kluge are often anecdotes, interspersed in the argument. The relationship between theoretical text and stories varies constantly, even in the textual arrangement. Stories occasionally appear as footnotes to the text, but sometimes a theoretical reflection forms a footnote to a story. There is no firm hierarchy between these registers, nor are the stories simply illustrations to the theory, but often, particularly in the footnotes, they are subversive: the feet that run in another direction from the one pointed out by the main text.

While the coherence of the system needs limits, delineates borders, and defines, the stories make the borderlines slip. Exclusions are revoked, but not denied. Habermas wants to exclude exclusion in the ideal model and is thus forced to rigorous exclusions in the discursive praxis.

Exclusion and inclusion are a central part of the exchange between public and private sphere. Habermas evokes such an economy with a particularly strong rhetorical pathos in the model of the Greek *polis*, the city-state, and its opposition to the *oikos*, the silent private sphere of the house. These two spheres are both strictly separated and mutually dependent. But it is not a symmetrical interdependence: the public life of the *polis* is grounded in the secret silence of the house. Only a master of the house (*oikodespotes*) can participate as a citizen in the life of the *polis* and speak in the *agora*. But the sphere of the house that grounds and guarantees the public speech remains silent outside of speech:

> The position in the polis is based on the position of the oikodespotes. The reproduction of life, the work of the slaves, the service of the women, birth and death, are carried out and occur under his protection; the realm of necessity and of evanescence remain immersed in the

shadow of the private sphere. In contrast, the public sphere, as the Greeks understood it, rises as a realm of freedom and of constancy. Being [*das, was ist*] comes into appearance, becomes visible for all only in the light of the public sphere. In the conversations of the citizens among each other things come into language and take shape; in the competition of equals among each other the best ones emerge and gain their essence—the immortality of fame. While the needs and what is necessary for the preservation of life are modestly hidden within the limits of the oikos, the polis offers a free field for honorable distinction. To be sure, the citizens associate as equals with equals (*homoioi*), but each one tries to distinguish himself (*aristoiein*). The virtues, as codified by Aristotle, are proved and acknowledged only in the public sphere. (S.W., 16)

The unusual rhetorical intensity of this passage indicates a strong affective investment. I suspect that the desire behind the Habermasian project is condensed in this Greek model. Despite the many interspersed Greek terms, the major metaphor belongs to the Enlightenment of the eighteenth century: it is the *light* of the public sphere that shines in the center. In this light things come into appearance, identity is constituted. The light wants to shine on each and all in order that nothing be excluded.

The passion to exclude nothing is grounded in the fear of being excluded oneself, and it generates the compulsion to exclude ever more. The *oikos*, the private sphere, becomes the scene of the ambivalence of exclusion. It is the secret place, excluded from the *agora* and yet its ground. Two models can be detected in Habermas's treatment of this exclusion. We can read the liberal public sphere as the light that redeems the obscure dark place of the private *oikos* without, however, doing away with it: the private sphere would constitute the public sphere. The house is no longer simply the secret place of the reproduction of life, but the scene of production and reproduction of public discourse.

Another possible reading is suggested by the metaphors of the text. The house, the secret place of the reproduction of life, immersed and modestly (*schamhaft*) hidden and in the shadow of the private sphere, resembles Habermas's understanding of Freud's id. For him, the id is at the same time the sphere of deformed private discourse, blocked off from the light and discourse of the public sphere. In this model, the private sphere, like Freud's id, is to be overcome and integrated in the public light and discourse. Freud's "Wo es war, soll Ich werden" is understood as an act of appropriation of the Other.

The Greek model leads to the formulation of the Habermasian project as the hope "to grasp systematically [*systematisch in den Griff zu bekommen*] our own society beyond a sociological clarification of its concept through one of its central categories" (*S.W.*, 17). The power that goes beyond the concept (*Begriff*) to a practical grasp (*Griff*) is reflection, a kind of meta-power that grasps all other power and dissolves it. The Freud chapter starts with that which is graspable: "Psychoanalysis is relevant for us as the only graspable [*greifbare*] example of a science that makes a claim for methodical self-reflection" (*E*, 262).

Habermas privileges the graspable in a field that in Freud's praxis and writing is marked by gestures of suspended attention, of receiving, assuming, accepting, acknowledging. Something might be grasped, but hardly in the instrumental grasp of the "hard" sciences. The implicit argument in Habermas would be that this is true for the analytical praxis, but that the result of this praxis would be the double grasping of a social praxis and a metapsychological theory.

Freud could never completely separate metapsychology from the process that produces it and of which it speaks. It is not by chance, then, that Habermas ultimately must reject Freud's metapsychology as Freud's misunderstanding of his own praxis. It is not a matter of debating specific theoretical contents, but a difference in the fundamental conception of the psychoanalytic scene, marked by two dominant terms: Habermas declares psychoanalysis to be a *discipline* that moves in "the element of *self-reflection*" (*E*, 262). To the degree that psychoanalysis has developed historically into a discipline and a school that demands discipline and control, it has demonstrated over and over again that it is not in control. It is the scene of those conflicts for which it provides a stage. This drama, in which the analysts perform a text they cannot control, can be read from the beginning of psychoanalysis to the tragicomedies of the *Ecole freudienne*. These dramas are not unique to psychoanalysis, but are the necessary effects of disciplines and institutions that cannot escape the antagonisms of the exclusions on which they are founded. In identifying psycho-analysis as a discipline, Habermas stages the conflict of his project: as discipline, psychoanalysis participates in the antagonistic battles of exclusions, at the same time that it is supposed to be the medium of non-exclusion.

Self-reflection is the magical power that makes psychoanalysis this privileged medium. Habermas thus introduces as a central term a category that plays no role in Freud's texts. Indeed, Habermas calls it the *element* in which psychoanalysis moves and before which it must legitimize itself. In contrast to Freud, the psychoanalytic process is not the court that questions the self-consciousness. Self-consciousness asserts itself beforehand as the highest judging agency. Habermas stages his book as a kind of trial: "If one were to reconstruct the philosophical discussion of modern time in the form of a court trial . . ." (*E*, 300). When Habermas chooses as judge in this trial that agency whose competence is questioned by psychoanalysis, the outcome is already predetermined. And indeed we read at the end of the chapter the judgment that psychoanalysis has denied its true mas-ter, origin, and goal: "The structural model denies the origin of its own categories in a process of enlightenment" (*ibid.*).

The text preceding the judgment is prescribed. The reading comes after the predetermined interpretation, as the positions of quo-tations indicate: they are almost invariably the illustrative end point of an argument, rarely the beginning from which the text unfolds its reading and explication. That can produce the unintended effect, however, that the subsequent quotation starts to interpret the preced-ing text. Quotations can say what the text discreetly hides.

Interpretation is the major theme of Habermas's text: "Psycho-analysis appears first only as a special form of interpretation" (*E*, 263). Psychoanalysis is thus doubly predetermined: it moves in the *element* of self-reflection, and the form of its movement is a special kind of interpretation.

The insistence on self-reflection and interpretation presents itself as an emancipatory gesture. It wants to understand psychoanalysis as a process toward the actualization of subjectivity and thus defend it against a degeneration into pure psychotechnology. It is important to understand the passion of this gesture in order to understand Habermas and to perceive the dialectical irony in this claim. The effects of this dialectic become noticeable in the ruptures and in the gliding of the text, above all in that which is excluded or bracketed in order to exclude exclusion.

In a confrontation of Dilthey and Freud, Habermas sketches the similarity and difference between philological and psychoanalytical interpretation:

> Like Freud, Dilthey is aware of the unreliability and confusion of subjective memory; both see the necessity of a critique that purifies [*reinigt*] the mutilated text that is transmitted [*den verstümmelten Text der Überlieferung*]. But the philological procedure differs from the psychoanalytical critique in the fact that it takes recourse, through an appropriation of the objective spirit, to the intentional coherence of subjective opinion as the ultimate basis of experience. (*E*, 265)

Habermas does put his finger on the crucial difference between the two hermeneutical models: while distortions and displacements are of an accidental nature for Dilthey, Freud treats them in a systematic mode; they are not merely the hiding of the truth, they are its *locus*. Yet despite this observation made with a consenting affirmative gesture toward Freud's model, the praxis of Habermas's method remains closer to Dilthey. The necessity of interpretation is seen as an act of purification (*reinigen*). That seems somewhat odd given the description of the text: the text transmitted by memory or on paper has been damaged; more precisely, mutilated (*verstümmelt*). Purification (*reinigen*) is in essence a negative act: taking something away, something that does not belong there in order to find the "pure" authentic essence. A mutilated body is one that has been deprived already of some of its parts. To respond to that situation with a further deprivation might sound a little excessive; but perhaps it is a surgeon's dream.

One might object that we are taking metaphors too literally. Habermas is obviously thinking of the philological model of critical text editing. The philologist who is confronted by various versions of a text with no original authentic document available will indeed generally see his major task as a labor of purification. Through meticulous detective work, he will try to remove everything that seems the result of later additions, "corrections," falsifications, and so on.

This very model has been questioned within that field where it has its firmest basis: in classical philology. The text editions developed by a group of classicists in Lille under the direction of Jean Bollack are no longer "purified" texts presenting an authentic original, but rather an archaeology of textual history with their own significance. These editions are the philological counterpart to Freud's hermeneutics.

Despite his nod in the direction of Freud's interpretive model, Habermas remains in his metaphors and praxis in the tradition of a philology that dreams of an original, authentic text to be reconstructed through a process of purification. Its paradigm is the coherence of a horizon of meaning guaranteed by an ideal of totality and closure. Coherence draws the borderlines that define what is inside, outside, or on the margins. The marginal case becomes the test case where Habermas draws his line:

> The grammar of everyday speech regulated not only the coherence and interrelation [*Zusammenhang*] of symbols but also the interrelation of linguistic elements, patterns of acting, and expressions. In the normal case [*Normalfall*] these three categories of expression complement each other so that linguistic utterances "fit" together with interactions, and both fit together with expressions, although there is always some necessary flexibility left for indirect communication through incomplete integration. In the marginal case, however, the language game can disintegrate so much that the three categories no longer fit together. (*E*, 267)

This model and ideal of an integrated communication where all registers fit together—speech acts, gestures, and actions—clearly identifies with Dilthey and not with Freud. The little play that is left to "indirect communication" can only emphasize the borders; the transition from "incomplete integration" to "disintegration" is a threat that will narrow the play for the former more and more, just as the anxiety to protect the democratic order infringes ever more violently on the civil liberties that constitute the democratic order.

What differentiates the "marginal case" (*Grenzfall*) from the "normal case" (*Normalfall*)? That differentiation might depend on how we understand the "normal case." The German word *Normalfall* could be read in two ways: either as that which is normally, generally, i.e., most often, the case; or we could read it as the normative case, that which should be the case. In the everyday use of the word the first meaning clearly dominates. But if Habermas really means that his model of integrated communication is the *Normalfall* in the first sense, he is a bad listener to everyday conversation and communication whether it be in mixed or not so mixed society. One does not need recourse to psychoanalysis in order to observe that there is hardly a language game in which rules and motivations of the most variant and often contradictory kind compete with each other.

Psychoanalysis has at its basis what is already the "normal" case in everyday speech. Whatever Freud observed in his patients, in the pathological, "abnormal" case, he would eventually detect as the normal case in everyday speech, life, and thought. Habermas wants to isolate the "pathological" elements and exclude them. His syntax performs a consistent operation of isolating: "The psychoanalytic interpretation deals with such symbolic relations in which the subject deceives himself." It "is concerned with texts that indicate authorial self-deception"; "such texts document the latent content of a piece of orientation not accessible to the author." "Such texts" are thus emphatically and consistently separated from another kind where these things do not happen. In order to mark them unmistakably they are designated as a class themselves: "Symbolic utterances that belong to this class of texts can be recognized through certain special qualities" (*E*, 268).

Habermas ends his work of isolating and delimitation with a quotation from Freud that starts with the transgression of a limit: "I certainly transgress the usual meaning of the word." Freud too draws this limit, but his line runs a different course: between a form of expression that is "foreign to us" and one that is "familiar to our mode of thought." Where Habermas separates two classes of texts, Freud differentiates between two modes of expression that can be at work in a single text. The difference in the borderlines marks the difference between two concepts of the analytic process. Freud's metaphor for this process is "translation," while Habermas speaks of "reconstruction." Reconstruction implies that something that once was complete is made complete again. Translation is a different process: while it might point to the ideal of an original text, it offers an equivalence that is never without loss. And where translation and the task of the translator are thought through in their implications, the very notion of the original text is radically displaced.

The problem of the Habermasian interpretation is the fixation of *one* text as norm. This text is regulated by the grammar of everyday language. For Freud, it is this grammar that is shaped by the rationalizing secondary processes. Habermas avoids the problem by another act of isolating: he posits the grammar by itself and pursues rationalization as separate from it. "This rationalizing activity tries to systematize confused contents, to interpolate gaps, and to smooth contradictions" (*E*, 271). The activity of rationalization thus consists in the tansformation of a confused text into an orderly (systematic, smooth, clear, logical) text. At this point Habermas seems to agree fully with Freud.

But if that is so, we have to raise some questions concerning the place of this ordering/distorting agency. It points suspiciously closely in the direction where Habermas at the very beginning positioned his judge: to (self-)consciousness that operates in the grammar of everyday language. It seems we find ourselves in the situation of Kleist's comedy *Der zerbrochene Krug*, where the same person who broke the jug holds court to find the guilty party.

The secondary work starts, in Habermas's paraphrase of Freud, "after the dream memory has emerged as an object before the consciousness of the awakened dreamer" (*ibid.*). Consciousness acts here as the representative of public intercourse: "This intercourse consists in the habituated interactions that are tied to the public sphere of everyday communication. The institutions of social intercourse license only certain motives of action; other dispositions of need, also tied to everyday-language interpretation, are blocked off from manifest action" (*E*, 273). Redemption, judgment, and distortion seem to be entangled in one agency. Habermas tries to avoid the entanglement by positing everyday language as a kind of neutral meta-agency in which censoring and repressing institutions as well as censored and repressed needs are at play. Yet it is not a playground in the language of Habermas, but above all an agency that "ties" (*bindet*) and fixates (*festmacht*). Everyday language is a *grammar* that ties and knots according to a uniform norm that censors any deviation as a fault (*fehlerhaft*).

According to Habermas, dream language has no grammar: "The sequence of visual scenes is no longer ordered according to syntactical rules because the differentiating linguistic means for logical relations are lacking; even elementary basic rules of logic are canceled. In the degrammaticized language of the dream, relations are constituted by fading over and by condensation of the material" (*E*, 274). The lack of common logical rules is identified with degrammaticization. Grammar is thus reduced to a specific class of syntactical relations.

Freud's description of the possibilities of dream language points in another direction. To be sure, he also notes the fact that the dream has no words for logical relations that would be equivalent to the syntactical conjunctions "if," "because," "although," "either-or." Freud takes recourse to his translation metaphor. The lack of the logical signs is not considered as a degrammaticization but as a problem of different media of representation. Freud uses the relationship between literature and painting as a paradigm:

> The plastic arts of painting and sculpture labor, indeed, under a similar limitation as compared with poetry, which can make use of speech; and here once again the reason for their incapacity lies in the nature of the material which these two forms of art manipulate in their effort to express something. Before painting became acquainted with the laws of expression by which it is governed, it made attempts to get over this handicap. In ancient paintings small labels were hung from the mouths of the persons represented, containing in written characters the speeches which the artist despaired of representing pictorially. (*G.W.* 2/3:317; *S.E.* 4:312)

Painting has its own order of representation, just as film has its own syntax. The same is true for the dream. The syntax Freud discovers in the dream is closer to the tropes and figures of rhetoric than to the syllogistic figures of logic. As such it represents a kind of language that cannot be relegated to the exceptions and margins of "poetic license." It is very much part of Habermas's favorite grammar of everyday language, it is a constitutive part of real speech situations, and its effects are no less at work in political debates and juridical battles than they are in informal conversation. On the other hand, Freud can describe and classify a pathological phenomenon such as paranoia in the form of syntactical variations of one sentence (G.W. 8:299ff.; S.E. 12:63ff.).

Habermas postulates a model of communicative praxis that is ruled by a uniform grammar, free of contradictions: "Every *deviation from the model language game of communicative praxis,* in which motives of action and intention expressed in language coincide, is faulty in a strictly methodological sense" (*E*, 277). Habermas is now forced to declare as the normative case what he called earlier the normal case: "Such a model can of course only find general application under the conditions of a non-repressive society; deviations from the model are therefore the normal case in all social conditions we know" (*ibid.*).

The backbone of this model is a self-identical subject in full control over all his/her discourses. The agency of the ego appears in Freud's writings in a rather fragile and fluctuating position; at best at times as a "constitutional monarch" with limited power, more often as the "servant" who begs for the love of his master.[10] Habermas's model wants to declare it an absolute master. The goal of psychoanalysis according to Habermas is therefore the unified discourse of one self-identical subject. The analyst is the teacher and guide who "teaches one and the same subject to grasp its own language. The analyst guides the patient so that he learns to read his own texts, mutilated and distorted by himself, and to translate the symbols from a deformed private language into the mode of expression of public communication" (*E*, 279f.). Precisely at the point when Habermas takes over Freud's metaphor of translation, it enters into a problematic relation to the preceding text. Public communication, which is here the goal of translation, appeared earlier as the cause for the internal communicative disturbances: in order not to disturb "the appearance of an intersubjectivity of a free communicative praxis it is necessary to erect barriers of communication within the subject" (*E*, 279).

Habermas dreams of a *Bildungsroman* ending with the subject in harmony with himself and with society. Yet, in the classical model of the *Bildungsroman*, *Wilhelm Meister*, Goethe problematizes rather than glorifies emancipation and self-reflection. From the beginning to the end Wilhelm's self-reflective attempts turn out to be self-deceptions. The story of his life is written by the tower-society; he has to find himself in that script if he does not want to give himself up. Despair and happiness are so close together at the end that only the authoritative dictate from the outside saves the promise of Wilhelm's happiness from his despair.

It is not arbitrary to evoke *Wilhelm Meister* at this juncture. The novel has been long petrified into the model of the bourgeois ideology, and Habermas too quotes it in order to exemplify his model of the bourgeois liberal public sphere. But the passage he quotes, Wilhelm's differentiation between bourgeois and aristocrat, articulates the rupture between bourgeois ideal and reality. The bourgeois subject *is* not, he *has*. Only as an owner who possesses and has is he a subject who can sign a contract with his name. And because he is subject only to the degree that he has, the bourgeois subject who believes in his possession has been had.

Where the *Bildungsroman* insists on the appearance of emancipation and autonomy, it cannot do without an authoritative agency that prescribes the text for the subject. Psychoanalysis is for Habermas even more clearly than for Eissler (see Preface) a kind of tower-society that organizes the desire of the subject. Yet Habermas is not insensitive to this danger, and he searches for safeguards against an authoritarian abuse of psychoanalysis. Thus he emphasizes the affective dimension of the analytic process, and he tries to ground his concept of self-reflection in the affects and the desire of the subject. The analyst's constructions are legitimated only in the patient's memory. This is the point where Habermas makes an explicit connection with Critical Theory (in the sense of the Frankfurt School: as a dialectical social theory that includes aesthetics as much as economics): based on the analysis of existing conditions and sufferings, Critical Theory articulates hypothetically the causes of suffering and the latent "true" needs. The critique is itself entangled in the object of its analysis: "The critique would not have the power to break down false consciousness if it were not driven by a *passion of critique* [*Leidenschaft der Kritik*]. At the beginning there is the experience of suffering and need, and the interest to find relief from the encumbering situation" (*E*, 286).

The intentions are laudable. The implications of the argument and its actual articulation are a different matter. Habermas speaks of the "passion of critique," but not of the passion of the critic. Wherever his text moves away from the cognitive realm, the personal subject disappears. It is curious that the process that is supposed to constitute the self and the subject ends in a narrative without a subject: "At the end of the analysis it should be possible to tell the story [*narrativ darzustellen*] of the events of the forgotten years that are relevant for the case history and which were not known at the beginning of the analysis either by the doctor or the patient" (*E*, 282). Who tells the story? Who is the narrator? The particular subject doesn't matter, because there is only one story and one grammar that can be recited *unisono* by doctor and patient.

At the end the absolute spirit reveals itself as the absolute grammar. If the not-knowing is identical at the beginning for doctor and patient, their knowledge is different from the start. The knowledge of the doctor (the critic) is already at the beginning a knowledge "for us," in the sense of Hegel's *Phenomenology*. The patient has to work his way through to that knowledge. The translation of the process in the language of Hegel is at this point *almost* identical with Freud's formulation quoted by Habermas: "Our knowledge in this part [*Stück*] is then also his knowledge" (*E*, 283). But Freud speaks of a certain piece (*Stück*) of knowledge, whereas Habermas points immediately to the virtual totality of a knowledge revealed in the model of ideal communication:

> The virtual totality, ruptured by fissures, is represented in the model of pure communicative praxis. According to this model all habituated interactions and all interpretations, which have consequences for the praxis of life, are accessible to free public communication on the basis of the interiorized apparatus of a non-restricted everyday language, so that the transparency of the remembered life story is preserved. (*E*, 285)

The model has a rather vague temporal and spatial status. As a "virtual totality" it is an atemporal postulate and a future possibility, but it also has a past: it existed once and is now ruptured (*zerschnitten*). It is marked by the three temporal elements that structure fantasizing according to Freud: unfulfilled presence, fulfilled past, projected future. The spatial topology has a similar movement: the subject, constituted as interiority against an exterior, is conceived of as a preexisting totality, yet it becomes whole only through a process of interiorization, emphasized by the German words *eingewöhnt, verinnerlicht, erinnert.* Whatever the subject expresses at the end first had to be taken in.

The subject who does not acknowledge and accept whatever s/he interiorized must be punished until s/he accepts the interiorized text. While the first translation into a Hegelian teleology transforms pieces of knowledge into the totality of knowledge, the second translation leads to a criminal trial. The suffering of the patient is also his/her motivation to be cured. This motivation now turns into an instrument of the moral law: the patient becomes a criminal who has disturbed the moral order because he has not yet acknowledged what is his:

> The one and only insight to which analysis should lead is that the *I* of the patient recognizes itself in its Other, represented by the illness, as its own alienated self and identifies with it. As in Hegel's dialectic of morality, the criminal recognizes in his victim his own corrupted self, a self-reflection through which the abstractly isolated parts recognize the destroyed moral totality as their common ground and return back to it through this recognition. (*E*, 288)

Self-reflection becomes self-accusation. Peter Handke's *Kaspar* is the theatrical parable of this process: how a Kaspar, stuttering in his deformed private language, is changed by nice prompters and teachers into a linguistically well-organized Kaspar who can tell the story of his life in grammatically correct sentences.

In its urge to exclude nothing the model excludes that which is in the center of Freud's work: sexuality. Only once, Habermas refers to it—within parentheses: "Developmental processes that deviate from the model (and Freud leaves no doubt that under the conditions of a twofold sexual development with a forced latency *all* socialization processes have to occur anomalously) are rooted in the oppression by social institutions" (*E*, 285). This seems to indicate that the condition for the ideal model would be no less than the disappearance of the latency period, a revolution of truly anthropological dimensions if one can imagine it. It would eliminate a rupture and discontinuity in sexual development and turn it into a homogeneous and continuous development: the classical ideal of *Bildung*. Given the implications of latency for human memory, the organization of human time (see chapter 7 on "Belatedness" [*Nachträglichkeit*], the consequences of the disappearance of the latency period can hardly be guessed. It probably would mean a radical change of the human species.

Rather than speculating about the good or bad results of such a change, I would like to comment on the position of this condition in Habermas's text. The question of sexuality is touched upon, yet it remains syntactically strangely marginal, without any grammatical interaction with the rest of the sentence, which speaks of the "model." It is cut off from the rest by parentheses and thus excluded from discussion. The parentheses *isolate* Freud's condition, and thus they perform something that Freud described very precisely. In the sixth chapter of *Inhibition, Symptom, and Anxiety* he discusses two "activities of the ego which form symptoms": "*undoing what has been done* and *isolating*" (G.W. 12:253; S.E. 17:240). Freud sees both activities as surrogates of repression. Isolating appears mainly in obsessional neuroses:

> We know that in hysteria it is possible to cause a traumatic experience to be overtaken by amnesia. In obsessional neurosis, this can often not be achieved: the experience is not forgotten, but, instead, it is deprived of its affect, and its associative connections are suppressed or interrupted so that it remains as though isolated and is not reproduced in the ordinary processes of thought. (G.W. 12:255; S.E. 17:242)

Freud immediately adds that this pathological phenomenon has its "normal" equivalence which serves as a basis:

> The normal phenomenon of concentration provides a pretext for this kind of neurotic procedure: what seems to us important in the way of an impression or a piece of work must not be interfered with by the simultaneous claims of any other mental processes or activities. But even a normal person uses concentration to keep away not only what is irrelevant or unimportant, but, above all, what is unsuitable because

it is contradictory. He is most disturbed by those elements which once belonged together but which have been apart in the course of his development. (*Ibid.*)

If we now look back at the parenthetical clause in Habermas's text, Freud's description seems very fitting. Sexuality and its position in Freud's oeuvre are not forgotten, but cut off from the flow of the argument. Once isolated, sexuality will not reenter the argument. It will not be reproduced and thus it will not disturb the ideal model, although it might have a lot to do with it. It rather is unsuitable because it contradicts *pure* communication, in which pure reasonable discourse is distracted by no desire, no speaking lips, no body. Because such "distractions" are at play in every communicative situation, in every moment of intersubjectivity, because they belong (all too much) to communication, they must be excluded as disturbances.

Both activities, undoing what has been done and isolating, are symptomatic activities of the ego according to Freud. They are thus located in that agency seen by Habermas as the guarantor of free and unrestricted communication:

We have all found by experience that it is especially difficult for an obsessional neurotic to carry out the fundamental rule of psychoanalysis. His ego is more watchful and makes sharper isolations, probably because of the high degree of tension owing to conflict that exists between his super-ego and his id. While he is engaged in thinking, his ego has to keep off too much—the intrusion of unconscious fantasies and the manifestation of ambivalent trends. (G.W. 12:256; S.E. 17:242)

It is specifically the watchful (*wachsame*) ego that is at work here. The attempt to keep away "unsuitable" tendencies puts the ego into a compulsive situation in which it becomes the agency of compulsion. A communicative situation that makes it its condition that all modes of expression converge, "fit together," free of contradictions—the Habermasian "normal case"—is the ideal case of a compulsive situation in which everything unsuitable must be kept out.

Habermas might perhaps object that he is thinking of a "weak," immature ego. But what does "weak" mean when the energy of resistance is so strong? In analytical as well as in everyday experience there seems to be little evidence that a "strong" ego displays the qualities of flexibility, playful freedom, and unrestricted openness. After a lifelong analytical experience, Freud describes in the late essay "The Infinite and the Finite Analysis" (1937) the strong and matured ego mainly as a builder of dams and dikes: "These new dams have quite a different firmness from the earlier ones; one can trust them that they will not give in easily to the high floods of increased drives" (G.W. 16:72; S.E. 23:228). Freud's metaphor touches upon a phantasm of anxiety that comes in many variations and that has recently been related specifically to a patriarchal setting: floods that must be dammed in, swamps to be dried out, the Zuider Sea that must yield the land.[11] In this setting, the ego is the engineer who appropriates the land from the swamps of the id. It is a fantasy not only of ego psychology, but also of a political rhetoric that borrows from Faust's last (violent and deadly ironic) project to settle and build only on land gained from the sea.[12] The enthusiasm of such rhetoric generally forgets what Freud articulates with it: the conditions of closure and exclusion. The denial takes revenge on the blindly emancipative discourse: the emancipative urge *acts* in the form of ever more exclusive anxiety.

Habermas's interpretation of Freud is not totally without a basis in Freud's texts. The problem is rather how to *read* those texts. Habermas wants to extrapolate firm and well-defined concepts. We are thus back to the initial problem we noticed in the Habermasian mode of storytelling: Habermas wants to subsume the stories of the ego to a teleological history of the ego told in terms of self-identical concepts.

Freud takes up the problem at the beginning of his work on "Drives and Their Vicissitudes": "We often have heard the claim that a science must be built on clear and sharply defined basic concepts. In reality, no science starts with such definitions, not even the most exact ones" (G.W. 10:210; S.E. 14:117). Freud immediately adds that this does not mean that science can develop purely on the basis of observation and experience, but that the experience already takes place in a context of preunderstanding and of conventions, which are at the same time shifted and displaced by new experience. We then try to fixate these shifts in definitions. The word Freud uses here is *bannen*, which means not only to fixate, but also to spellbind. We are then in the realm of the witches where Freud locates metapsychology. The spellbinding, however, is not the end. "The progress of knowledge does not tolerate the rigidity of definitions." The spellbound concepts can be redeemed by the shock of experience.

The particular status of psychoanalytical concepts is well illustrated by the attempt of Laplanche and Pontalis to present the vocabulary of psychoanalysis. [13] Each entry begins with an approximative definition of the term followed by a brief history of the term in Freud's writing. It is not a teleological history in which a term moves from initial uncertainty and vagueness to its final definition, the kind of story we often read in popular stories about science. These terms have their vicissitudes in the sense that Freud describes the drives. They have their fates, their truth, their functions, at a given place in a given text, and move on from there without ever completely giving up whatever their former positions might have been.

The entanglement of the analytical discourse in the constellations of the analytical process touches both the language of its reconstruction and the language of theory. There is no discourse for Freud that is free of the effects of the unconscious. And while we would get nowhere without theory, theory moves on ghostly wings: Freud must call the witch "the witch metapsychology. Without metapsychological speculation and theorizing—I was almost going to say: fantasizing—one doesn't get anywhere" (G.W. 16:68; S.E. 23:224). This is said in the essay that sums up Freud's experience of analysis as a process that is constitutionally infinite, open-ended. There is no point where I can say once and for all: "Here I am."

This is the point where the radical difference between Freud and Habermas becomes most manifest and is articulated in Habermas's critique of Freud's metapsychology:

> The derivation of the structural model from the experience of the analytical situation connects the three categories ego, id, and super-ego with the specific sense of a communication into which doctor and patient enter with the goal to bring about an enlightenment process and to lead the sick person to self-reflection. Therefore it does not make sense to describe the same complex to which we had to recur for the explication of ego, id, and super-ego in terms of the structural model. That is what Freud does. He interprets the interpretive work of the doctor in the theoretical terms of the structural model. (E, 299)

Habermas demands a theoretical language that is independent of the effects it tries to understand. *Control* becomes the dominant term in the last sentences of the Freud chapter: sublimation as "control of the ego," "not only by means of ego, but under the control of the ego" (*E*, 300).

At the end, Freud has disappeared. In a more recent book by Habermas, *Zur Rekonstruktion des historischen Materialismus*,[14] Freud's place is taken by Piaget, whose work seems to fit better with a model that aims teleologically at the unrestricted control of the cognitive ego. The path "from Hegel through Freud to Piaget" (*R.H.M*, 14) leads to a "system of ego delimitations" (*Ich-Abgrenzungen*; *R.H.M*, 18). The knight who rode out to conquer positivism has staked out his territory, and its name is positivism, although a more subtle and more sophisticated version.

IV

DRINKING THE WITCH'S BREW:
NIETZSCHE AND THE
(K)NOTS OF RESENTMENT

One of the many seductive traits of Nietzsche's writing is the apparent clarity and decisiveness of his valorizations. The popular image of Nietzsche is characterized by sets of dichotomies with clearly marked hierarchies. Thus, the metaphysical depth and essence of the Dionysian is opposed to the illusionary appearance and surface of the Apollonian; the Dionysian/Apollonian artistic forces are opposed to the destructive cyclopean eye of the Socratic intellect; aristocratic morality confronts slave morality in a rhetoric and vocabulary that leaves the reader little doubt as to which he should identify with. More than any particular content or idea, it is this rhetorical strategy of valorization that has made Nietzsche's texts so susceptible to political use and abuse.

The seductiveness is intensified by a seemingly contradictory phenomenon: the slipperiness and subversiveness of Nietzsche's valorizations which could lend support to rather contradictory Nietzsche images.[1] If Nietzsche's pathos of negation and subversion appeals to the discomfort of the authoritarian mentality, at the same time it appeases the authoritarian anxiety and need for security by an offering of new sets of exclusionary opposites.

Can we escape this machinery? Am I not already caught in it by my cautious introductory qualification of the clarity as being "apparent"? Calling it apparent, I have implied an original, genuine, authoritative text and thus am already operating in the network of the Apollonian surface and the Dionysian depth. What is at stake, then, is not simply Nietzsche's politics, but the politics of reading. Much of the politicization of Nietzsche is indeed also a cover-up of the politics of reading.

More subtle readers have of course been working for a long time to either liquidate the oppositions into a dialectical process or to subvert and deconstruct them through the text's own rhetorical troping. The latter strategy has particularly marked the more recent French or French-oriented Nietzsche reception[2] and has led to genuinely new readings, among them Derrida's *Spurs* (*Eperons*) and Paul de Man's *Allegories of Reading*.[3] But curiously, although not surprisingly, these deconstructions of oppositional constellations have effected at the same time all the more rigid dichotomies on the institutional level.[4] Even the simple uttering of a term like "deconstruction" places us firmly and inescapably within an institutional machinery of exclusion and inclusion. Thus, in the search for an escape from the ontological and metaphysical dichotomies, we find ourselves in the concrete(ness) of institutional walls. If this seems to lead us farther and farther away from the philosopher who ultimately stepped outside the institution, it brings us at the same time to the core of a philosophy of conflict, opposition, exclusion and inclusion, radical no and jubilant yes. This violent struggle of yes and no, of decisions, indecisions, and revisions, is condensed in the somewhat unappetizing (k)not of resentment. To unravel that knot, some detours will be necessary. But then, according to Nietzsche, resentment is essentially a detour.

Let us look back, then, briefly at that text of Nietzsche which for the first time sets into motion a strong—and, as far as the Nietzsche reception is concerned, perhaps the most enduring—oppositional machinery: *The Birth of Tragedy*. The simple, straightforward valorization of the Dionysian needs hardly any rebuttal today. Nietzsche's text, as much as its rhetoric, gestures toward such a valorization, enters the opposition of the Dionysian and Apollonian into such a dialectical exchange that a careful reading will have a hard time not being destabilized. Even the most innocent reader is apt to pause reflectively when Nietzsche, after establishing and valorizing the Dionysian force as the true ground of being which produces the Apollonian appearance, suggests a strategy of approach which asks the reader to translate Beethoven's *Ode to Joy* into a painting, in order to come closer to the Dionysian music (1:29).[5] But such reversals or strategies of detours can still be explained relatively easily within a dialectical economy of the manifest text. Even Paul de Man's more radical deconstructive reading can support itself to a large degree on Nietzsche's own manifest deconstructive moves.[6]

Instead of retracing the dialectical or perhaps deconstructive logic between the Dionysian and Apollonian, I would like to shift my focus toward the economy of pleasure and pain operating in and through these relations, and particularly through the Dionysian. It soon appears that the Dionysian, this all-embracing force of unification, is strangely split in itself. It is a place both of horror (*Grausen*, 1:28) and pleasureful ecstasy (*wonnevolle Verzückung, ibid.*). Nietzsche thus encounters at a very early stage of his writing a problem that will turn out to be one of the knottiest problems of Freud: the disquieting interrelation between pleasure and pain. But like Freud, Nietzsche can escape the problem at least initially by a topological distribution: what is experienced as pleasure in one place can be pain and displeasure in another place. The dissolution of individuation is experienced as horror in the Apollonian sphere, but as ecstasy in the Dionysian. Thus, the Dionysian does not need to be split, the split occurs reassuringly between two topologically separated agencies. But just as later in Freud's further probing, the topological solution and distribution are shaken. It will take Nietzsche only a few more pages.

After a curious speculation about the shape and colors of ancient Greek dreams, Nietzsche introduces, somewhat abruptly, a new oppositional constellation, shaped by an enormous cleavage (*ungeheuere Kluft*, 1:31). And while the supposedly clearly delineated shapes of Greek dreams can only be guessed at, there is no doubt about the shape of this new opposition which separates the Dionysian Greeks from the Dionysian barbarians. Thus, the very force of all embracing unity, Dionysus, is split by an enormous cleavage; or, to be more precise, the human agents acting out the Dionysian agency form a constellation of radical mutual exclusion. Indeed, the very word *barbaros* is not so much the designation of a particular entity, but the name of the *other* as the other, which allows the Greeks to be "Greeks."

However, if we try to delineate the exact shape of the difference, some problems arise. Nietzsche begins with the characterization of the barbarian Dionysian festivals. Their relation to the Greek festivals is equivalent to the relation of the bearded Satyr and goat to Dionysus "himself" (1:32). This suggests that Dionysus himself is embodied in the Greek festivals, while the barbarians cling to a fetishized, perverted attribute of him. At this point, Nietzsche's rhetoric assumes a highly unusual and uncharacteristic Victorian, moralistic tone. The barbarian festivals are characterized by floods of sexual licentiousness which destroy the bonds of the family and its sacred laws, and—I now quote literally—"the wildest beasts of nature are let loose [unchained] here to the point of that abominable mixture of blissful pleasure [*Wollust*] and cruelty, which always seemed to me the actual 'witch's brew'" (*ibid.*).

If we compare this characterization, marked by the spell of a horrifying threat, with the earlier introductory remarks on the Dionysian, we notice dreamlike similarities and shiftings. Nietzsche introduces the Dionysian in two oddly contrasting paragraphs. The first resumes Schopenhauer's rhetoric of horror which accompanies the dissolution of the principle of individuation; but, as we have seen, this horror coexists with blissful ecstasy. Nietzsche illustrates this interrelation by a phenomenon which would lend itself, it seems, as a paradigm of a barbarian Dionysian festival: the ecstasy of medieval orgiastic St. Vitus dances. But at this point, Nietzsche's rhetoric has nothing but contempt for those who would denounce such phenomena: people who abhor these events as sick and despicable do not know how sickly and ghostly their own health looks compared with the glowing life of the Dionysian crowds.

The second paragraph transforms the image of the Dionysian in a shift not unlike the transformation of the condemned criminals in Kafka's "Penal Colony," when their suffering, after hours of torture under the machine, is transformed into an expression of ecstatic blissfulness. The Dionysian horror turns into magic (*Zauber*) which reestablishes the bonds between man and man, and man and nature; an alienated, hostile, and subjugated nature celebrates its festival of reconciliation with humanity. The beasts of nature approach peacefully, panther and tiger are guided by Dionysus (1:29). In a strange way, this idyllic setting with the typical requisites of the Golden Age contains all the major ingredients of that which Nietzsche calls later the "witch's brew," except that everything appears in a different light. The sphere of the witches lures as beneficial magic, the transgression of all family bonds is presented as the constitution of a much larger and universal bond, and the threatening beasts of nature are tamed by the agency in whose name they have come. It thus seems that the scene of horror and the scene of paradise are one and the same.

In the magical transformation of horror into paradise, it is Dionysus himself who tames the beasts under his yoke. But under the threat of a barbarian form of Dionysus, it is no longer Dionysus but the rigidly erected shape of Apollo which protects the Greeks from the barbaric onslaught. However, it turns out not only that the threat comes from the outside, the barbarians, but that the Other is already within. And again it is the Delphic god who makes peace with the threatening force of Dionysus. It is ultimately not Dionysus who tames the beasts, but Apollo who tames Dionysus. Dionysus, it seems, is the very name of the witch's brew, the name of a scene where blissful pleasure and cruelty are indistinguishably one and the same. Only a distribution onto two different scenes and names can relieve the threat. But even then there is no full escape from the brew: the mixture of pleasure and cruelty might have lost its force, but there remains a trace of it: "Only the miraculous mixture and doubleness in the effects of the Dionysian enthusiasts remind us of it [the witch's brew]—like the remedy reminds us of the deadly poison" (1:33).[7] The remedy, of course, is more than just a reminder and metaphor of the poison it is supposed to cure; it is the poison. And the doubleness in the phenomenon "that pain evokes pleasure and jubilation unleashes painful screams" is not just a reminder of the nauseating witch's brew: it is the brew. Only the dosage might be slightly weakened.

But why the horror? Why this strong rhetoric of rejection and its moralistic overtones? To explain it with Victorian prudery won't do. It is not the sexual licentiousness and the threat to the family bonds that Nietzsche is moralizing about: the strongest adjectives of rejection, *abscheulich* and *scheußlich,* are connected with the twice-repeated formula of the witch's brew of *Wollust und Grausamkeit.* The threat to be rejected is the undecidability between pleasure and cruelty, or between pleasure and pain. At this point we might remember that the title of the essay is the *Birth of Tragedy.* What is most puzzling about tragedy as a genre is not so much death and suffering as such, but death and suffering as aesthetic pleasure. Thus, all theories of tragedy and tragic effects have to do with the rationalization of the phenomenon that we take pleasure in cruelty and pain: in watching it, in inflicting it, in suffering it.

But what, precisely, constitutes the horror of this phenomenon, particularly for a writer and philosopher who has set out on a path which leaves no taboos unquestioned? In approaching this question, allow me another detour, but one indicated by the signposts of Nietzsche's text, more specifically by his metaphors. Witch's brew and remedy/poison are things to be consumed or not consumed, incorporated or not incorporated, taken in or rejected. They are either appropriate or inappropriate to the body; and perhaps it is only the quantity that decides between proper and improper. Witch's brews usually consist of ingredients rejected by civilized and toilet-trained society; but one of their main effects is the desire for universal incorporation, as Mephisto says to Faust after the latter has tasted the witch's brew: "With this brew in your body you will soon see Helena in every woman." There will be no more rejection, only the jubilant *yes.*

My phrasing of the implications of Nietzsche's metaphors might have already evoked the text toward which and through which I would like to take my detour: Freud's brief and dense essay on negation.[8] Freud's starting point is a phenomenon which has scandalized and horrified people as much as Nietzsche seems to be horrified by the witch's brew of cruelty and pleasure: the phenomenon that in the psychoanalytic discourse yes and no are no longer clearly distinct, because no can mean yes. This phenomenon, probably much more than the topic of sexuality, constitutes one of the strongest elements of resistance and might perhaps be the source of the most insistent resentment against psychoanalysis.[9] The force of this resistance will not be diminished by pointing out that there are many everyday situations in which we know to take a no for a yes. The purity of the scientific discourse will, for the sake of its identity, exclude the impurity of everyday experience and ordinary language. All the more intriguing is the fact that one of the most radical purists and one of the founders of modern logic, Gottlob Frege, comes to conclusions according to which "negation has no place in the realm of thought."[10]

But the resistance against this thought also remains insistent. After all, somewhere the operation of negating does and has to take place. And of course neither Freud nor Frege are negating negation (which would have an intriguingly curious logical status), they displace it. In addition, Freud traces its genealogy and with it the genealogy of judgments and propositions in general. Judgment, according to Freud, makes two kinds of decisions: either to affirm or negate a quality or property of a thing or to affirm or negate the existence of a thing. In the first case, the most basic decision is whether something is good or bad, useful or harmful. Freud immediately translates this decision into the language of orality: "I want to eat this or I want to spit it out," which can be translated again into the more general expression: "This I want to introduce into me, this I want to exclude," or in another modification: "It should be within me or it should be outside me." Freud ascribes these decisions to the pleasure-I (*Lust-Ich*), whereas decisions about the existence or non-existence of a thing are made by the reality-I which develops out of the pleasure-I and functions in the service of the reality principle. Thus, reality judgments are secondary, but they have something in common with the first kind of judgments: they draw a boundary between what is inside and what is outside. Or, in other words, the reality judgment already presupposes the constitution of an inside/outside dichotomy which is established on the oral level.

If we now return to Nietzsche's texts, our attention will be sharpened for the recurring oral metaphors and their extension to a digestive system of taste, smell, hygienics, diets, all in the service of an economy of exclusion and inclusion. The witch's brew and the poison/remedy in the *Birth of Tragedy* set up that metaphorical economy. Poison and poisoning (5:392 passim), bad odors (5:277, 281, 368 passim), and indigestion (5:371) characterize resentment in the *Genealogy of Morals*. Aristocratic morality, in contrast, is blessed with a healthy digestion, partly because of highly differentiating organs for taste and smells.[11]

But before we enter further into this digestive system and its economy of incorporation and rejection, we must dwell for a moment on its constitutive elements, particularly the question of what determines the decision to take something in or to spit it out. The most simple answer, of course, is that we take in what we like, that which pleases us, that which tastes and smells good, and we reject the opposite. Thus, Freud, as we have seen, locates the agency of this decision in the pleasure-I, which originally is only interested in whether something causes pleasure or displeasure. And Nietzsche too writes in section 18 of *Human All Too Human* that "originally nothing is of interest to us as organic beings in a thing except its relation to us in terms of pleasure and pain" (2:39). And in the second section of the *Genealogy of Morals*, yes and no are constituted in an organic necessity: "With the necessity with which a tree bears its fruits, our thoughts, our values, our yeses and noes, grow out of us" (5:248). The economy of remembering and forgetting appears in an explicit analogy to corporeal digestion: "Forgetfulness is not simply a *vis intertiae* . . . but in the strongest sense a positive faculty of inhibition to which we owe it that whatever we experience, what is taken in by us, enters our consciousness in the state of digestion . . . no more than the manifold process in which our corporeal nourishing takes place, the so-called 'incorporation'" (5:291).

It is seductively self-evident to think that, even if all things and all knowledge are questionable and uncertain, we know at least with absolute certainty whether something hurts or pleases. If it hurts it hurts, pain cannot be debated. Perhaps we might find in some cases the relationship between cause and pain incommensurate, but nobody can deny the fact of pain. Even if we talk about "imagined" pains, we are only locating the pain in a different sphere from bodily pain;

and it might hurt no less for all that. The neurotic probably suffers as much or more than the physically tortured being.

And yet it is this certainty and this fundamental facticity which is destabilized already in the *Birth of Tragedy*, even, as it appears, against the writer's resistance. We might now begin to understand that forceful rhetoric of rejection directed at the witch's brew, because that brew undercuts all attempts of stabilization on all levels. Not only do all epistemological foundations become shaky according to the genealogy of negation and judgment as Nietzsche and Freud see it, but also our biological survival seems threatened if we can no longer trust our gut feelings and instincts that supposedly tell us what to take in and what to spit out.

Nietzsche's conflictual entanglement in this problem, throughout his work, can be noted most clearly in the tension between the use of a highly valorized biologistic vocabulary of stabilizing instincts and a movement of argumentation which radically destabilizes any possibility of a firm ground. This affects most of all the usage of language. Indeed, my own usage of certain terms could be criticized for some imprecisions. Thus, perhaps I carelessly used the terms "pain," "displeasure," and "cruelty" almost interchangeably as terms opposed to pleasure. A more rigorous argumentation could point out that if we clearly distinguish between pain and displeasure, we could possibly unravel our knot quite logically. We could then perhaps say that while pain always remains pain, it can be experienced as either displeasure or pleasure. In the case of cruelty, the differentiation is even easier and clearer: cruelty is causing pain in another being, and, as unpleasant as it might be to admit it, there is certainly no logical reason to see a contradiction between that and my own pleasure. But it is exactly the rigorous attempt by both Nietzsche and Freud to come to such clear distinctions which unsettles them and relegates them to a secondary although to some degree necessary construct. Readers of Freud know the painstaking labor of his attempt to unravel the knots of sadism and masochism and the many revisions and reversals on that tortuous path,[12] where even the seemingly clear difference of cruelty and suffering pain becomes blurred when the pleasure of sadism is located not primarily in the act of causing pain but in the introjection of the pain of the sufferer.[13]

We will find the analogy to this tortuous path in Nietzsche's discussion of resentment. But already before that, another constitutive threshold and necessary boundary has been shattered. Again its symptoms can be found in an apparent lack of precision, again also in my own use of terms. I referred earlier to Nietzsche's witch's brew and poison/remedy as metaphors. That seems reasonable enough, since Nietzsche is evidently not talking about an actual, real witch's brew or poison. The only problem is he explicitly says the opposite when he refers to that "detestable mixture of pleasure and cruelty, which always seemed to me the *actual* 'witch's brew.'" The German word is *eigentlich*, which also means "proper" and is commonly used as the oppositional term to the metaphorical *uneigentliche* usage of words. But then again, Nietzsche put the word "Hexentrank" in quotation marks, which would indicate that the word is to be read metaphorically. Thus, metaphor and proper use are mixed together indistinguishably in a concoction which seems to me a real witch's brew of language.

Nietzsche's brief essay on "Truth and Lie in the Extra Moral Sense," dictated shortly after the publication of the *Birth of Tragedy*, states the problem explicitly and in the most radical form: language as a whole and truth are nothing but a "mobile army of metaphors, metonymies, anthropomorphisms" (1:880). If all language is figurative, the distinction between proper and figurative usage collapses. And yet, if we want to communicate, the distinction is essential. How can I understand you, if I don't know whether to take your words literally or figuratively? And yet do I understand you, if I don't ever take you literally? Or figuratively? We are all familiar with a certain dialogical scenario centered around the apologetic "I didn't mean it literally." To accept such a statement might avoid a few conflicts, not to accept it might create some resentment. But then, how much resentment is in the well-known triumphant and malicious gesture of phrases such as "That's what you think you say, but actually you mean . . ." It's mean, indeed, to speak in such a vein. But don't we all, especially as critics in various positions? The psychoanalytical discourse lends itself to such gestures; so does the discourse of ideology critique; so does any language with the gesture of "unmasking." And whose rhetoric was sharper in that respect than Nietzsche's?

Indeed, whose resentment are we talking about? But at least we are now talking about resentment. At last I am coming to the point. But the point is a knot, or perhaps a witch's brew of many strange and familiar ingredients. [14] Through the long detours, we have already gathered all the threads which are knotted to Nietzsche's texts on resentment and all the ingredients to brew our own witch's brew.

It began, it begins, with distinctive opposition. Let's make them perfectly clear: the opposition of slave morality to aristocratic morality as the very spirit of resentment. Thus Nietzsche himself characterizes the first part of the *Genealogy of Morals* in *Ecce Homo* (6:352). But in the same text he gives a little warning about beginnings: "Each time a beginning which is supposed to lead astray" (*ibid.*). We find a few more familiar ingredients in this self-characterization: the second chapter, Nietzsche says, deals with the psychology of conscience, which is the "instinct of cruelty which turns backward" (*ibid.*). The third chapter analyzes the ascetic ideal, which one could understand as a form of diet.

Aristocratic morality is based on direct, active affects, unconcealed aggressivity, and clear and sure instincts, and blessed with a fine and differentiating nose. In short, the hero of the aristocratic morality might be dangerous, but he can be trusted and he is never deceptive. Slave morality, on the other hand, is based on reactive affects, indirect aggression, duplicity, envy, etc. In short, it stinks. Such oppositions have led to the charge of irrationalism against Nietzsche. This was the focal point of Lukács's Nietzsche critique in his *Destruction of Reason*. Although Lukács does not use the term, his consistent analysis of Nietzsche's philosophy in terms of a reaction of anxiety against the contemporary socialist movements (which Nietzsche himself interprets as the most recent historical manifestation of resentment) transposes Nietzsche's characterization onto his own philosophy.

It is easy to see that such a line of argumentation will soon lead to an impasse. The mutual reversals of the resentment charge can go on *ad infinitum*. Nietzsche is the first one to ask the question about the possible ingredient of resentment in his own undertaking, although he puts the question explicitly to the English philosophers and moral critics and their tendency always to find the *partie honteuse* in our values and morals. Isn't that also Nietzsche's project? Is not the question he asks the English philosophers relevant for his moral critique too? "What is it," he asks, "that drives these philosophers always in this direction? Is it a secret, malicious, mean, and perhaps unadmitted instinct to belittle humanity? Or perhaps a pessimistic suspicion or mistrust of disappointed, gloomy idealists turned poisonous? Or perhaps a little subliminal hostility and rancor against Christianity (and Plato), which perhaps has not even reached the threshold of consciousness?" (5:257f.). This passage contains indeed all the major qualities Nietzsche ascribes to resentment: secretiveness, maliciousness (*hämisch*), meanness, a tendency for belittlement, pessimism, suspicion, mistrust, disappointment, rancor, poison, and—especially important—all this is subliminal, unadmitted, unconscious. It also contains the major objects of Nietzsche's unmasking project: standard morality, Christianity, and Plato. Is this why he listens to his own questions "with resistance" (5:258)? Is this why he does *not want* to believe in it, why he wishes it were different, wishing these philosophers and "micrologists of the soul were basically courageous, magnanimous, and proud animals, who know how to restrain their heart and pain, and who have taught themselves to sacrifice wishfulness to the truth" (*ibid.*)? This last phrase is a paradigm of Nietzsche's skillful, cunning style in the way it undoes the wish through its very uttering: wishing that wishfulness be sacrificed. Such cunning turns of style should make us watchful, even if Nietzsche had not warned us himself that beginnings might lead astray.

Thus we have to begin again. Resentment is essentially negative, a reactive activity of negation, in its most global form a no to life (5:252). It is noteworthy, however, that Nietzsche locates this no first in Schopenhauer, who, in a certain sense, was his philosopher-father. Now, a fundamental suspicion (*ein immer grundsätzlicherer Argwohn*, *ibid.*) speaks in Nietzsche against Schopenhauer's no. But *Argwohn* too is part of that vocabulary which Nietzsche ascribes to resentment and which he wishes away from the English moralists. Against this no, Nietzsche would like to posit the jubilant yes of the positive aristocratic spirit. But there is no symmetry between yes and no. If, on the level of the unconscious, the no does not exist, we find the asymmetry in a mirror reversal on the manifest level of expression. The famous *fort/da* game of the little boy in Freud's story is asymmetrically dominated by the *fort;*[5] every yes is constituted by a determinate negation. The affirmative figure of the rigidly erected Apollo is constituted by the Dionysian threat of dissolving the principle of individuation, just as the phallus is erected on the story of castration.

Thus, in order to keep the economy of yes and no, of resentful and aristocratic spirit, in balance, Nietzsche has to introduce a difference into the no, just as he was forced to split the Dionysian into two modes. In the fourth section of the introduction to the *Genealogy*, Nietzsche sets himself off against the study on the origin of moral values by his former friend Paul Ree: "Perhaps I have never read anything to which I have said so decidedly no, sentence for sentence, conclusion for conclusion, as to this book: but completely without ill humor or impatience" (5:250), and he continues, saying that he referred to this book occasionally, but never to refute it—"What have I to do with refutation," he exclaims—but simply to posit the more probable in the place of the improbable "as it befits a positive spirit" (5:251). Thus, Nietzsche establishes himself as a "positive spirit" not by simply opposing a yes to a no, but by a differentiation of the no. In a similar way, the aristocratic spirit in general is not simply constituted by a yes, but by a fundamental attitude, which Nietzsche evokes emphatically throughout his work as the "pathos of distance."[16]

This differentiation within the no is exemplified in the differentiation of revenge. Already in the "Wanderer and His Shadow" (section 33, 2:564–566) Nietzsche distinguishes revenge as an instinctive, defensive response of self-preservation from a mode of revenge which is the product of reflection upon the vulnerability of the enemy, and is directed by the will to hurt the Other. Thus, a temporal delay and a sense for equivalence are involved in the second mode. At this point, this second kind of revenge seems to be clearly valorized over the first one. But already here the difference is blurred, the two meanings of revenge come into conflict with each other, because the actual motivation is undecidable or a construct after the fact (2:566). In the *Genealogy* we find a shift in the valorization: since aristocratic morality is based on direct, straightforward action, the delayed action moves

closer to the sphere of resentment. (In German the close relationship
is already indicated in the words *nachträglich*, after the fact, delayed;
and *nachtragend*, bearing a grudge, resentful.)

At the beginning of section 10 of the *Genealogy* (5:270),
Nietzsche summarizes once more the opposition of resentful slave
morality and aristocratic morality. The first emanates from a lack of
power which forces a delay and transformation of revenge. "While all
aristocratic morality grows out of a triumphant yes to oneself, slave
morality says *a priori* no to any 'exteriority,' to any 'other,' to any 'not-
self.'" Thus, slave morality always needs an outside world as an *other*
and *counter*, while aristocratic morality acts and grows spontaneously;
it looks for its opposite only to say *yes* with even more jubilation.
There is a curious discrepancy in this passage between the strong
rhetoric of contrast and inversion (*das Umgekehrte ist der Fall*) and a
content which has some difficulties in upholding the opposition. We
find a parallel here to the emphatic insistence on the difference between Greek and barbarian Dionysian, where it was also somewhat
difficult to pin down any real difference in content. The oppositional
pairs do not pair symmetrically. The triumphant aristocratic self-affirmation does not stand in a logical contradiction to the slave's no to
the Other; they could even be seen as mutually constitutive. At the
most, Nietzsche can insist on a difference in emphasis and degree.
And indeed, that is what happens; the inversion (*das Umgekehrte*)
turns out to be a matter of degree. Aristocratic morality also searches
for its opposite, although supposedly "only" to be even more trium-
phantly affirmative. But why search at all? Perhaps the affirmed self
is not that self-sufficient after all and needs the Other too to constitute
itself. How else are we to explain the pathos of distance?

Slave morality, as well as aristocratic morality, is operating within
an economy of yes/no, inside/outside, and self/other. What constitutes
such an economy? All signs in the *Genealogy of Morals* point in the
direction of resentment, or, to be more precise, the genealogy of
resentment is intimately involved in the constitution of an interior/
exterior and self/other opposition. We have already noted that the
aristocratic self-affirmation is not purely affirmative; there is an element of impurity, an element of no mixed in. With this vocabulary,
I have already shifted grounds: pure/impure is an opposition which

Nietzsche ascribes to the priestly caste, which forms as a subclass within the aristocratic class in order then to become its radical opposite. In this process, a crucial transformation takes place: in the beginning, Nietzsche says, the terms "pure" and "impure" can still be understood quite literally and unmetaphorically as clean versus dirty. But then the priestly aristocracy managed "to interiorize and sharpen these value oppositions in a dangerous way" (5:265). This interiorization brings with it a chain of qualitative changes, condensed, on the linguistic level, in the change from literal to metaphorical meaning.

But what does "metaphorical" mean here? An adjective describing something "physical" and "exterior" is now used to describe something "metaphysical" and "interior." However, this interior itself is not a literal interior, since physiologically/spatially I can go as far "inside" the body as is possible and still find nothing but physical organs to which the adjectives "pure/impure" can be applied in a completely exterior sense. Interiorization thus constitutes metaphorization, and metaphorization constitutes the possibility of positing an inside versus an outside, a self against an Other. Through this process, Nietzsche writes, "abysses have finally opened up between human being and human being, which even an Achilles among free spirits will not cross over without shuddering" (*ibid.*). The German word *Schauder*, which Nietzsche uses here, is semantically very close to the words *Schauer* and *Grausen*, with which he described the effect of the dissolution of the principle of individuation in the *Birth of Tragedy*.

Interiorization appears as constitutive for individuation, but it is also described as dangerous and above all unhealthy. Medical and hygienic vocabulary dominate the description: there is something "unhealthy in such priestly aristocracies from the beginning on"; these priests suffer "unavoidably of intestinal illnesses and neurasthenias"; the medicines they invented against these illnesses are "a hundred times more dangerous than the illnesses themselves"; humanity itself is still sick from the effects of these priestly cures, particularly dietetic prescriptions and asceticism (*ibid.*). But after all this is said, Nietzsche adds, for the sake of justice, "that only on the ground of this *essentially* dangerous priestly mode of existence, human beings have become *interesting animals*, that only here the human soul has acquired *depth* in a higher sense and has become *evil*—and these are the two basic forms which so far distinguish human beings from other animals" (5:266). We find here, in other words, the origin of humanity and human culture as we know it so far; in other words again: humanity, as we know it so far, has the same origin as resentment. Drinking the witch's brew has made us into human beings; but the witch's brew is also a product of human culture.

At this point again, some striking parallels to Freud's thoughts on the origin of culture might be tempting to pursue. However, more interesting than some obvious similarities to *Civilization and Its Discontents*, and also more fruitful for an "immanent" understanding of Nietzsche's text, is the problem of "instinct" and interiorization. A superficial reading of the *Genealogy of Morals* could easily construe the opposition of aristocratic morality versus the slave morality of resentment as an opposition between spontaneous, instinctive action and the perversion of the natural instincts through delay, detours, and inversions. Indeed the inversion of "instincts" changes their quality. Again, interiorization is the crucial moment of this change: "All instincts which are not discharged toward the outside world turn inward—that is what I call the interiorization of the human being: with this only something grows onto the human being [*wächst an den Menschen heran*] which has later been called 'soul'" (5:322). The inversion and perversion of instinct is described as constitutive for the human species. "Instinct" thus occurs in at least two distinctive senses: in the biological sense as a natural behavior pattern with clearly determined objects and aims; and after the inversion as a "dangerous" force with no clear direction, object, and aim. In this second sense, Nietzsche's "instinct" moves into the position and function of Freud's "drive" (*Trieb*), in which object and aim have become flexible and can be substituted by equivalences; thus Freud can talk of their "vicissitudes."[17] But on another level this distinction starts to be blurred again by Nietzsche. We have already noticed that the opposition of aristocratic and slave morality is not stable; it is hardly an opposition at all, certainly not along the lines which Nietzsche's vocabulary sets up, except if we are ready to relegate the aristocratic class to a prehuman, humanoid animal species. The aristocrat perhaps as a kind of a Neanderthal? But even if we were ready to go that far, we will find Nietzsche's text there blocking our way back to nature. In section 12 of the second part of the *Genealogy of Morals* we read: "The whole history of a 'thing,' of an organ, of a custom, can thus be a continuous chain of signs of ever-new interpretations and manipulations whose causes do not necessarily cohere among each other. . . . The form is liquid, the sense is even more so. . . . Even within each individual organism it is no different: with each growing of the whole, the 'sense' of each individual organ is displaced [*verschiebt sich*]" (5:314–315). Nature partakes already in a signifying chain of interpretations, already the "natural" organs have their vicissitudes.

In an analogy to an inversion that Peter Szondi made in regard to Schiller's famous opposition of naive and sentimental, declaring "the naive is the sentimental" as its product and construct,[18] one could say that the spontaneous, instinctive, natural morality is the fictive sentimental construct of the inverted and perverted slave morality.

The clearest sign of this indefinite delay and displacement of nature is again that "real" witch's brew of Nietzsche, the undecidability of pain/cruelty and pleasure. Pain is no less a result of interpretation than the witches themselves, as Nietzsche reminds us in regard to the witch trials: "Not even the most intelligent and most humane judges doubted that there was guilt, not even the 'witches' themselves doubted it—and yet there was no guilt. And, to expand this premise, 'suffering of the soul' [*seelischer Schmerz*] is for me not a fact, but an interpretation of facts" (5:376). One could perhaps say that Nietzsche is explicitly only talking here of psychological pain, not physical pain. But where else do we *feel* pain, physical or not, but in its psychic representation? And Nietzsche himself points out in an earlier section of the *Genealogy* (section 7, part I, 5:303) that physical pain too is subject to interpretation and a product thereof. This is not a denial of pain and suffering: the interpretation is a fact, even if the "fact" is an interpretation.

It is now perhaps possible to map the detours of our reading and to describe the structural transformations in the economy of resentment. It is in its most general form a transformation of oppositional pairs. Nietzsche himself gives us the paradigm for this mode of transformation. He begins with the origin of the concept and judgment "good." In the beginning, he posits an original good-bad opposition, in which the terms can still be understood in an extra-moral sense as "This is good for me," "This is bad for me." It is the same pairing on which Freud later bases the genealogy of negation. Through the intermediary opposition of pure/impure, the first pair is transformed into a second pair, "good/evil." It is, as we have seen, the product of a metaphorization and interiorization. The moralistic opposition good/evil will from now on be the characteristic mark of the Judaic-Christian slave morality. Thus the two pairs now form together a new oppositional pair: the good/bad opposition of the aristocratic morality versus the good/evil opposition of slave morality. The opposition of these two value systems constitutes, according to Nietzsche, the conflictual battlefield of the history of the last millennia. And the battle is not over yet. But a new element, a fourth stage has formed: "One could even say that the battle has been carried up to ever-higher regions in the meantime and therefore has become ever deeper, ever more spiritual, so that there is perhaps today no more decisive mark of a higher, more spiritual nature than to be ambivalent [*zwiespältig*] in that sense and to be really a battlefield of these oppositions" (5:285–286). Remarkable in this passage is the repetition of a new familiar process of interiorization: the first interiorization creates ever-new ones by doubling the pairs "within."

Joel Fineman has found the same process and transformation in what he calls "the structure of allegorical desire."[19] There too the same transformation of oppositional pairs takes place, in all probability for the same reasons. "Distanced at the beginning from its source, allegory will set out on an increasingly futile search for a signifier with which to recuperate the fracture of and at its source, and with each signifier the fracture and the search begin again: a structure of continual yearning, the insatiable desire of allegory."[20] Fineman can point toward an even more formalized and general paradigm for the constitution and working of binary systems: Jakobson's phonological system.[21] Jakobson traces the phonological opposition back to an original maximum opposition of full openness in the vocalic /a/ and complete closedness in the labial stop /p/. But "in order to build a structure, at least two sets of opposition are required."[22] The second set is introduced through a kind of "plugging up" of the movement from /a/ to /p/, resulting in the nasal /m/ which can be seen as being contained within the original opposition and becoming a differential mark in itself for further oppositions.

What seems to me specifically significant for our discussion of resentment in all these oppositions and transformations is the moment which Nietzsche already emphasized: the moment of interiorization of the "original" opposition and conflict. In this process the nature of the opposition changes. Signification and articulation take place, just as the new phonological difference turns the babble of p-a-p-a-p-a into language and meaning. What is first posited in Nietzsche's opposition as an external dichotomy of inclusion and exclusion, securing a desired identity (individual or collective), becomes the scene of an internal conflict within that identity and thus threatens it. Resentment reacts to the threat by trying to externalize the conflict again. Thus, wherever identity is claimed, be it of the individual, of a group, of an institution, of a discipline, of a nation, etc., the economy of resentment is involved. But the very economy that constitutes both interiorization and resentment also sets the scene for a differentiation, a very fragile one, to be sure: resentment tries to displace the interiorization of conflict, it tries to avoid being the scene of conflict by externalizing part of the internalized pair, ascribing it to the other, the *barbaros*, whoever (s)he might be. Overcoming resentment, then, would mean not to reject it, not to negate it, but to acknowledge and accept it as a necessary ingredient.

Such an acceptance, however, can only be the result of a "working-through": working through all the knotted threads of denials, negations, and nots, not simply as individual work, but as work within institutional frameworks. The politics of discipline building and their relation to the politics of resentment are today as relevant as at Nietzsche's time. The rhetoric with which Wilamowitz ended his devastating critique of Nietzsche's *Birth of Tragedy* still has a familiar ring: "May Mr. N. keep his word, may he grasp the thyrsos, may he wander from India to Greece, but may he descend from the professorial chair, on which he is supposed to teach scholarship [*Wissenschaft*]; may he collect panthers and tigers around him, but not Germany's philological youth who must learn to work in the asceticism of self-denial, to search everywhere nothing but the truth."[23] Nietzsche's text on resentment also has a lot to say about asceticism and self-denial, perhaps more than Mr. Wilamowitz would have liked to know, and about scholarship, perhaps more than some of us might want to know.

V

BRECHT'S THEATER
OF CRUELTY

Die Menschen handeln nach ihrem Hunger und empfan-
gen ihre Belehrung vom Tod.

(Brecht)

kann die lehre die gewalt zerstören?
möge die gewalt nicht die lehre zerstören!

(Brecht)

Zugrunde gehen heißt hier immer:
auf den Grund der Dinge gehen.

(Walter Benjamin)

A widespread consensus in literary and
theater criticism, particularly among Brecht scholars, differentiates

two traditions in modern theater: one is derived from Antonin Artaud, the other from Bertolt Brecht. The former, marked by violence, excess, irrationalism, and absurdity, is pitted against the cool, distanced, ascetic, political, and rational theater of Brecht. Since any reading of Artaud and Brecht undermines an opposition of the two in those terms, the force of conviction that feeds the opposition must come from somewhere else. It has its own tradition which has created, with the force of a repetition compulsion, ever-new oppositional pairs since the Enlightenment: Kant and Sade, Marx and Nietzsche, Brecht and Artaud.

This is not the place for a detailed discussion of the relationship between Brecht and Artaud.[1] My critique is directed at the terms of the opposition and principle from which they emerge. This critique does not come from the outside, it operates already within the texts of Brecht and Artaud. The opposition is not so much between them as immanent in their work. While it has often been said that playwrights of a younger generation—Peter Weiss, Heiner Müller, Edward Bond—have brought together Brecht and Artaud in a new kind of theater, it would be more accurate to say that they have always already been together in a conflictual setting within themselves. To move the opposition from an "in-between" to a "within" changes the fundamental quality of that opposition. It can no longer be grasped in terms such as "rationality" versus "irrationalism."

Yet theater lives from opposition and conflict and projects them into its own typology. Other pairs have marked the typology of modern theater, among them the opposition of voice and body.[2] The theater of the voice reduces the theatrical corporeality to that phenomenon in which the body fades away. Theater turns into dramatic dialogue. Peter Szondi's *Theory of the Modern Drama* sees the essential development of the theater since the Renaissance in an increasing emphasis on dialogue and a reduction of the whole body as acting agent on the stage.[3] Artaud's rebellion against traditional theater can then be seen as a reintroduction of the body in the theatrical space. Brecht's theatrical revolution points in the same direction. The circus and the sports stadium are Brecht's exemplary models for theatrical space; gestures (*Gestus*: a characteristic ensemble of gestures) are the medium in which his plays unfold.

There is, however, something odd about the invocation of the body. The non-identity of the material body with the imaginary, the erotic, and the symbolic *corpus* undermines any simple opposition between a sublimated theater of speech and a sensual-naturalistic theater of the body. Brecht's *Gestus* paradigmatically shows the difference *in* the body: *Gestus* is the sum of concrete bodily gestures, facial expressions, tones of voice, and rhythm and figures of speech, but is not identical with any of these. It contains the *relation* to another body and *Gestus*. It is structured by the symbolic code of a specific social situation. The body does not have the identity of its wholeness in itself. It provides the ideal and idol, the *Gestalt*, of wholeness, which it only finds in the distribution along a symbolic chain.

This status of the body has its consequences for theatrical corporeality. The emphatic invocation of the body does not exclude extreme violence, it even seems to act out a certain hostility against the body. The theater of the body is above all the theater of the mutilated and dissected body. Oppositional paradigms, such as Beckett's theater of the voice versus Artaud's theatrical corporeality, are therefore rather fragile. The disembodiment in Beckett's theater takes place in the medium of pantomime and clownish corporeality; in a similar way, Handke's *Sprechstücke* (speech plays) move more and more toward the silence of the gestural body. Yet the opposition of voice and body is not completely wrong. Their mutual interpenetration forms the scene of violent conflict.

Brecht's *Lehrstücke* (teaching plays or learning plays, but in a very particular sense, as we will see) are shaped by violence and cruelty such as the dismemberment of a body in the clown scene of the *Badener Lehrstück*. The emphasis on the political content of these plays from the late twenties and early thirties has obscured their striking tendency toward cruelty. The simplistic dichotomies of the cold war mentality that affected the discussions about Brecht, pitting the "poet" against the political activist, effectively paralyzed any serious investigation of the interrelation of politics, violence, and aesthetics. The exploration of this interrelation does not fit in the traditional political ideological discourse. In Brecht's *Lehrstücke*, violence is not merely "content," but form, an inseparable linking of the aesthetic with the pedagogical elements. The trinity of art, teaching, and politics forms the conflictual unity of these plays.

The explosiveness of these elements shows its effect even in the reception, where it produces an excess of dichotomies, oppositions, and separations. The general contradictions and debates provoked by Brecht's theater are condensed in the discussion about the *Lehrstücke*. The critical vocabulary is dominated by oppositional pairs such as abstract-concrete, reason-emotion, individual-mass, didacticism-aesthetic pleasure, and so on.[4] In the German discussion about Brecht, there are two major studies that make an attempt to overcome these dichotomies. Jan Knopf's polemical review of Brecht criticism as well as his *Brecht Handbuch*[5] endeavors to take seriously Brecht's claim as a dialectical writer and to trace dialectics as a form of writing as well as thinking. Knopf is thus able to move beyond the all too familiar and simplistic oppositions.

One of the most influential and consequential turns in the discussion about the *Lehrstücke* was achieved by Reiner Steinweg. He interprets the *Lehrstücke* as Brecht's most radical attempt at a political-aesthetic education, the project of a "Great Pedagogy."[6] Steinweg places Brecht's experiments within the context of the revolutionary–avant-gardist tendencies of the twenties and thirties. The great ambition of the artistic and political avant-garde of that period was directed toward a radical restructuring and reshaping of the relationship between aesthetic production and reception. The passive art consumer was to become an active participant. According to Steinweg, this is the major aim of Brecht's *Lehrstücke*: they are not didactic in the sense that they present political content to an audience, but rather as theatrical pedagogy for the actors, experimental practices of an aesthetic-political nature, and exercises in sociopolitical behavior and dialectical thinking.

Beyond their differences in method and aim, Knopf and Steinweg share a tendency toward a harmonizing totality, be it in the name of "dialectic" or in the name of the "Great Pedagogy." The question is to what degree Brecht's *Lehrstücke* are test cases of dialectic and pedagogy in delineating the constitutive margins of dialectic and pedagogy, and perhaps transgressing them. Knopf and Steinweg still feel compelled to integrate all violence, antagonisms, and negativity into the totalizing machine of a dialectic or of pedagogy. If our reading now follows the traces of death, violence, and suffering that cannot be sublated, it might seem that we are returning to the unreflected "bourgeois" oppositions and the clichés of existential rhetoric. There is, however, a small and yet radical difference between that which cannot be integrated after working through the dialectic of things and the sentimental contradictions before that work has taken place. In Brecht criticism, and in the discussion about the *Lehrstücke* in particular, there are only a few beginnings in this direction.[7]

Steinweg's thesis about the *Lehrstücke* met strong resistance in East and West. His claim that Brecht had reached the most progressive form of a revolutionary socialist theater with these experiments implied that Brecht's later "mature" plays were compromises with the inadequate cultural politics and reality of the German Democratic Republic. Western critics, on the other hand, could not reconcile themselves to the glorification of a form of theater that goes against the grain of the most deep-seated sentimentalities of the sacred bourgeois individual.

But Steinweg's theory did lead beyond critical debates to an experimental pedagogical praxis based on the form of Brecht's *Lehrstücke*.[8] In these practical experiments, the implications and limits of Steinweg's interpretation become most clearly visible. The majority of these experiments come closer to the Habermasian model of a symmetrical communication, free of violence and antagonistic conflicts, than to the violent conflicts of Brecht's plays.

Brecht's *Lehrstücke* are "teaching plays," i.e., not merely plays that teach, but also plays about teaching, in the form of teaching. Contrary to well-meant ideologies, the teaching situation is never a matter of symmetrical communication between "equals." Brecht stages such a communicative constellation in the theatrical relation between text, actors, and listeners/viewers, whereby the actors are ideally also the audience.

Paul Hindemith, who composed the music for Brecht's earliest *Lehrstücke* experiments, saw the relationship of the actors to the text as that of free agents improvising on the basis of the text. Brecht contradicted this vehemently and called Hindemith's notion a shallow harmonization (*St.* 2, 59). The text of the *Lehrstücke* stands in relation to the "free" actor like language to the speaker: it rules. The smooth functioning between rule and freedom is not necessarily the result of a dialectical sublation of the master-slave conflict; it could be the symptom of a total interiorization of the rules: the beautiful soul as beautiful speaker and agent with the graciousness of the marionette. The attempt to mediate between the freedom of the actor and the prescribed text occasionally forces even Brecht to compromise formulations worthy of any politician: freedom "within the frame of certain determinations" (innerhalb des rahmens gewisser bestimmungen; *St.* 2, 165). The question is, what is the "determinate" status of those "certain" determinations? In the idiomatic usage, both in English and German, "certain" is that which is not certain and therefore all the more certain. It invokes the agency of an implicit understanding that does not need or even permit an explicit naming—you know those certain things, those certain limits.

An "immense variety" (ungeheuere mannigfaltigkeit) is possible in the *Lehrstücke*, according to Brecht. He immediately gives an example: "During the performance of the *Badener Lehrstücke*, the author and the composer were present on the stage and constantly intervened" (*ibid.*). The constant interventions of those who prescribe guarantees the immense variety. To be sure, freedom is not limited to the interventions of the author in the narrow sense of the word: "The form of the *Lehrstücke* is rigorous, but only in order that parts of one's own invention [*Teile eigener Erfindung*] and of a topical nature [*aktueller Art*] can all the more easily be introduced" (M, 252). There remains the indeterminateness of the relation between "one's own" (who is the proprietor?) and the authority of the rigorous form (who authorizes it, by what legitimation?). Who determines the parts, who conceives the whole?

Under the gaze of a critical reading, Brecht's own theory of the *Lehrstücke* seems to open up to something that it wants to hide rather than enlighten. Such a conclusion would then be in agreement with those critics who have claimed for a long time that Brecht's theory of the *Lehrstücke* was only a rationalization after the fact in order to distract from the terrorist content of the plays. There certainly is a great deal of rationalization in Brecht's writing. But the matter is not as simple as some conservative critics would think, in order to distract from their own rationalizations. It does not help to throw away the theory in favor of the pure praxis of the plays "in themselves." The truth is not to be found "behind" the covering belatedness of rationalization. It is rather in the conflict between theory and praxis, in *their* process of covering up. The plays are not simply the "other" of their theory, they also double it. *The Measures Taken (Die Maßnahme)*, for example, is not simply the staging of a violence covered up by a rationalization process in the form of a trial; the theory "itself," on the other hand, is also a representation of violence. Critics who gleefully think they can hang Brecht by his own words offer themselves the paradigm of rationalization when they cover up their own entanglement in the violence of authority with sublime statements about freedom and individuality. When the critics, as in many cases, are also (academic) teachers, they, that is we, cannot escape the pedagogical implications of the *Lehrstücke*. What they reveal is the repressed part of the official dogmas about teaching.

The general assumption that *Lehrstücke* are didactic plays that communicate a certain knowledge or opinion is based on a reduction of the idea of teaching and learning to a mere cognitive process. The modern discussion about "didacticism" seems to have forgotten a very different notion of pedagogy from Plato to Nietzsche and Lacan, as well as the tradition of *Lehre* as apprenticeship. The reduction of teaching to a purely cognitive "communication" since the Enlightenment is part of the phenomenon that Freud calls "isolating."[9] Teaching is isolated from its affective entanglement—from pleasure on the one hand, from violence on the other hand one might be tempted to say, were not the "on the one hand" and "on the other hand" already part of the idiom of isolating that wants to neatly separate what belongs inseparably together. The separation of pleasure and violence is the first step of the separation of both from teaching as a pure, cognitive communication.[10] Violence covers itself as objective reason, pleasure is degraded to a simple means for the weak and less talented ones; a sugarcoating of the bitter pill of knowledge is one of the favorite images of the eighteenth century.

Brecht's *Lehrstücke* break through the isolation and reconnect the teaching with a praxis and with the body (*Einübung in Haltungen*: practicing attitudes, modes of behavior), with pleasure, and with violence. All three elements participate in the dramaturgy of these plays.

Brecht's polemics of the twenties against "culinary" theater are directed above all against a specific form of bourgeois consumer mentality and the reduction of pleasure to consumption. In his later writings, Brecht emphasizes more and more the element of pleasure in teaching, learning, and producing. It might seem that the *Lehrstücke* replace pleasure with violence, but only in order to stage all the more intensely the disturbing concoction of pleasure in violence and of violence in pleasure. In a short text from the fragmentary *Fatzer* complex, Brecht offers his version of the witch's brew of cruelty, terror, and pleasure:

> They are wrong who present sexuality to the pupil as something clean, harmless, and understandable. They are right who demonstrate it as unnatural, that is, as dirty, dangerous, and ununderstandable. . . . This is not in order to deter the pupil from love, when one presents love to him as dirty and unnatural, rather in order to teach him merely the truth. It is not in order to incite disgust in him, but to teach him terror. The best way to teach sexual love is therefore the way boys do it among themselves: they talk about sexual things with giggling and hot faces, and they draw large, dirty symbols on walls and on houses, resembling those symbols that are used by the religions of the most wise in all races. This mode of teaching is good also, because it takes place among those who touch each other not only with words but also with their hands.[11]

The scene of the *Lehrstücke* also is the obscene where the sacred and the filthy meet in the carnival and the terror of the taboo. Only in this silent center does their full political implication unfold. Their relationship to the Japanese No plays is more than a formal one.

There is still another, although related, pleasure in these plays: the pleasure in the mechanical (a pleasure that is explicitly presented as sexual pleasure in Fellini's version of *Casanova*): "There is a specific joy in the mechanical, in the well-timed entrance, in precise coordination, in the participation in a mathematical exercise, a kind of "cue-word pleasure" [*Stichwortgenuß*]: each of four players is subjected to the same numerical system, and each prepares his entrance like a cardplayer his trick [Stich] or as each part of a machine does its specific beat."[12] "Cue" and "trick" in German are both based on Stich, literally a stab. The pleasure machine of the Lehrstücke works with stabs and beats.

According to Brecht, exercises in attitudes (Einübung in Haltungen) are the major aim of the Lehrstücke. But what is Haltung (attitude, posture; from halten, to hold, a way of holding oneself)? A text from the Keuner stories elaborates the term:

> Often I see, said the thinking one, that I have my father's attitude/ posture [Haltung], but I don't do my father's deeds. Why do I do different deeds? Because there are other necessities. But I see that the attitude endures longer than the mode of action [die Haltung hält länger]: it resists the necessities. Many a one can do only one thing if he does not want to lose face. Because he cannot follow the necessities, he easily perishes. But he who has an attitude can do many things and does not lose face.[13]

In this text Haltung seems to be a kind of substance in the literal sense: that which subsists and remains under all transformations, and yet is itself a principle of transformation. Haltung as a substanceless substance represents the place of the subject and his identity. It is also the place of the father, as the thinking one says; he sees himself as the subject in the Haltung—that is, also in the hold—of the father. He who has a Haltung does not lose face. Is it because his father guarantees his face, just as the name of the father guarantees his name? The term Haltung leads into an ideological minefield. It is the favorite word of the authoritarian character, under the motto Haltung bewahren (the German version of to "stay the course"). Its paradigmatic bodily expression is the one called for by the military command for "attention!"

Brecht's texts enter this minefield and cause a few explosions that set the term vertiginously spinning. In the conservative character ideology, the stiff backbone of inner character creates a Haltung, and from this Haltung action emerges. In Brecht's text it works the other way around: "Our attitude comes from our actions, our actions come from need and necessity [Not]" (St. 2, 47). But there is another turn:

"When need and necessity have been brought to order, from where do our actions then come? When need and necessity have been brought to order, our actions come from our attitude" (*ibid.*). Character as a substance has disappeared. There remains a reversible effect (although not symmetrically reversible) between action and attitude, which is extended to the relation between expression and expressed, and between signifier and signified: "Just as moods and chains of thought lead to attitudes and gesture, attitudes and gestures lead to moods and chains of thought. The tension of the neck muscles and the holding of one's breath are observed to accompany anger. By straining the muscles of one's neck and by holding one's breath one can also bring forth anger" (*St. 2,* 141). The gesture, expression and sign of an interiority, in turn produces interiority.

According to Brecht, the gestural signifier has three qualities: it is meaningless, corporeal, and mechanical. It constitutes meaning and the subject through these three qualities:

> whatever you think, keep it secret
> go out with us mechanically!
> go like someone greets: because it is customary
> perform the movements that
> mean nothing. [14]

Brecht puts an end to a tradition that goes back to the eighteenth century, and in some sense he returns to an older one. While rhetoric, poetics, and rote learning have been denounced since the eighteenth century in favor of the free, creative, personal expression of an interiority, Brecht relocates meaning in the corporeality of the material signifier and in the mechanism of a symbolic machinery.

The relationship to a technical apparatus stands at the beginning of Brecht's *Lehrstück* production. *Der Ozeanflug* (*The Flight Across the Ocean,* first entitled *The Flight of Lindbergh*) is a radio play experimenting with a new technical medium. Like many of his contemporaries, Walter Benjamin among them, Brecht considered the radio to have the most advanced technical potential to revolutionize not simply the contents but the structure of communication. *Der Ozean-*

flug was first performed at the music festival in Baden-Baden in 1929. It was the representation of a radio play, the musical-theatrical representation of a new relationship between human producers and technical apparatus. The play thematically repeats that relationship.

During the performance in Baden-Baden, "the radio orchestra with its apparatus and singers stood on the left side of the stage, the audience was on the right side." The actors representing the audience sang the part of Lindbergh. In an actual radio performance the listeners are supposed to read the Lindbergh text along with the radio voice.

In this setting, the apparatus represents the general, the state, and the richness of the whole to which the individual is not simply opposed but into which it integrates itself through speaking: "Pursuing the following principles: the state is supposed to be rich, man is poor, the state must be obliged to have a lot of potential, man should be permitted to have little, the state should be able to produce everything concerning music, everything that needs special capabilities and apparatuses, but the individual should produce an exercise."[15] The introductory appeal (*Aufforderung*) of the play invokes such a relationship:

> The community asks you: repeat
> the first crossing of the ocean
> By singing together
> The notes
> And by reading the text.[16]

The apparatus is the voice of the community. The individual speaks only by repeating the language of the community. Brecht's words for "singing" and "reading" are not simply *singen* and *lesen*, but *Absingen* and *Ablesen*, which emphasize the mechanical aspect of singing or reading "off" of a prescribed text. *Absingen* and *Ablesen* exclude any notion of singing and reading as personal expression. The individuals who sing and read the prescribed text stage the symbolic bond that constitutes them. Brecht points to the pedagogical effect of the paradox that people sing and read *together* in the form of "I."

In a reductive reading one could summarize the theme of the play as: man masters nature with the help of the technical apparatus. But Brecht's text raises the question: who masters whom? An odd

entanglement of speaking agents and roles is typical for the *Lehrstücke*.
In the distribution of various roles to various speakers, fixed identities
are dissolved. The technical apparatus speaks the part of nature, the
airplane is both helper and enemy: "In flying / I fight against my
airplane and / Against the primitive." And it is also a battle "Against
myself" (*W.S.* 2:576). The battleground is apparently Hegel's dialectic
of self-consciousness and its Marxian extension toward a humaniza-
tion of nature and a naturalization of man: "Let us fight against nature / Until we have become natural ourselves" (*W.S.* 2:573).

The dialectic works almost smoothly. But there is something left
over that needs to be covered up. In the sixteenth scene the exhausted
but successful pilot wants to be carried into the shed: "I am nomatterwho. Please carry me / Into a dark shed so that / Nobody sees my /
Natural weakness" (*W.S.* 2:584). Why must the natural weakness be
pushed aside, covered in darkness? Within the framework of a dialectic
it does not make sense. Dialectic would insist and remain in the face
of the negative in order to turn it around, not hide it. There is apparently a surplus of negativity that does not participate in the economy of dialectics. The text leaves it there and claims that there was
no mistake in the work. But the fact that it articulates, be it only for
one moment, the shadow of repression testifies to another knowledge
and to a knowledge of the Other.

There is an additional implicit cover-up at work in the strange
naming of the pilot: "I am nomatterwho (*Ich bin Derundder*). This
no-name replaces the name of Lindbergh, who was originally also
named in the title. Brecht explains the erasure of the name was a
result of Lindbergh's fascist tendencies and his fraternalization with
the Nazis. Thus the main speaker no longer says, "My name is Charles
Lindbergh," but, "My name does not matter," and "I am nomatterwho." But if the name does not matter, why is there an effort to erase
it? Apparently it does matter and therefore it must be erased. But
erasing it also changes the matter. The dialectic has broken down
when it gets rid of that which disturbs by erasing it instead of working
through it by asking: what does it matter, when fascism participates
in that which matters to me?

On July 28, 1929, a day after the *Ozeanflug*, another *Lehrstück*,
Das Badener Lehrstück vom Einverständnis (*The Baden Teaching Play*

of Agreement), had its first performance. It is one of the most disturbing and enigmatic Brechtian texts. It literally begins with the end of the *Ozeanflug*, quoting its epilogue as a prologue. The trial is reopened in the face of the fliers whose plane has crashed. Their weakness is no longer hidden in the darkness of a shed. While the *Ozeanflug* celebrates victory as the result of the collective effort of the pilot and the mechanics, the *Badener Lehrstück* splits the four fliers into the three teachable mechanics and the unteachable pilot who is erased at the end.

As in the *Ozeanflug*, chorus and orchestra on the left side of the stage are confronted with the human voices, the four fliers, on the right side. Already in the *Ozeanflug* the play was centered around *Einverständnis* (agreement, understanding, consensus) between apparatus and human voices/listeners/speakers. Brecht's staging of *Einverständnis* in the *Badener Lehrstück* unfolds the dimensions and implications of consensus that the philosophy of Habermas avoids. In the *Badener Lehrstück* the *Gelernte Chor* (educated chorus) represents the community. Like Hegel's *We* in the *Phenomenology*, the *Gelernte Chor* already possesses the knowledge through which the fliers must work. So far the dialectical configuration works, but it is brought to its most extreme limit—and perhaps beyond it.

Brecht polemicizes sharply against any harmonious interpretation of understanding and agreement:

> Even if one would expect that "the individual integrates himself into something" or that certain spiritual and formal congruences are developed on a musical basis, such an artificial and shallow harmony would never be able to create a counterweight even for a minute on the widest and most vital basis against the collective formations that tear apart people with quite another violence.[17]

The artificial, shallow harmony is confronted with violent collective formations that tear apart. Tying together (collective formations) and tearing apart are intimately knotted together in such a way that they have to be countered with an equally strong, rending violence. This is the scene of the *Badener Lehrstück vom Einverständnis* that relegates any liberal theory of consensus to brutal impotence, uncovering at the same time the hidden violence in such theories. "Let us be reasonable," says the voice that is already in the more powerful position in a conflictual situation. Brecht indicated this in a fragmentary scene:

> T(EACHING): How does one recognize the ruling species?
> M(ASSES): One recognizes the ruling species when they say that violence is not necessary. [18]

Instead of denying violence, the play doubles and intensifies it to the point of the grotesque clown scene where a man is sawed to pieces in the name of helping him. Since help is necessary only where there is violence, "help and violence are one," and the helper is the accomplice of violence. Such is the logic of the play.

The teaching play about consensus is also a teaching play about dying. It is an attempt to integrate the most radical negation into the dialectical economy. Dying is an exercise in *Einverständnis*: "If the thinking one overcame the storm, he overcame it because he was in agreement with the storm. Therefore, if you want to overcome dying, you will overcome it when you know dying and when you are in agreement with dying." [19] To a certain degree, this is still in agreement with Hegel's dialectic: "Life is not that which fears death and wants to preserve itself from devastation, but that which bears it and sustains itself in death." [20] Truth is only gained by him who "finds himself in the absolute rending" (*in der absoluten Zerrissenheit*). *Einverständnis* becomes the power that "faces the negative." Thus, Brecht can write: "To be in agreement means also: *not* to be in agreement" (*St. 2, 62*).

In the *Badener Lehrstück* the three mechanics come to *Einverständnis*, but the pilot refuses it. He is the stumbling block to a smooth dialectic. *Einverständnis* is preceded by an expulsion. It is not simply an Other that is expelled, but the Other in the form of "us": "one of us / thoroughly like us / In face, form, and thought." Brecht tried later to minimize the death motif: "There is probably too much weight attributed to death in comparison with its small use value" (*St. 2, 57*). Death seems to disturb the economy.

In the *Jasager* and the *Neinsager* (*He Who Says Yes* and *He Who Says No*) Brecht explicitly returns to the theme of *Einverständnis*: "Important it is above all to learn agreement / Many say yes, and yet there is no agreement," sings the great chorus (no longer a learned one) at the beginning of both plays. The situation seems simple. A boy wants to accompany his teacher and a group of students on a voyage across the mountains, in order to get medicine for his gravely ill mother. In the mountains he falls ill. The great custom demands that the sick person be thrown to his death into the valley. The boy is asked whether he agrees and, following the custom, he says yes in the *Jasager*; he refuses in the *Neinsager*. Most critics read the *Jasager* as an example of blind submission to traditional authority which is then criticized in the *Neinsager*. Yet already the first verses of the chorus, quoted above, clearly state that *Einverständnis* is not identical with saying yes. Furthermore, Peter Szondi has shown in his afterword to a critical edition of the two plays that the relationship between *Jasager* and *Neinsager* is far more complex than had been assumed. There are two very different versions of the *Jasager*. In the first version, the major aim is a research trip to the great teachers beyond the mountains. When the boy falls ill he is thrown into the valley because the great custom demands it. In the second version the situation has changed: the aim of the trip is now to get medicine for the whole town suffering from an epidemic. When the boy falls ill, attempts are made to carry him across. Only after these attempts fail and the ill boy endangers the whole trip and thus the recovery of the whole town is he asked to agree to his death. If the *Neinsager* is a negation of the *Jasager*, it negates only the first version.

The second version of the *Jasager* differs from the first mainly in the rationalization and secularization of the motifs. The model is a Japanese No play. Brecht's co-worker Elisabeth Hauptmann had translated Arthur Waley's English version into German. The rigorously ritualized form of the No theater has a strong affinity with the rigor of the *Lehrstück* form. The religious mythical substance of the No plays, however, seems to be in utter contrast to the secularized political substance of Brecht's theater. Yet a theatrical genre where the form of presentation is so constitutive of the substance (its substance being a *Haltung*) cannot simply discard that which is sedimented within the form by tradition. In that form, the sacred and the ritual are insistent. The *Jasager/Neinsager* complex as a whole is not simply the secularization and rationalization of a religious paradigm, but the representation of the process of secularization as dramatic conflict.

Already Waley's English version of the No play eliminates large parts of the ritual and religious aspects of the original and even more of its magical and lyrical aura. Like the No theater in general,[21] the Japanese play *The Throw Into the Valley* is marked by a mixture of the hieratic rigor of ritual language, lyrical and magical invocation of local names, and a great many puns.[22] In the witty slipperiness of puns the firm margins of language dissolve, producing unexpected new meanings and displacements. Together with the evocative force of local names that often form dense sequences like litanies, they stand in contrast to the hieratic ritual form. Such contrasts contribute to the theatrical force of these plays.

Elisabeth Hauptmann closely follows Waley's English translation, which had discarded many religious and lyrical elements. Brecht's first version of the *Jasager* takes over Waley's plot but with a new emphasis on the motif of *Einverständnis*. The second version seems to transpose the problem into a completely secular setting where rational decisions have to be made. Death is no longer the consequence of an old sacred custom but motivated by the situation at hand: if the boy is not sacrificed the whole town might perish. Once rational motivation is introduced as a principle of legitimation, everything must be justified in these terms, otherwise the rational process is incomplete and the whole becomes irrational.

Brecht's second version is thus confronted with serious problems. While the sacrifice of the first version is fully motivated as long as one accepts the sacred tradition, the rational motivation produces holes that threaten its base. Question after question arises: if it is the aim of the trip to get medicine in the city beyond the mountains, why does the boy have to go along? If he goes along because he insists on it, why does the reasonable authority of the teacher not prevent him from doing so? Even if he goes along and falls ill, is it not possible for a member of the group to stay with him while the others continue their trip? and so on. The discussions among students after one of the performances, documented in the critical edition of the play, demonstrate that these are indeed the questions that are raised and that they can be continued infinitely, like all rationalizing questions. The rational legitimation finds no ultimate ground, only provisional reasons that are displaced by the next question. The "use value" of death becomes most questionable where it seems most reasonable. There are always the shadows of other motivations. The remark of one student in the discussion of the play indicates a sensibility for such other shadows: "One could almost think that the boy agrees with the wishes of his comrades because they are his wishes which he cannot express" (*J.N.*, 60).

The student's question points toward layers of the play that are only implicit in Brecht's text, but indicated in the Japanese original as far as I can judge on the limited basis of a translation. There is above all the intense relationship between the boy and the mother on the one hand and between the boy and the teacher on the other hand. In both cases love and authority are enigmatically intertwined. The love and tenderness of the teacher toward the boy is so strong in the No play that the teacher is in danger of betraying his vows and has to be admonished by his students. Brecht's play contains only faint traces of all this, but the traces point to other motivations than those articulated. *Einverständnis* has its center not necessarily where the yes is spoken, as indeed the first verses of the play already have shown. The *Lehrstücke* that speak most radically in the name of historical materialism confirm Benjamin's parable of historical materialism and theology in the image of the chess automaton and the hidden dwarf.[23]

While the *Neinsager* opposes the yes of the No play and the *Jasager*, the *Maßnahme (The Measures Taken)* performs a new inscription of the negated prescriptions. It confirms that the *Neinsager* did not take back the *Jasager*, but only modified it. Brecht planned the *Maßnahme* as a concretization of the *Jasager*. The burial scene of the first version of the *Maßnahme* literally repeats part of the scene of the throwing into the valley from the *Jasager*.

Die Maßnahme is the representation of a represention, or the performance of a performance: "Show [perform/represent] how it happened" (*Stellt dar, wie es geschah*), the chorus (now called *Kontrollchor*) sings at the beginning. The command for a presentation is preceded by *Einverständnis*: "We are in agreement with you" (*Wir sind einverstanden mit euch*). But the agreement is stopped by a caesura: "Stop! We have something to tell!" The presentation emerges from a caesura in the agreement, as a rupture in the continuity of praxis and theory. At the end *Einverständnis* is reconstituted. The theatrical presentation forms the transition from a blind agreement to one that has been worked through.

This transition is marked by two striking formal particularities: momentary standstill and repetition. The "Stop!" at the beginning of the play marks the moment of a blockage which the aesthetics of the eighteenth century knew as a moment of the sublime.[24] The natural imagination and the physical nature of man have come to a limit where they meet a moment of total standstill in the face of imminent annihilation. Only the intervention of another, "higher" force or faculty turns the situation around and lets a new sphere emerge. The relationship to Brecht's *Lehrstücke* is closer than it might seem. The concept of the sublime is that which cannot and must not be thought in the concept of beauty: violence and unreconciled, antagonistic conflict. While the beautiful soul has internalized the power of authority and the moral principles to the point that she seems to act from pure nature,[25] the sublime opens up the abyss and an unreconciled battle between two powers for mastery. Brecht's *Lehrstücke*, and *Die Maßnahme* in particular, stage this battle. They turn around the process of interiorization in their theatrical and gestural exteriorization of violence.

Since antiquity inversion and repetition have been stylistic marks of the sublime. *Die Maßnahme* continues that tradition on the level of syntax as well. Normal syntactical sequence is inverted in favor of the "high" style: "Wir werden anerkennen euer Urteil" instead of "Wir werden euer Urteil anerkennen" (we will accept your judgment). It is not by chance that Roman Jakobson demonstrated the principles of inversion and repetition in the grammar of poetry (and in the poetry of grammar) in a chorus song of *Die Maßnahme*, where the principle rules "down" to the level of the letter.[26] Repetition as parallelism and antithesis as repetition of the same in the inversion are the ruling principles on all levels of the text and of the performance, as a brief example can show.

The young comrade introduces himself as a subject thoroughly inscribed by the ideals of the revolution: "My heart beats for the revolution. Seeing injustice brought me among the fighters. I am for freedom. I believe in humanity. But I know that the classless society

can be brought to reality only through the dictatorship of the prole-
tariat, and therefore I am for the radical execution of our slogans."[27]
The sequence of these sentences of self-presentation can be read as a
phenomenology of a consciousness. "My heart beats": the first subject
is a physical organ that marks, linguistically as metaphor, the transition from the sensual to sense. But there is still feeling. Perception
(*Anblick*) drives the subject out of himself (*trieb mich*) toward a being
for ("I am for"). Consciousness splits into two opposite forms: "I believe" and "But I know," from which it returns to the form of praxis:
"therefore I am for the radical execution."

The subject thus inscribed is erased like a written leaf of paper
together with his comrades in order that they become "empty leaves
on which the revolution writes its commands" (M, 11). This inscription of the revolutionary script turns out to be a reinscription of the
erased script. To each sentence of the young comrade a scene of
reinscription responds:

> *My heart beats*—Scene 3: "The stone." Compassion and spontaneous
> feeling are at stake. But spontaneity is coded. Nothing is more stereo-
> typical than what comes from the heart. The spontaneous feeling be-
> comes a contradiction to itself; in following his heart, the young
> comrade betrays his heart.
>
> *Seeing injustice*—Scene 4: "Justice." Driven by the perception of in-
> justice, the young comrade wants to create justice and thwarts it by his
> single-handed attempt.
>
> *I am* —Scene 5: The self-confident assertion of the subject, "I am," is
> confronted in this scene by the critical question: "What is man?" and
> once more at the end of the scene: "Who are you?"
>
> *I believe*—Scene 6: Faith is put into question by the rebellion against
> the teaching. The representation of this rebellion wants to confirm,
> however, the faith of those who perform it. The representation of the
> erasure reinscribes that which was erased.
>
> *But I know*—Scenes 7, 8, 9: "The time of extreme persecution," "Anal-
> ysis," "Burial." Knowledge constitutes itself in the extreme, at the limit,
> by dissolving the limit (analysis). According to Brecht people learn from
> and in death.

The repetition as parallelism is both an erasure of that which is
repeated and its reinscription in a different place. In this displacement

the quality of that which is repeated changes. We are still in the realm of dialectics. Brecht's play does not hide this rest that is silence; it was criticized for this reason by the orthodoxy.[28] Brecht responded with some thematic and stylistic changes and compromises. Thus, the "sublime" style of the first version was toned down in the name of more realism. It could be argued that this was the beginning of idealization.

The conflict between the desire for totality and all-embracing integration that motivates the *Lehrstücke* (as it does all teaching) and the infallible eye for that which cannot be integrated intervene violently within the *Lehrstücke* and fragment them. The finished ones are not finished in Brecht's eyes; others, like the *Fatzer* fragments, remained fragments in the literal sense. Still others, like *Die Ausnahme und die Regel* (*The Exception and the Rule*) and *Die Mutter* (*The Mother*), are at the borderline between *Lehrstück* and drama and raise the question of genre, which is also a question about the whole and the parts.

This question is the theme of *Die Ausnahme und die Regel*. The play is based on the general rule that the exception confirms the rule. Exception and rule constitute each other, they confirm each other even in conflict: the exception wants to contradict the rule, the rule wants to annihilate the exception. They thus establish a system of increasing totalization. Schiller presented this totaling force in his ballad *Die Bürgschaft* as a touching scene of human integration. Because reason wants to occupy the heart too, the heart can no longer have any reasons that reason does not know. Even the tyrant wants to be included in all-embracing brotherhood and friendship. The unheard-of exceptional behavior of a friend transforms the ferocious tyrant into a human being.

The first seven scenes of Brecht's play have the balladesque character of an adventure story with some direct allusions to Schiller's ballad, such as the threatening attack of robbers, the dangerous flooding of a river, and the threat of dying from thirst. But at the moment when the touching deed of the poor man, who is ready to share the last drops of water with his master, is supposed to appeal to the universal law of humanity and establish it on earth so that from now on everything will be fair, Brecht blocks the edifying conclusion with a violent shot. The master cannot believe in an act of selfless sharing and interprets the move of the servant as a threat to kill him. So he shoots him. The trial that follows proves him right: he acted reasonably. Reason and its immanent violence are at stake. "To assume that the servant did not want to kill the master would have meant assuming that the servant was not reasonable." Fear, defense, and violent exclusion are the mark of reason: "The fact that they have fear proves that they are reasonable."

The play shows that reason is not the whole, but the exclusive power of a partial interest, a piece that claims to be the whole. It is the irrationalism of reason.

Brecht's theater is usually seen as a theater of rationality, because Brecht often suggested that himself with specific references to the Enlightenment and to Diderot in particular.

But Brecht's plays, and his *Lehrstücke* most radically so, are also a critique of reason. Some verses in *Die Ausnahme und die Regel* indicate the particular mode of Brecht's critique of reason:

> Observe closely the behavior of these people:
> Find it strange [*befremdend*], although not foreign [*fremd*]
> Inexplicable, although normal
> Incomprehensible, although it is the rule.[29]

These verses can be read first as one of Brecht's many formulations of his *Verfremdungseffekt*. Something is taken out of its familiarity and appears now strange, inexplicable, incomprehensible. But because it is no longer familiar it becomes recognizable. Hegel already describes the process in the *Phenomenology* as the work of analytic reason (*Verstand*). In contrast to synthesizing reason, *Verstand* analyzes, i.e., dissolves; it dissects and dismembers. Hegel calls this work of analytic reason "the most miraculously astounding [*verwundersamste*] and greatest or rather the absolute power."[30] Brecht's plays (to which he refers most often as *Stücke*, pieces) stage this work of the analytic power to the point of actual dismemberment.

The work of distancing and defamiliarization is not finished with the text and the performance. It is also the work of the readers and audience to whom the demand is directed: "Observe closely," "Find it strange." One could compare the Brechtian audience to the analysand in psychoanalysis: it is the patient who is called upon to do the work. But to invoke such an analogy immediately raises the question of transference and its processes of identification.

It would seem that the relationship between audience/reader and text/performance is at least negatively clear for Brecht: no identification. That answer, however, is clear only if there is a concept of identification. Yet the process of identification has largely remained obscure in literary criticism despite the popularity of reception theories.[31] Brecht criticism in particular repeats over and over the same old clichés about V effect and non-identification without ever seriously investigating the process of identification.

A beginning for such an investigation might open up in the difference between Lehrstück and drama (what Brecht calls Schauspiel). If we understand the Lehrstücke as plays for performers, not for viewers and passive consumers, the role of the audience becomes that of a participant who is, so to speak, dismembered and disseminated into the various Haltungen, postures, of the piece. As participant the audience becomes one with the performance so that this strangest and most defamiliarizing type of Brechtian drama paradoxically becomes the place of the most intense identification. There is, however, a substantial difference from the kind of identification as it is generally understood since the eighteenth century and brought to its most articulate theory by Stanislawski. This more familiar form of identification is based on the imaginary wholeness of the Gestalt of the other and it presupposes an interiority. Identification in this sense means to enter into the other, to immerse oneself into the character and to speak and act out of the other. Before Brecht began the experiments of his Lehrstücke, he had already dissolved the presuppositions of such a form of identification in plays like Im Dickicht der Städte (In the Jungle of the Cities) and Mann ist Mann (Man Is Man). Already these early plays reject the basis of traditional bourgeois drama: motivation. They dissolve the ground of identification, by purposely "flattening" the "round" character. Brecht's theatrical technique in these plays has less to do with behaviorist theories than with the formation of a new poetics of modernism that has its parallels in the writing of Kafka and Beckett.

The identity of audience and performer in Brecht's *Lehrstücke* is not based on an immersion into a character, because his characters have no interiority. They are rather dismembered and disseminated into a sequence of postures. They unfold into the chain of the gestural rhetoric.

In the drama (*Schauspiel*, a play to see, to watch) the audience remains physically in front of the events and their sequence of rhetorical gestures. There is a spatial distance, a gap that is filled in traditional theater with the imaginary space of the stage.

Die Ausnahme und die Regel and *Die Mutter* are located on the threshold of *Lehrstück* and *Schauspiel*. The command "Observe!" appeals to a viewer. In reference to *Die Mutter*, Brecht writes that it was "written in the style of the *Lehrstücke*, but in need of actors [*Schauspieler*]" (*St 2*, 138). What is the "style of the *Lehrstücke*"? A brief comparison with the later drama *Mutter Courage und ihre Kinder* can delineate the difference. Both plays are dominated by a strong central maternal figure, and both direct their force at the same time against the immanent traditional power of such a figure whose affective force is supported by mother tongue, mother myths, and mother wit. She is the topos of a figure, a place where the delirium of identification finds its primal scene: to return to and enter into the womb.

The two plays work in different ways against this force without annihilating it. Roland Barthes has formulated the difference between the two plays most succinctly: In *Die Mutter* the audience learns and sees together with the main figure; they are on the same level. In *Mutter Courage* the figure remains blind, the audience seeing her blindness sees.[32]

Again it seems that the *Lehrstück* is more prone to identification than the *Schauspiel*, and yet that contradicts all experience. *Mutter Courage*, despite its V effects, produces by the very distance between viewer and figure the speculative desire of identification. In *Die Mutter* the dual relationship is expanded in a triadic shape: the cathexis between mother and son (and between mother and audience) is transferred to the *dritte Sache* (third thing) where mother and son meet without devouring each other. This *dritte Sache* takes the literal form of ABC: the letters that the mother learns from the teacher, and the

ABC of the class struggle that the teacher learns from the mother. In this double alphabetization, the imaginary body of identification is spelled out and dismembered.

In the violence of this dismemberment the dichotomy of an identifiable "rationality" opposed to an equally identifiable "irrationalism" is dispelled, and with it the simple opposition of Brecht and Artaud, who both rearticulated the relationship between reason and its other. Brecht's own commentary on the *Lehrstücke* points out that "the most rational form, the *Lehrstück*, produces the most emotional effects" (*St* 2, 169). Artaud's apparent emotionalism searches for a new intellectuality: "Une intellectualité nouvelle et plus profonde, qui se cache sous les gestes et sous les signes élevés à la dignité d'exorcismes particuliers"[33] (A new and deeper intellectuality that is hidden under the gestures and under the signs elevated to the dignity of the particular exorcisms). One could read this sentence as a characterization of Brecht's *Lehrstücke*.

VI

PAUL CELAN:
CONFIGURATIONS OF FREUD

Under the title *Frankfurt, September* the second poem of *Fadensonnen* invokes the name of Freud:

Blinde, licht-
bärtige Stellwand.
Ein Maikäfertraum
leuchtet sie aus.
Dahinter, klagegerastert,
tut sich Freuds Stirn auf,
die draußen
hartgeschwiegene Träne
schießt an mit dem Satz:
"Zum letzten-
mal Psycho-
logie."
Die Simili-
Dohle
frühstückt.

Der Kehlkopfverschlußlaut
singt. (2:114)[1]

(Blind, light- / bearded display wall. / A maybug dream / illuminates it. /
Behind it, lamentation-screened, / Freud's forehead opens up, / the tear /
hard-silenced outside / shoots up with the phrase: / "For the last / time psy-
cho- / logy." / The simili- / jackdaw / eats breakfast. / The glottal stop /
sings.)

The name appears in the inflected genitive form: syntax changes it,
rules over it, and marks it at the same time as a place of property and
origin. The subject of the sentence—*Stirn*—belongs to Freud and
originates with and in him. It opens up, reflexively: "tut . . . sich
auf." It seems to fulfill Danton's wish and desire for knowledge, as
expressed in Büchner's play:

JULIE: Du kennst mich Danton.
DANTON: Ja, was man so kennen heißt. Du hast dunkle Augen und
lockiges Haar und einen feinen Teint und sagst immer zu mir: lieb
Georg. Aber (*er deutet ihr auf Stirn und Augen*) da, da, was liegt hinter
dem? Wir müßten uns die Schädeldecken aufbrechen und die Gedanken einander aus den Hirnfasern zerren.[2]

To recall this text is to recall Celan's major poetological statement,
Der Meridian, where Büchner's text plays a major role.

But what is Freud's role in the poem and the poetics? Does the
opening of Freud's forehead indicate a promise?

Indeed, it seems that Freud's psychoanalysis promises the opening and penetration that Danton desires so violently: to break open
the skull and pull out the hidden thoughts. And is that not also the
desire and promise of Celan's poetic language, as stated in an often-
quoted poem?

Weggebeizt vom
Strahlenwind deiner Sprache
das bunte Gerede des An-
erlebten—das hundert-
züngige Mein-
gedicht, das Genicht. (2:31)

(seared away by / the ray-wind of your language / the colorful babbling of the aped / experience—the hundred-tongued my-perjured / poem, the non-entity)

Language that cleans away the walls and covers of false language in order to open the path to a place of truth appears with the seductiveness of a common place between Freud and Celan. But then, they also share a radical displacement of common places.

Freud's place in Celan's poem is not easy to locate. In order to locate a place, some kind of topology is necessary. Most of the metaphors point toward a familiar spatial paradigm of inside/outside that also belongs to an old metaphysical topology according to which the truth is located "behind" or "beneath" a deceptive surface, which has to be broken through or penetrated. This paradigm informs literary criticism as much as a certain—more Jungian than Freudian—understanding of psychoanalysis as "depth psychology."

Celan's poem seems to suggest such a topology. There is a wall—*Stellwand*—a kind of display wall, as Celan probably saw it at the Frankfurt book fair, where the Fischer publishing house would display portraits of its most famous authors, among them Freud and Kafka. The title of the poem "Frankfurt, September" points at these "data." But what is thus "given" by the real is no ground. It opens up with Freud's forehead and marks something "behind" (*dahinter*). There is also an outside: "die draussen hartgeschwiegene Träne." This tear, hardened through silence, sets up a vertiginous displacement of the date and the data that the title indicates to us. In accepting this "gift" from the real, we believe to have found an authentication of the poem's meaning, authorized by the authorial eye that actually saw a setting of a configuration of the authors Kafka and Freud. But the eye that saw is metonymically displaced by the tear that in turn points metaphorically at a loss. If tears are supposed to speak and to testify for the authenticity of mourning and loss, this tear also refuses to "speak," hardened in silence. It does not enter into or penetrate something, but shoots or rushes up to a violent confrontation with Freud's opening forehead: "Zum letzten- / mal Psycho- / logie."

The quotation points to an outside of the poetic text signed by Celan, referring to another signature, another proper name: Kafka, who wrote this sentence into his notebook.[3] While the first two parts

of the poem (4 + 2 lines) lead to the name of Freud and are dominated by him, the last three parts (6 + 3 + 2 lines) belong to three
epiphanies of Kafka in the form of a quotation, in the form of his
name (*Dohle*: *kavka* in Czech means jackdaw, the bird that Kafka's
father used as an emblem for his business, a kind of *Warenzeichen*,
trademark), and finally in the form of his illness, the laryngeal tuber-
culosis, the *Kehlkopfverschlußlaut*, which sings while it silences the
carrier of the name.

The configuration of Freud and Kafka seems to take the form of
a confrontation. Kafka's phrase, spoken by the hardened tear, seems
to reject the sphere opened up by Freud's forehead. This presupposes,
of course, that psychology and Freud's psychoanalysis belong to the
same sphere. Freud, however, has distanced himself, at times very
emphatically, from the field of psychology, to the point where he
declares that even a discussion with those working in the field of
psychology would be impossible.[4]

On the other hand, there is Kafka's well-known entry in his diary
on September 23, 1912, after the night when he wrote *The Judgment*,
a text written "mit . . . vollständiger Öffnung des Leibes und der
Seele" (with complete opening of body and soul): "Gedanken an
Freud natürlich."[5]

Thoughts of Freud that come naturally are not necessarily
thoughts about or by Freud. One might even say that they exclude
Freudian thought because Freud's thoughts are unnatural to the degree that they go against that second nature which makes certain
culturally conditioned thoughts "natural." When thoughts of Freud
come naturally, they have entered general discourse and participate
as such in a secondary process, the target of Freud's analytical intervention, which ultimately dissolves it.

Thus, the encounter of Freud and Kafka in Celan's poem does
not take place where thoughts of Freud are natural, but in the act of
taking leave, forever, from psychology.

That this poem, and especially its middle part, is indeed the scene
of an encounter, and not merely a confrontation, is indicated in several ways by the text. Not only is one front, *Freuds Stirn*, opening
up, but also the syntactical transition is an open one. Moreover, the
semantic dimension of *schießt an* implies not only the violent rushing

up against, but also a spontaneous connecting up with, as in a crystallization process, where one particle shoots up to the next to form a firm and necessary pattern.

The screen of lamentation (*klagegerastert*) that marks Freud's opening forehead shares a sphere of mourning with the hardened tear. Freud and Kafka meet in the process of *Trauerarbeit*. But do *they* meet? Celan's text forces us to reformulate this scene. In a certain sense, what connects Freud and Kafka is their absence, their silence. They are replaced. They do not speak and act, but something else speaks and acts in their place and name. Even Kafka's own phrase is ascribed to the hardened tear rather than to him: it speaks in the name and place of Kafka.

Freud and Kafka have entered the land of fable. And as often happens in fables, animals speak and act in the place of humans. A *Maikäfer* (cockchafer or may bug) and a *Dohle* (jackdaw) are the agents of the scene. Yet this is obviously not a simple fable, where animals represent human agents, because the animals are themselves displaced in a compound word formation: *Maikäfertraum* and *Simili-Dohle*.

The *Maikäfertraum* is told by Freud in his *Interpretation of Dreams* as an example of *Verdichtungsarbeit* (work of condensation).[6] It is not Freud's dream, but the dream of a patient. Freud is less interested in the latent thoughts of this dream (the relation between sexuality and cruelty), than in a particular mode of work: *Verdichtungsarbeit*. And this is perhaps the point that seized the attention of Celan the poet.

To be sure, *Verdichtungsarbeit* and *Dichtungsarbeit* are not identical, yet they share more than a phonetic similarity. Long before Freud it has been claimed that the etymologically faulty connection between *dichten* and *verdichten* was nevertheless grounded in the act of *poesis*. But, particularly after Freud, we should not overlook the prefix *ver-*, one of the strangest and most elusive prefixes in German. Where it connects with a verb it changes the activity in an often unpredictable and not clearly definable way.[7] One could say, perhaps, that in its displacing function, all the displacements psychoanalysis talks about are condensed: *versprechen, verhören, vergessen, verlieren, verneinen*. . . . It names all those activities which in English have assumed the proper name of Freud, Freudian slips, and more. At first glance the *ver-* seems to imply a certain negation of the verbal activity it modifies, to make it false, incorrect, untrue. It indicates that something went wrong. *Versprechen* is to mis-speak, *verhören* to mis-hear, etc. But this is also the point where Freud inverts the function on another level: the mis-speaking turns out to be the actual speaking of the truth, and the mis-hearing to be the hearing of another truth, not heard in a "correct" hearing. The linguistic usage supports this: *versprechen* is also to promise, which is an appeal to a truth in the future; and *verhören* is also an activity of interrogation, an attempt to penetrate through a supposedly false screen of speaking. In some cases the affirmative function prevails, as in *vermehren* and *verdichten*. Negation and affirmation meet in the *ver-* as in a *Verneinung*, which is a (de-) negation. A general quality of language seems metonymically operative here: to uncover by covering up.

One of Celan's poems not only refers to this, but stages it also as *Verkenntnis*:

> Du durchklafterst
> Farbenstoß, Zahlwurf, Verkenntnis,
> viele
> sagen:
> Du bists, wir verwissens,
> viele verneinen sich an dir,
> der du sie dir einzeln
> erjast,
> aufständisch wie
> der dem Handgesagten geschenkte
> Steinmut,
> der sich hinhob zur Welt
> am Saum des gewendeten Schweigens
> und aller Gefahr. (2:375)

(You fathom through / color-push, number-throw, mis-cognition, / many / say: / It is you, we mis-know it, / many denegate themselves with you / who affirms [literally, yeses] them / singly / rebellious the stone-mood offered to / the hand-said / that lifted itself to the world / at the seam of the turned silence / and of all danger.)

The *ver-* does not simply shift the scene from a (false) surface to a (true) depth or vice versa, but rather indicates a shift in the topological system. The new space opened by the *ver-* and by the poem can only be approached at this point by its two major marks, *Saum* (seam, limit, border, margin, threshold) and *gewendet*. We know the crucial importance of *Wende* in Celan's poetics from the *Meridian* speech as well as from his poetry. We will come back to the twisted moves of this *Wende* (turn) and its transformation of *Wände* (walls) later.

The convergence and difference between *dichten* and *verdichten* represents a scene that both fascinated and troubled Freud. He invoked the poets as recorders and guarantors of a knowledge he had to explicate in scientific language, only to find that many of his explications and case studies again approached the forbidden register of the poetic text.[8]

While the *Maikäfertraum* illuminates the processes of *Verdichtungsarbeit*, in Celan's poem it illuminates a "Blinde licht- / bärtige Stellwand." The *Stellwand*, a surface to place things, to order or to display them, as, for example, at the Frankfurt Book Fair, where Celan might have seen portraits of Freud and Kafka together displayed at the booth of the Fischer publishing house, but also a wall to cover or hide something, is marked by the same qualities as the surface of a text. Thus, Celan's poetry speaks of "Redewände, raumeinwärts" (2:211). The scene of illumination, in this case, is a surface that is itself blind and yet *lichtbärtig*. At the same time, there is a *dahinter* where Freud's forehead opens up and seems to indicate another scene of illumination of cognition, which, however, is projected on the screen of the *Stellwand*. To be more precise, it remains utterly undecidable which is the actual scene of illumination and which is the projection.

If we compare this Freudian scene of *Verdichtung* in the first part of the poem with the scene of *Dichtung* under the hidden name of Kafka in the later part of the poem, we first notice a shift from the visual register to the oral and aural: "Die Simili- / Dohle / frühstückt. / Der Kehlkopfverschlußlaut / singt." And while the Freudian scene is marked by indicators that point, metaphorically at least, toward a cognitive activity (*leuchtet aus, tut sich Freuds Stirn auf*), Kafka's scene seems to be one of pure events: *frühstückt, singt*. This coincides, of course, with the major thrust of each of these two writers: Freud's interpretive, explicatory, scientific discourse as opposed to what I would call Kafka's radical surface writing, i.e., a writing that seems to know no interiority, only gestures, bodies, surfaces, that drive the reader into a delirious despair of interpretive searches for "deeper" meanings behind or beneath the maddening surface of the written text.

But remarkable parallels also emerge in the shift from Freud to Kafka. There is, first of all, the transposition to the animal world. Yet it is not the world of the classical fable where the animal agents represent human agencies. Freud's scene of *Stellwand* and *Maikäfertraum* makes it impossible to locate the actual agency of illumination and thus undercuts the traditional metaphorical hierarchy of tenor and vehicle.

The *Simili-Dohle* puts us in a similar uncertainty. At first glance, things seem to be simple enough. All we need is a little information and knowledge about Kafka and we know that it is his name that appears in this form. Yet there are two problems that complicate things. About whom are we speaking when we say "Kafka"? The obvious answer would be: the man who wrote *The Judgment* and *The Metamorphosis*, the man who wrote in his notebook, "Zum letztenmal Psychologie," and the man who also wrote a short text "über die Gleichnisse." But this answer is obvious only because the texts mentioned, and others as well, have turned the name Kafka into a literary trademark, a kind of *Warenzeichen*. But before the author of these texts effected this trademark, a kind of *Dohle* and the name Kafka were a trademark and name that belonged to another man: Franz Kafka's father, Hermann Kafka. It was he who used the jackdaw on a branch as an emblem for his business of fancy goods and trinkets.

Just as the *Maikäfer* appears on the Freudian scene in the deceptive realm of the dream, where identities shift and fluctuate, the *Dohle* appears in the deceptive form of a *Simili-Dohle*. Simili in German designates an artificial false gem (the kind of object one might have found in Hermann Kafka's *Galanteriewarengeschäft*.[9] The *Dohle*, then, is false. But which one? The father or the son? Both made a claim on the name Kafka and the sign of the *Dohle*.[10] Yet, as far as the sign is concerned, the claim could be considered false in itself, since, as Binder points out, the connection of the name Kafka to the Czech word *kavka* is probably a false folk etymology.[11] It is more likely that the name derives from the Ashkenazic or Low German diminutive form of the name Jakob (Kobs, Köpke), which was also the name of Freud's father.

The *Dohle*, which seemed to explain the origin of a name, would then cover up another origin. But that might be just another trace leading to no tangible origin. Thus, we can only speculate about Celan's knowledge of these possible relations when he wrote the poem, just as any literary criticism that grounds the poetic text in the known or deduced motivations and intentions of an author can only produce *Simili-Dohlen*. The fact that this particular *Dohle* eats breakfast places it at the end of a night of which we know nothing.

Where the origin remains a riddle, the question of genuine and false has to be shifted to another level. The *Simili-Dohle* might then also become a simile in the sense of those *Gleichnisse* that *are* Kafka's texts, while, at the same time, Kafka's writing investigates them in a vertiginous interchange of turns, of *Wenden*, that leave no side in the fixed, privileged place of significance and truth.

Yet there is something that emerges, something that sings. If Freud and Kafka take leave, forever, of psychology and its unquestioned faith in origins and motivations, the singing takes leave of Freud and Kafka. Singing is grounded, abysmally, in the erasure of a glottal stop, which marks the physical death of Franz Kafka, as well as the unbridgeable caesura, the *Atemwende* that turns the babbling of the child into the articulation of language and speech acts into the song of poetic language, [12] that sphere which has been characterized by one of the most thoughtful readers of Celan, Winfried Menninghaus, as "Intention auf den Namen." [13]

Our reading of the configuration of Kafka and Freud under the name of Celan has already been punctuated at some points by other names, Büchner and Hölderlin, for example. [14] This latter name is subtly suggested within the text. It is a hint that inscribes Freud's name even more deeply in Celan's poetics. The word *lichtbärtig* has to my knowledge only one modified predecessor in Celan's poetry, in a poem that invokes Hölderlin: *Tübingen, Jänner* (1:226), which speaks of the "Lichtbart der / Patriarchen." An awareness of this connection opens up other striking parallels: both titles are composed of the name of a city and a month, both start with blindness, both end in an utterance of the poets that marks the end of their legal person, and both are arranged around a quotation from the poet.

Hölderlin's "ein Rätsel ist Reinentsprungenes" shoots up, from the outside, to Kafka's "Zum letztenmal Psychologie" and comments on it, grounds it in what one could call an un-grounding. It simultaneously removes and acknowledges that ground that psychology takes for granted. The two quotations point in the same direction, where Freud's analysis of dreams locates a spot, the "navel" of the dream, that can no longer be grounded: "Jeder Traum hat mindestens eine Stelle, an welcher er unergründlich ist, gleichsam ein Nabel, durch den er mit dem Unerkannten zusammenhängt."[15]

The acknowledgment of an enigmatic, unknowable spot, not as a negation of knowledge, but as its irreducible grounding in the abyss, where, as Freud puts it, the dream sits on and is taken for a ride by the unknown (dem Unerkannten aufsitzt),[16] radically shifts the metaphorical space of knowledge and discourse. A new topology is needed; in the words of Celan, one that appears in the light of the non-topos: utopia.

While this enigmatic spot cannot be specified further, we will have to specify its poetic and poetological consequences in Celan's writing. I will approach this question first through a reading of one of Celan's earliest poetological reflections, "Edgar Jené and der Traum vom Traume".[17]

At first glance, it seems that this early text is still a straightforward staging of a spatial setting structured according to surface and depth and a desire that sees the penetration through the surface as the poetic-aesthetic goal. The vocabulary of the first two sentences evokes such a structure: "Ich soll ein paar Worte sagen, die ich in der Tiefsee gehört habe, wo so viel geschwiegen wird und so viel geschieht. Ich schlug eine Bresche in die Wände und Einwände der Wirklichkeit und stand vor dem Meeresspiegel" (I am supposed to say a few words which I have heard in the deep sea, where there is so much silence and where so much happens. I made a breach into the walls and inwalls/objections of reality and stood before the seasurface [literally: sea-mirror]) (3:155). The first sentence locates a place where something is heard and in which words are supposed to originate. It is a place in the deep sea, a favorite topos for the unknown from romanticism to symbolism. But if the utopian topos of the deep sea as the ground and abysmal origin of a language richer and more resonant than the linguistic coins of everyday speech has itself become a rather familiar poetic commonplace,[18] Celan's text distances it again via an approach that dissolves its all too familiar appearance. The first move is still familiar enough, breaking through the deceptive wall and surface of a reality: "Ich schlug eine Bresche in die Wände und Einwände der Wirklichkeit." The little pun, however, transforming *Wände* into *Einwände* performs a turn that complicates the spatial structure. Puns belong traditionally to a sphere where silliness and profundity, the dead letter and the living spirit, *Kalauer* and *esprit*, are entangled in an undecidable and irritating knot.[19] Disregarding all boundaries, they occupy the private realm of our dreams and circulate with ease in the public sphere of sophisticated society, constituting at the same time the very boundaries they break.

The I that clears the way through the *Wände* and *Einwände* is moved by a play of words. The "superficial" externality of the signifier becomes the instrument of breaking the surface. The result is another space, not under the surface, but "in" it: while the most common meaning of *Einwände* is a non-physical concept (objections, oppositions), its parallel position to *Wände* inscribes it in the spatial sphere and makes us read it as *Ein-Wände*: "in-walls." The space of a turned, twisted, or folded surface is suggested.[20]

Such a reading points in the direction of Celan's later poetry where such turns of the walls constitute the poetic movement:

Redewände, raumeinwärts—
eingespult in dich selber
grölst du dich durch bis zur Letztwend. (2:211)

(Speech-walls, space-inward— / inreeled into yourself / you bawl yourself through to the last-wall.)

The movement, although seemingly inward, toward an interior space, remains still one along the walls, from wall to wall.

The first space that opens up after the breaking through the *Wände* and *Einwände* is another surface: *Meeresspiegel*. Thus, another surface has to be broken before an interior world opens up: "Ich hatte eine Weile zu warten, bis er zersprang und ich den großen Kristall

der Innenwelt betreten durfte" (I had to wait for a while until it shattered and I could enter the great crystal of the interior world). Both
penetrations are acts of violence—*schlug, zersprang*—but while the
first is an act of the I, the second opening takes place by itself, the I
can only wait for it to happen. The interior world (*Innenwelt*), the
space through which and in which subjectivity represents itself to us,
is thus not directly accessible to the subject as I. But at least interiority
is claimed again, and the familiar topology seems to have returned.
Yet, already at this point, the movement of the text indicates less a
change in place (from surface to depth, from outside to inside) than
a change in the mode of perception. Each of the new streets on which
the subject travels offers another pair of eyes ("jede von ihnen bot mir
ein anderes Augenpaar"). The major obstacle in this world is the old
eyes ("meine alten eigenwilligen Augen") that see in terms and forms
of the familiar world. A new pair of eyes from the bottom of the soul
is prescribed. This advice is itself the effect of an inversion of the
familiar up-down topology: "Mein Mund aber, der höher lag als
meine Augen und kühner war, weil er oft aus dem Schlaf gesprochen,
war mir vorausgeeilt und rief mir seinen Spott zu" (My mouth, however, which lay higher than my eyes and was bolder, because it had
often spoken out of the sleep, had hurried ahead of me and called its
mockery toward me). This inversion of the position of eyes and mouth
suggests the desire of Büchner's *Lenz* to walk on his head, which Celan
recalls as one of the *Gestalten* of the poetic *Atemwende*.[21]
      Another topology starts to emerge from the familiar space. At no
time can the re-presentation of this other topology, which is also a
topology of the Other, get rid of the spatial metaphors of depth and
surface, inside/outside, just as the poetic intentionality toward the
name can constitute itself only in and through the binary system of
language and its differential play. Thus, through Celan's latest poetry,
the vocabulary of depth, interiority, and exteriority remains part of
the poetic universe. But it is reinscribed in a constellation and movement which twists, flattens, and opens the familiar three-dimensional
space in a way that could perhaps be compared with the flat hierarchical space of Byzantine paintings.
      This new perspective and topology is that of the language of the
name capable of shaking the foundation of the familiar world, "wenn

ich die Dinge bei ihrem richtigen Namen nännte" (if I would call things by their right name).[22] The text cannot describe this other language—to do so would imply being in it—but only the approach toward it. And like the approach toward the interior world at the beginning of the essay, it is a mediated approach, this time through another text, Kleist's essay on the *Marionettentheater*. First we hear the interpretation of a friend, who sees the return to original grace as well as the future paradise "auf dem Wege . . . einer vernunftmäßigen Läuterung unseres unbewußten Seelenlebens" (via . . . a purification of our unconscious psychic life according to reason) (3:156). The friend's vocabulary resembles a certain understanding of psychoanalysis, mainly that of ego psychology and its continuation in a Habermasian communication theory.[23] Its difference from Freud is subtly indicated in a slightly modified Freudian metaphor: the friend talks of the "Königswasser des Verstandes" which will purify (*reinwaschen*) words, things, and events, thus returning their original significance to them. The difference between Freud and the *Freund* is small, but significant: Freud calls the interpretation of dreams the *via regia* to the knowledge of the unconscious.[24] Freud's walking of the royal road of dream interpretation demands the persistent following of the twists and turns of the dreams, no matter how mad and unreasonable they seem: it is a *Maikäfertraum* that illuminates the *Stellwand*. The friend wants the royal water of reason to wash away and tear down the wall instead of illuminating it: "Die Mauer, die Heute von Morgen trennt, sei niederzureißen."

Against this tearing down of the wall, Celan intervenes with one of his *Einwände*: "Hier kündigte sich der erste meiner Einwände and und war eigentlich nichts anderes als die Erkenntnis" (Here, the first of my objections announced itself and it was actually nothing else than the recognition). Thus, the *Einwände* of the beginning, which the writer wanted to clear away, return now in the form of *Erkenntnis* itself: the wall as in-wall. This knowledge consists in an acknowledgment that the events (*Geschehenes*) are not accidental covers and attributes of the actual truth, but essential transformational elements of the actual truth itself: "ein dieses Eigentliche in seinem Wesen Veränderndes, ein starker Wegbereiter unausgesetzter Verwandlung" (something that changes that which is proper in its essence, a strong

pioneer of continuous transformation). The walls of reality, the distortions of the surface, the sinful Fall of the language of arbitrary
signs, appear as the *felix culpa* of a language that is the *via regia* to
Erkenntnis.

But the rhetoric of the depth insists and speaks through the mouth
of the friend who remains *hartnäckig* (stubborn): "Er könne, behaup-
tete er, auch im Strom der menschlichen Entwicklung die Konstanten
des Seelenlebens unterscheiden, die Grenzen des Unbewußten erken-
nen, und alles sei getan, wenn die Vernunft in die Tiefe stiege und
das Wasser des dunklen Brunnens an die Oberfläche fördere" (3:157).
In this insistence, the rhetoric of the depth displays its major operating
terms: boundary (*Grenze*) and ground (Auch dieser Brunnen habe
seinen Grund) (this fountain too had its ground). The voice of the
friend is thus the voice of the "Identitätskrämer" (3:155). In asserting
firm boundaries and an attainable ultimate ground, he claims an identity for that which is brought from the depth to the surface: "wenn
die Vernunft in die Tiefe stiege und das Wasser des dunklen Brunnens
an die Oberfläche förderte" (if reason would descend into the depth
and would bring to the surface the water of the dark fountain).

The metaphor of the dark and deep fountain has a resonant
tradition especially in symbolist poetry. Hofmannsthal evokes it as a
ground of lost knowledge in the poem *Weltgeheimnis* (1894):

> Der tiefe Brunnen weiß es wohl,
> Einst waren alle tief und stumm,
> Und alle wußten drum.[25]

(The deep fountain knows it well, / Once all were deep and mute, / And all
knew of it.)

The knowledge of the deep fountain in Hofmannsthal's poem is intimately tied to its muteness: it was known by all insofar as all were
"tief und stumm." Uttered in language, it is no longer known:

> Wie Zauberworte nachgelallt
> Und nicht begriffen in den Grund,
> So geht es jetzt von Mund zu Mund.

(Like magic words, echoed by a stammer / And not understood into the
depth, / Thus it now goes from mouth to mouth.)

Yet it is not simply outside of language: it is in it ("In unsern Worten liegt es drin"), but it is not "it" as language, but as language's mute abysmal grounding. This non-identity of the depth brought to the surface is even more directly articulated in a passage in Maeterlinck's "Le trésor des humbles" (1898), which Musil used as a motto for his first novel *Die Verwirrungen des Zöglings Törless* (1906):

> Sobald wir etwas aussprechen, entwerten wir es seltsam. Wir glauben in die Tiefe der Abgründe hinabgetaucht zu sein, und wenn wir wieder an die Oberfläche kommen, gleicht der Wassertropfen an unseren bleichen Fingerspitzen nicht mehr dem Meere, dem er entstammt. Wir wähnen eine Schatzgrube wunderbarer Schätze entdeckt zu haben, und wenn wir wieder ans Tageslicht kommen, haben wir nur falsche Steine und Glasscherben mitgebracht; und trotzdem schimmert der Schatz im Finstern unverändert.[26]

To recall these topoi of the non-topos of the constitutive ground of language brings the friend's desire into sharper contrast: his faith in the identity of that which is in the depths and that which is brought to the surface makes him a spokesman of that psychology from which Freud and Kafka, together with the major writers of modernism, have taken leave.

The writer's response to his friend's declaration is first a subtle shift in the topological relations from the vertical to the horizontal, from surface/depth to the interior/exterior of a prison: "die Welt mit ihren Einrichtungen als ein Gefängnis des Menschen und seines Geistes" (the world with its institutions as a prison of man and his spirit). This would hardly be a shift, since the vertical and the horizontal model belong essentially to the same epistemological and metaphysical tradition, were it not immediately followed by a second shift through which the prison itself is moved into the interior of language: "Ich war mir klar geworden, daß der Mensch nicht nur in den Ketten des äußeren Lebens schmachtete, sondern auch geknebelt war und nicht sprechen durfte—und wenn ich von der Sprache rede, so ist damit die ganze Sphäre menschlicher Ausdrucksmittel gemeint—weil seine Worte (Gebärden und Bewegungen) unter der tausendjährigen Last falscher und entstellter Aufrichtigkeit stöhnten" (It had become clear to me that man not only languishes in the chains of his exterior life, but that he was also gagged and was not allowed to speak—and when I speak of language, the whole sphere of human means of expression is meant—because his words (gestures and movements) moaned under the thousand year old weight of false and distorted honesty) (3:157). Again there is a muteness within language, not the "original" muteness of Hofmannsthal's poem, but a silencing and an interdiction to speak.

Yet there is a remarkable inversion in the effect of these mute spots of language. The muteness of Hofmannsthal's poem effects a language that resonates from its remembrance of a loss; the fullness of this language is grounded in the knowledge of its inadequacy and of a silence that cannot be mastered. The gagged language in Celan's text, however, is paradoxically a language of honesty and straightforwardness (*Aufrichtigkeit*). This honesty *is* the gag and the interdiction. What makes it a false and displaced honesty is precisely its faith in a language that could ever say honestly and straightforwardly what it means, i.e., a language that has renounced the mute u-topos from where it speaks and which displaces all self-identity of the word: "was war unaufrichtiger als die Behauptung, diese Worte seien irgendwo im Grunde noch dieselben" (what was more dishonest than the assertion that these words were somehow essentially still the same).[27]

Im Grunde, in or on the ground, the identity of the word has already been shifted. But it is not a ground that can be uncovered or recovered—that would be the fallacy of an empty, deceptive honesty—but only the effects of the displacement *in* language: the ashes of burnt-out signification (*die Asche ausgebrannter Sinngebung*). In the acknowledgment of these ashes, the universal ground of language, its constitutive silence, meets with the singularities of historical experience. The ashes in a text of 1948 must include the ashes of the human bodies in the German concentration camps. No fundamental ontology or semiology can circumvent the intervention of these ashes into the *Sinngebung* of any utterance.

". . . Und nicht nur diese!" And that is not the only intervention our language has to acknowledge and to trace if it wants to be more than *une parole vide*.

The difference between a *parole pleine* and a *parole vide*, to use the terms of a distinction which Lacan developed from his reading of Freud and the analytic experience,[28] can be traced in Celan's work in the difference between *sprechen* and *reden*, which might be translated, perhaps a little arbitrarily, as "to speak" and "to talk."[29]

The text that most intensely traces this difference stands under the title of a *Gespräch: Gespräch im Gebirge* (3:1169–73), written about ten years after the Jene text. In an almost literal echo, the first sentence evokes precisely the passage in the Jene text acknowledging the burnt-out ashes "und nicht nur diese." The *nicht nur diese* is a determinate negation that marks a silence that cannot otherwise be spoken. The *Gespräch im Gebirge* begins: "Eines Abends, die Sonne, und nicht nur sie, war untergegangen" (One evening, the sun, and not only it, had gone under). Something has gone under (one could say, since it is the sun, it "burned out"), but not only it. Such is the situation in which a meeting and a *Gespräch* take place. One might be tempted to describe it as a dialogue between two Jews meeting in the mountains. But that would be misleading. The point of this text is precisely that a *Gespräch* is not a dialogue between I and Thou. The I-Thou model of dialogical speech presupposes a transparent relationship between two self-identical agencies: I am I, you are you; I speak to you, you speak to me; I hear you, you hear me; we hear each other, we speak to each other.

From the first sentence on, Celan's text radically displaces such symmetries. Two Jews meet in the mountains and talk to each other. But are they two or is there one, splitting into two voices; or are they many, coalescing into two voices? The first figure that emerges from his house is more than one already: "der Jud, der Jud und Sohn eines Juden, und mit ihm ging sein Name, der unaussprechliche" (the Jew, the Jew and the son of a Jew, and with him went his name, the unspeakable one). A trinity walks up into the mountains. The first person bears the mark imposed by the Nazi vocabulary, which does not recognize a diverse plurality of Jews, but only the Jew: *der Jud*. Bearing the stamp of the slaughterers, his first identity is that of a suffering people, a collective name of a people and of a condition. The second person is marked by the stamp of singularity emerging from another singularity: "Sohn *eines* Juden." And then there is the third name, not the name Klein, by which this man is called and described, but the unspeakable name, a silent mark that accompanies the two.

Before Klein meets his cousin Groß and talks to him, there are already three: two who can talk—*der Jud und Sohn eines Juden*—and the silent third. When the two figures, described and named as Groß and Klein, talk to each other, there is again a silent third agency present, and it is there where it speaks, from the silent stone: "Er, der Stein, redet nicht, er spricht, und wer spricht, Geschwisterkind, der redet zu niemand, der spricht, weil niemand ihn hört, niemand und Niemand" (It, the stone, does not talk, it speaks, and he who speaks, cousin, speaks to nobody, he speaks because nobody hears him, nobody and Nobody). The silent stone who talks to no one and No One, makes the difference between *reden* and *sprechen*. The *Gespräch* in the mountains is thus not the dialogue between the two figures, not between I and you, but the resonance before the silent third.

Celan's *Gespräch* is closer to the scene of the joke and its three persons, as Freud describes it, than to the transparent fallacies of two honest talkers.

A poem from the second part of *Schneepart* again invokes the scene of *sprechen*:

> Mit den Sackgassen sprechen
> vom Gegenüber,
> von seiner expatriierten
> Bedeutung:
> dieses
> Brot kauen, mit
> Schreibzähnen. (2:358)

(To speak with the dead-end streets / of the one vis-à-vis, / of his expatriated / meaning: / to chew / this bread with / writing teeth.)

The exiled meaning of the other, the one sitting across (*gegenüber*), being on the opposite side, the subject's object, comes into speech in speaking with the Other: the dead-end streets that interrupt the continuous intercourse of traffic. The form this speaking assumes is the silent scene of writing, which has its own teeth, to join the *Simili-Dohle* at breakfast. He who writes talks to no one, like the stone, he only chews the words until the exiled meaning emerges. Kafka too felt the desire for writing in the teeth and the lips: "das, mit allen Zähnen, in allen Lippen, ersehnte Schreiben" (the writing desired with all the teeth, in all the lips).

The scene of writing is thus the scene of *sprechen*. Its location in the teeth and thus in the mouth recalls the inversion of the mouth *above* the eyes in the Jene text. It is confirmed in Celan's most authoritative poetological text, *Der Meridian*: "Die Aufmerksamkeit, die das Gedicht allem ihm Begegnenden zu widmen versucht, sein schärferer Sinn für das Detail, für Umriß, für Struktur, für Farbe, aber auch für die 'Zuckungen' und die 'Andeutungen', das alles ist, glaube ich, keine Errungenschaft des mit den täglich perfekteren Apparaten wetteifernden (oder miteifernden) Auges, es ist vielmehr eine aller unserer Daten eingedenk bleibende Konzentration" (The attention that the poem seeks to devote to all that occurs, its sharper sense for the detail, for outline, for structure, for color, but also for "vibrations," for "hints," all this is, I think, not an achievement of the eye that competes or tries to keep up with the ever more perfect instruments, it is rather a concentration that keeps a faithful memory of all our data) (3:198). There is again something "above" and beyond the eye, this privileged organ of the Enlightenment,[31] something related to the scene of writing and the mouth: *das Gedicht* and its concentration. Concentration has some similarity with *Verdichtung*, but is not exactly the same. If the scene of *Verdichtung*, the *Maikäfertraum*, illuminates the blind wall, as its *Einwand* and in-wall, it might be seen as an illumination of the scene of writing, where the *Simili-Dohle* eats breakfast, and the *Kehlkopfverschlußlaut* silences all talk, so that ein *Gespräch* or perhaps even *Gesang* might appear.

The appearance of the name of Freud in Celan's poetry does not allow us to translate that poetry into the language of psychoanalysis. Such a translation would not only be a *Verkenntnis* (to use Celan's own word, 2:375) of the poetry but also of Freud's texts. To call it a *Verkenntnis* implies, however, according to the logic of the *ver-*, also a *veritas*, an actual truth in the mis-cognition. But this truth cannot be located in an act of translation, as this term is most commonly understood. Translation, in the common use of the word, posits a hierarchy of original and imitation, of actual truth and metaphorical mimesis. Thus, the translation of a text into a foreign language usually involves the attempt to render the original as faithfully as possible; the original is the master text. In the interpretive translation of a literary text into a cognitive discourse, in terms of philosophy, religion, sociology, or psychology, the hierarchy seems to be inverted: the interpretive translation tacitly assumes that its terms state directly what the literary text metaphorically and symbolically veils. The interpretive translation thus gives itself the status of the original. Yet it cannot say so, because it would violate philological humility and its reverence for poetic truth.

There is, indeed, often an inverse relationship between an abundant rhetoric of reverence and humility in regard to the "work of art" and a ruthless praxis of hierarchical translation for which the literary text is only an allegorical veil that must be lifted in order to present the naked truth in unveiled terms. Thus, the most schematic psychoanalytic or Marxist critics are the most effusive in their rhetoric about how "deep" and "inexhaustible" the work of art is. Wherever this rhetoric appears, one can be sure that the bad conscience of the opposite praxis speaks.

The ambivalence of interpretive translation in regard to the question of original and secondary language points toward a basic problematization of such hierarchies that nevertheless constitute the very concept of translation. Walter Benjamin's essay on "The Task of the Translator" develops a different concept: the original is not any given, positive language; each such language is already a translation, a metaphorical space of displacements and approximations of an original which itself is not an existing language.

Freud's interpretations of dreams are translation in this other sense: translation of something that is already translation, because "it" is never where "it" speaks. The translation of the manifest dream into the latent dream thoughts is still a translation into a language shaped by secondary elaboration, not the language of the primary processes. And yet the being of the subject is affected by this language, which it effects through all the detours of displacement.

Poetic language is per se neither closer to nor farther from the origin than any other register of language. As is said of the spirit that blows where it wishes, "it" speaks where it wants to—and can do so; and it is not in our will to decide. Hölderlin, a major poetic presence in Celan's poetry, conceived the task of the poet as that of an interpreter and translator:

> der Vater aber liebt,
> Der über allen waltet,
> Am meisten, daß gepfleget werde
> Der veste Buchstab, und bestehendes gut
> Gedeutet. Dem folgt deutscher Gesang. (*Patmos, St.A.,* 2:172)

(the father, however, he who reigns over all, loves most that the firm letter be cared for, and the existing well interpreted. To this German song is obedient.)

> So hatten es die Kinder gehört, und wohl
> sind gut die Sagen, denn ein Gedächtniß sind
> Dem Höchsten sie, doch auch bedarf es
> Eines, die heiligen auszulegen.
> (*Stimme des Volks, St.A.,* 2:53; F.A. 5:596)

(Thus the children had heard it, and, to be sure, the legends are good, for they are a memory to the highest, but One is needed too to interpret the holy ones.)

This goes against a claim for poetry as an originary voice. The originary voice, if it could be heard, would probably sound more like the neighing of a horse than like human language. Celan's poetry tends toward that language, but still in the translation of poetic language:

> Bei Wein und Verlorenheit, bei
> beider Neige:
> ich ritt durch den Schnee, hörst du,
> ich ritt Gott in die Ferne—die Nähe, er sang,
> es war
> unser letzter Ritt über
> die Menschen-Hürden.
> Sie duckten sich, wenn
> sie uns über sich hörten, sie
> schrieben, sie
> logen unser Gewieher

um in eine
ihre bebilderten Sprachen. (1:213)

(With wine and forlornness with / both their declensions: / I rode through
the snow, do you hear, / I rode god into the distance—the nearness, he
sang, / it was / our last ride over / the human hurdle. / They ducked when /
they heard us above, they / wrote, they / lied our neighing / into one / of
their imaged languages.)

Although the poem speaks of "them" and "their" lying and translating
into "imaged language," it can itself only speak in translation.

It is important to remember this as I conclude with two of Celan's
poems that are marked by a Freudian vocabulary:

. . . auch keinerlei
Friede.
Graunächte, vorbewußt-kühl.
Reizmengen, otterhaft,
auf Bewußtseinsschotter
unterwegs zu
Erinnerungsbläschen.
Grau-in-Grau der Substanz.
Ein Halbschmerz, ein zweiter, ohne
Dauerspur, halbwegs
hier. Eine Halblust.
Bewegtes, Besetztes.
Wiederholungszwangs-
Camaieu. (2:201)

(. . . and no kind / of peace. / Gray-nights, preconscious-cool. / quantities
of stimuli, otterlike, / on gravel of consciousness / on their way to / a small
memory-bubble. / Gray-in-gray of the substance. / A half-pain, a second,
without / enduring trace, halfway / here. A half-pleasure. / Something
moved, something cathected. / Repetition compulsion / camaïeu.)

Offene Glottis, Luftstrom,
der
Vokal, wirksam,
mit dem einen
Formanten,
Mitlautstöße, gefiltert
von weithin

Ersichtlichem,
Reizschutz: Bewußtsein,
unbesetzbar
ich und auch du,
überwahr-
heitet
das augen-, das
gedächtnisgierige rollende
Waren-
zeichen
der Schläfenlappen intakt,
wie der Sehstamm. (2:388)

(Open glottis, airstream, / the / vowel, effective, / with the one / formant, / consonant thrust, filtered / by something visible / from afar, / protective shield: consciousness, / uncathectable / I and you too, / overtruth- / ed / the eye-greedy, the / memory-greedy rolling / commodity / sign / the temporal lobe intact / like the optic center.)

Like his name, Freud's vocabulary gives us no license to translate the poems into a psychoanalytic theory. Yet we cannot discard the signals set by this vocabulary. We have to take the poem on its own terms, which includes the recognition that its "own" terms are not entirely its own. We have to recognize the poem as a translation, not a translation from Freud's text, but a translation like Freud's text.

While the vocabulary of the two poems literally recalls Freud's words, the syntax is radically different. Celan's two poems do not contain a single predicative verb. In contrast to Freud's text, there is no predication, only constellation and juxtaposition. The radical reduction of syntax to juxtaposition moves the poetic texts closer to the language of the dream, which lacks certain grammatical signs.[32] But even if the poems speak syntactically, like a dream, this fact does not give them the status of an originary language; it is still another translation.

The two most obviously "Freudian" texts of Celan do not speak of the unconscious, they remain manifestly in what Freud called the system W-Bw (Wahrnehmung-Bewußtsein, perception consciousness).

". . . auch keinerlei / Friede." Three dots mark what most beginnings hide: the opening of the poem points back to something preceding it that remains silent. Articulation and consciousness emerge into a ruptured sentence, indicating the continuity of a discourse which remains partially submerged. The discourse of consciousness is fragmentary, the law of consciousness is coherence. The interpretive desire wants to fulfill that law and restore coherence by filling in the dots. The poet, subjected to the same desire, helps, perhaps, in the arrangement of the poems: the text preceding ". . . auch keinerlei / Friede" speaks of war and death:

> Die brabbelnden
> Waffen-
> pässe.
> Auf der übersprungenen
>   Stufe
> räkeln sich die
>   Sterberein. (2:200)

(The babbling / weapon- / passes. / On the skipped step / loll the / dyings.)

". . . auch keinerlei / Friede" seems then like a response. Even the three dots of fragmentation seem now to build a bridge of continuity, indicating the place of "der übersprungenen Stufe." Such smooth coherence is, of course, like the smooth narratives of dreams, the result of a secondary elaboration. And while it is false, it is still the only space of truth. The poems stage and provoke the work of consciousness. At the same time they mark the dotted line of another discourse, one that is left out and skipped over.

We will not find this hidden discourse in the depths by denying our narrative desire for coherence, but we might be able to circumscribe it by following it.

At first glance, it seems easier to connect the first fragmentary lines to the preceding poem than to the text of the poem itself, unless we connect it with the Freud text that is signaled through the vocabulary of the poem. *Beyond the Pleasure Principle*, with its speculation on repetition compulsion and death drive, has been inscribed, particularly in Germany, in an ideological constellation where thinking about such matters is already suspected of advocating war and destruction. So strong is this ideological force that recently 327 German psychoanalysts seriously and honestly believed they would serve the cause of peace by signing a manifesto renouncing the death drive and the repetition compulsion. That the courage not to think of such matters will help the peace movement is doubtful, but it will certainly provide the signers with the peaceful sleep of the just.

Celan's poem registers this constellation and is framed by it: ". . . auch keinerlei / Friede"—"Wiederholungszwangs- / Camaieu." There is, however, no grammatical indicator to specify the relationship between the first two lines with their denial of peace and the last two lines with the evocation of the repetition compulsion. But within this frame, the scene of consciousness, or more precisely, of the system W-Bw, is unfolded. The realm of this system is not the sunlit day, as the Enlightenment likes to represent it, but the gray night of the preconscious: "Graunächte, vorbewußt-kühl." Consciousness appears in this realm only in the form of fragmented pieces: *Bewußtseinsschotter*. To the degree that there is a movement or process (*unterwegs*), it happens through the medium of *Reizmengen*, which, according to Freud, constitute the great unknown X which remains part of any metapsychological theory.[33] In Celan's poem, these quantities of stimuli are given the shape of an otter, locating them in a slightly archaic and vague animal world. The word itself is ambiguous, designating an amphibious creature as well as vipers and adders. But it always implies something that creeps, crawls, sneaks, in brief: something creepy. The creepiness of the living organism on its way to a little memory bubble is opposed to the anorganic stuff of consciousness, which is gravel, hard and dead, as, according to Freud, *Bewußtsein* indeed is anorganic *Reizschutz*.[34]

The system thus outlined in the first stanza (if we consider the opening two lines and the last two lines of the poem as a frame) is given in descriptive and objective terms. The middle line of the poem, a stanza in itself, summarizes it in a kind of *camaieu* tableau, i.e., in monochrome gray-on-gray: "Grau-in-Grau der Substanz." The *camaieu* is the art of difference in the same, linguistically performed by the poem. The descriptive term for the gray substance of the brain is doubled as a metaphorical term for the gray nights that constitute consciousness as fading moments of light in the grayness of the pre-

conscious. In the same way, substance describes the physical mate-
riality of the brain as well as that which subsists in the phenomenon
of consciousness.

The evocation of the system W-Bw continues after the middle
line, but in terms of its felt effects, i.e., in terms of the subject:
Halbschmerz, Halblust, Dauerspur, Bewegtes, Besetztes. It is the
"same" as before, yet radically different: a *camaieu* of language. On
this side of the system, as we experience it in terms of *Schmerz* and
Lust, again a certain grayness prevails: nothing is full. There is only
Halbschmerz, Halblust, and only *halbwegshier*. This is far away from
those favorites of the gods as one of Goethe's poems sees them:

> Alles geben die Götter, die unendlichen,
> Ihren Lieblingen ganz,
> Alle Freuden, die unendlichen,
> Alle Schmerzen, die unendlichen, ganz.[35]

(The gods, the infinite ones, give everything to their favorites completely, all
the joys, the infinite ones, all the pains, the infinite ones, completely.)

But it is also said of these favorites of the gods that they die early.
Freud takes that up in *Beyond the Pleasure Principle*: consciousness
which is an anorganic, burnt-out surface is a protective shield against
the all too strong love of the gods and the energy of the world, which
would kill us instantly, as Zeus incinerated Semele, who wanted to
experience her lover and god in the fullness of his power.

The dissemination of fullness into sequential repetition of partial
moments that mark consciousness (*ein Halbschmerz, ein zweiter*) also
organizes the arrangement of the text. Beyond the semantic principle
of coherent meaning, the text is governed by the principle of repetition. It recalls words: *Graunächte, Grau-in-Grau*; vor*bewußt*,
*Bewußt*sein; unter*wegs*, halb*wegs*, *Bewegtes*; halb*wegs*, *Halb*lust. It
creates rhymes: *otter*haft, Bewußtseinss*chotter*. The rhyme of *otter* and
-schotter simultaneously produces a semantic opposition between living organism and anorganic matter. The sameness produces the difference that turns an *einerlei* into *keinerlei Friede*. The repetition
compulsion and its tendency toward undifferentiated sameness and
death is kept in the fragile suspension of a *camaieu*: monochrome,
but with a subtle difference.

The "gray-in-gray of the substance" that forms the axis of the poem is the scene of consciousness as a scene of difference in the same. The poem *Offene Glottis* is arranged around a similar one-line axis, marking the scene of consciousness: "Reizschutz: Bewußtsein." This is the most obvious echo of Freud in the poem, and its position as axis of the text gives it a special status.[36] It inscribes the Freudian terms in the sphere of language and, at the same time, differentiates that one sphere into two phenomenal realms: the physiological scene of language formation (before the axis) and the sociological scene of language effects (after the axis).

There is an opening at the beginning. Again Danton's wish seems to come true through a hole in the head. We might also remember that the first major dream Freud tells in the *Interpretation of Dreams* as an introduction to the method of dream analysis is his dream about Irma and how he looks down her throat: "Ich nehme sie zem Fenster und schaue ihr in den Hals" (I take her to the window and look into her throat).[37] In his analysis, Freud refers to the "little secrets" that are revealed in such occasions, although not pleasant ones (keinem von beiden zur Lust) (for neither of them a pleasure).

Celan's *Offene Glottis* opens up to the secret of language formation and seems to trace it to a physiological base where the opposition of vowel and consonant is formed. What is seen, then, through the opening in the depth of the glottis is not an interior, but the pure exteriority of language. Yet many of the language theorists of the eighteenth and early nineteenth centuries already emphasized what Sausurre and Jakobson confirmed later as the very basis of linguistics: the articulation of phonemic oppositions and differences is a radical break from a pure physico-physiological phenomenon. It is not the physical entity of the sound or the letter that constitutes language, but the differential relationship between them, a non-physical quality that organizes the physical letters and sounds.

One of the most thorough and systematic formulations of this law of language can be found in Wilhelm von Humboldt's study *Über die Verschiedenheit des menschlichen Sprachbaues und ihren Einfluss auf die geistige Entwicklung des Menschengeschlechts* (1830–35).[38] Certain passages sound like a subtext to the first two stanzas of Celan's poem. I will italicize some of the most striking parallels:

> Die Articulation beruht auf der Gewalt des Geistes über die Sprach-
> werkzeuge, sie zu einer der *Form* seines Wirkens entsprechenden Be-
> handlung des Lautes zu nöthigen. (p. 441)

(The articulation rests on the power of the spirit over the language instruments, to force them to a treatment of the sounds according to the form of
his [the spirit's] activity.)

> Die consonantisch gebildeten articulierten Laute lassen sich nich an-
> ders, als von einem Klang gebenden *Luftzuge* begleitet aussprechen.
> Dies Ausströmen der Luft giebt nach dem Orte, wo es erzeugt wird,
> und nach der *Oeffnung*, durch die es *strömt*, ebenso bestimmt ver-
> schiedne und gegen einander in festen Verhältnissen stehende Laute,
> als die der Consonantenreihe. In dieser aber liegen nicht, wie as nach
> unserer Art zu schreiben, scheinen sollte, zwei oder mehrere Laute,
> sondern eigentlich nur *Ein* auf eine bestimmte Weise herau*sgestosse-
> ner*. . . . Genau genommen, können auch die Vocale nicht allein
> ausgesprochen werden. Der sie bildende *Luftstrom* bedarf eines hörbar
> machenden An*stosses*. (p. 442)

(The consonant formed articulated sounds can only be pronounced accompanied by an airstream that gives resonance. This streaming out of the air
gives no less than the consonant series determinedly differentiated sounds
that stand in firm relations to each other according to the place where it is
produced and according to the opening through which it streams. Therein
lie, however, not two or more sounds, as it might appear in our way of
writing, but actually only one pushed forth in a specific way. . . . To be
precise, neither can the vowels be pronounced by themselves. The airstream
that forms them needs an initial push that makes them audible.)

If we turn to Celan's text, we may hear the echoes:

> Offene Glottis, Luftstrom,
> der Vokal, wirksam,
> mit dem einen
> Formanten,
> Mitlautstöße, gefiltert
> von weithin
> Ersichtlichem.

While Humboldt constitutes articulation in the power and violence
of the spirit (*Gewalt des Geistes*) that can be traced in its formative

effects (*Form seines Wirkens*), Celan connects both vowel and consonant with a modifier: "Vokal, wirksam," "Mitlautstöße, gefiltert." Celan no longer postulates a spirit, as Humboldt does, but like Humboldt, he locates the force of articulation not in the physical element as such, but in its qualitative differentiation.

Again the topological system has changed: the glance into the depth of the throat revealed the open mystery of the surface rather than a secret from the deep sea. But if language is a surface, the exteriority of the spirit, it is a differentiated, infolded surface, an "inscape," shaped by and leading to Freud's paradigmatic surface phenomenon: "Reizschutz: Bewußtsein."

The phenomenon of consciousness is juxtaposed with a realm of evidence: "weithin / Ersichtlichem," that which is visible from afar. But the clear evidence, the *weithin Ersichtliche*, is also that which filters, thus implying that it blocks out evidence as well. Visibility, clarity, evidence: the privileged metaphors of cognition in the Enlightenment appear in the function of covering rather than revealing. Every discourse already articulates its own limitations, and thus the ambivalence of seeing. Within the discourse of Enlightenment, the realization can be read that he who sees sees no more.[39]

With consciousness, the sphere of a personal agency is opened up. It is the sphere where I and you are located as agencies of the discourse. At this point, however, Celan's poem takes a curious turn: "unbesetzbar / ich und auch du." Once more, a central Freudian category is invoked, that of *cathexis*. It appears at first glance as a deceptively simple concept, describing the investment of a certain psychic energy in a concept, a notion,[40] an object, or part of the body. Yet how are we to understand this investment of energy: as an actual physico-neurological event? At some points, particularly in his earliest writings, Freud seems to suggest this. Later texts seem to indicate an analogy, and it seems that we can understand the term "only" metaphorically. Things become even more complicated when we look at the possible objects of cathexis: it seems that they can be objects, persons, ideas, or words. But in a literal and physical sense, a physical object or person cannot be cathected, only our *Vorstellung*, our mental representation of objects and persons, with the only apparent exception of our own body or parts of our body. Yet a more precise

analysis tells us that, to the degree that anything or anybody is per-
ceived as an object, that object has, by definition, the status of a
Vorstellung, i.e., it is an object for a subject to whom it is re-presented
as such. "My body" exists *for me* only to the degree as it is represented
to me; and the drives too have a psychological reality only through
the mediation of their representations, which include pleasure and
pain.

    I recall these psychoanalytical and philosophical truisms to point
out the specific structure of a sphere that is always already in a state
of representation and thus undercuts in a very specific way the separation of an "actual" from a "metaphorical" world. In other words,
we find ourselves again on the scene of the infolded surface that has
no depth.

    If we have thus arrived at a scene where psychoanalysis and po-
etry, in fact, seem to meet, Celan's two lines "unbesetzbar / ich und
auch du" seem to take leave not just from psychology but also from
the realm of psychoanalysis. *Ich* and *du* in psychoanalysis might be
more or less cathected, we might even conceive of a situation where
all cathexis has been withdrawn from the I, but one could never say
that the I and the you are uncathect*able*. In fact, one could argue
that the process of analysis depends on the cathexis of I and you
through the various modes of transference and countertransference.

    How can we read the *Unbesetzbarkeit* of *ich* and *du*? We might
first remark that Celan's poem uses the pronominal form, not the
allegorical nouns (*das Ich* and *das Du*) as they occur frequently in
psychoanalytic discourse. This difference is significant: for, although
Freud's use of *das Ich* (the ego) preserves the pronominal trace (more
so than the English Latinized terms "ego" and "id"), it nevertheless
suggests in the form of a noun a substantive agency, a kind of allegorical persona. It is the forgetting of the pronominal ground of the
Ich that has led to an ego psychology declaring the I as a kind of
permanent fortification, rather than a fluctuating function of discourse.

    Yet, even if we understand *ich* and *du* in their pronominal func-
tions, we have to assume them to be cathected to the degree that they
are functioning agencies of a concrete discourse.

    Since this phrase is part of a poetic text, we might then surmise that it is not to be read as a general assertion, as for example in a metapsychological text, but rather as the statement of a particular poetic instance and a singular lyrical I speaking only of its own situation, or at most perhaps of the particular historical condition in which we find ourselves. Yet such a presupposition leads again to insurmountable contradictions. Whatever the agency would be that could utter such a phrase, it could not be the agency of this discourse, which can speak only in some degree of cathexis. The phrase radically resists any possible existential reading, in terms of the individual subject or in terms of that collective subject so frequently invoked with a certain tremolo by many critics, when they talk about the "alienation of modern man."

The only place where *ich* and *du* are uncathectable is within language as such, within the *langue*; as soon as they enter a discourse they are, by definition of their function, in the position of an agency of the discourse, and as such eminently "cathectable." Even a strongly negated *ich* or *du* would not escape cathexis, since the phobic object is no less cathected than the beloved one. If *ich* and *du* cannot be read as a statement of an existential or lyrical I, their only place is in a metalinguistic utterance as the signs "ich" and "du" in language, where, indeed, they are completely empty.

Yet metalinguistic statements, as any other theoretical discourse, must enter into some relation with the poetic function. Contrary to some vulgarized applications of structuralism and poststructuralism, not every metalinguistic act is a poetic act. The notion that metalinguistic utterances should be privileged over other kinds of discourse in literary texts is partly due to the emphasis given by the Russian formalists to the self-referential function as a specifically poetic function. But there is often a confusion between self-referential and self-reflective: the self-referential linguistic act is not necessarily self-reflective, nor is self-reflective discourse more self-referential than any other. A poem that presents and stages certain devices and operations of language does not necessarily "know" or talk *about* them; and self-reflective texts that talk about themselves are often the blindest toward their own performance as linguistic acts.

We have to read the poetic sense and function of Celan's metalinguistic phrase within the poetics established through the constellation of his texts. We have condensed these poetics already in what Winfried Menninghaus, following Walter Benjamin, calls the *Intentionalität auf die Sprache* (intentionality toward language). This intentionality is not directed toward *a* language, but *the* language, language as such and thus never "there" in any specific language. Therefore, any language, including poetic language, can only be the realization of an intentionality toward it.

The uncathectable *ich* and *du* can then be read as one of the most direct utterances of this poetic desire and intentionality. Saying it delineates at the same time the limits of the discourse that says it. The asyntactical tendency toward mere juxtaposition in Celan's poetry can now also be read in a different way: not so much as an analogy to the language of a dream, as we read it earlier, but as an attempt to approximate *language*. Thus, one of the most essential markers of discourse, the finite verb, is completely missing. The minimal punctuation, reduced to the comma that separates and serializes a string of distinct units, points in the same direction.

The poem that speaks of this intentionality toward language is not language, but discourse. To be more precise: we read it as discourse, as a text that says something, anything. For, strictly speaking, our reading of the two lines "unbesetzbar / ich und auch du" silently inserted a verb not written in Celan's text, i.e., we read it as "unbesetzbar (ist/sind) ich und auch du"; we read the *unbesetzbar* in the grammatical position of a predicative.

If we would not read it as a text and discourse that says something, for example something about an intentionality toward language, we could not read it at all and we could not then say that there is such an intentionality.

The text moves along a threshold that it cannot cross. But being on or near the threshold, it also indicates the double nature of that which it desires: language, in the emphatic absolute sense it acquires in Benjamin's work as well as in Celan's poetics, carries the full weight of a long theological-mystical tradition, and yet it can be *thought* of and spoken of only as pure, meaningless non-sense. It is the double-faced image of the puppet and the god in Kleist's essay on the *Marionettentheater*.

On the other side of the threshold is the social sphere of commodity signs ("Waren- / Zeichen"). But if we read the preceding two lines as a predicative claim, that "ich und auch du" are uncathectable, there is no social sphere left. It and its emblematic condensation in the commodity sign are "überwahr- / heitet" (again we read predicatively without a predicative copula in the text). But in this case, the copula is to a certain degree replaced by a peculiar parallel conjunction: *überwahr-heitet, Waren-zeichen.* The parallelism in the breaking of the compounds is enforced by the internal parallels between the two pairs: the homophony of *-wahr-* and *Waren,* the consonance of *-heitet* and *-zeichen.* If the commodity (*Ware*), since Marx the privileged place of deception and illusion, is overcome by truth, "overtruthed" (*überwahr-heitet*), the homophonic relationship, brought forth by the textual constellation, indicates not that the relationship between the fetishistic deceptiveness of *Ware* and *Wahrheit* is simply one of opposition, but that one is enfolded in the other. The silent letter *h* marks the difference within the sameness of the signs.[41] If the truth is over (*über*) the commodity sign, it still emerges from the commodity and the vicissitudes of its exchanges.

Things enter into the traffic of exchange and turn into signs, commodity signs. Yet, if they are to be overcome by truth, it is only with the help of an empty sign, *heitet*; consonant with *zeichen* and a *Zeichen* itself, it is the formative element that affects the *Warenzeichen* with the quality *überwahr.* The suffix *-heit*, derived from an old high-German word indicating "kind" or "manner," has lost its independent meaning. It no longer designates anything, but marks the transformation of a "concrete" quality into an "abstract" entity (similar to the function of the English suffixes -ness and -ty, as in "illness," "beauty"). The overcoming of the commodity sign by truth, the move from the sign to the name, can only be indicated by a sign that no longer names.

That which is overcome is yet conserved: while the appeal of the commodity sign to the eye and to memory ("das augen-, das / gedächtnisgierige rollende / Waren- / zeichen") is overcome by truth, the physical places of seeing and memory remain intact: the *Schläfenlappen* (the section of the brain near the temple) and the *Sehstamm* (the optical center of the brain). The forehead seems to have opened up at last. Yet we do not find an interiority behind the surface; we find another surface, intact. Danton's wish, become true, does not open the truth. Interiority, a spatial metaphor, is reduced to pure surface when literally entered. Its metaphorical space opens up only along the folds of the surface in the exteriority of signs that always point elsewhere.

VII

BELATEDNESS:
HISTORY AFTER FREUD
AND LACAN

To be or not to be historical is a question frequently asked in that tone in which Gretchen asks Faust: "Heinrich, what about your religion?" The question put in this tone is not so much an appeal for an epistemological clarification as it is a demand for a moral commitment and confession. If, in the realm of literary criticism today, this appeal to history is most evident and urgent wherever a certain social claim and relevance is attached to the critical and academic activity, its moralistic implications cannot be confined to a single ideological corner. The ghost of Hamlet's father keeps appealing to us lest we forget him and pursue our own desires.

History and the humanities somehow seem to belong together. As Yosef Yerushalmi puts it: "For those reared and educated in the modern West it is often hard to grasp the fact that a concern with history, let alone the writing of history, is not an innate endowment of human civilization."[1] Yet it does not need much of the historical gaze, directed at itself, to recognize that historical thinking in an emphatic sense is a relatively modern phenomenon, emerging specifically in eighteenth-century Europe. Peter Szondi goes so far as to claim a radical rupture that separates Kant's still-ahistorical philosophy from the historical thinking of the post-Kantian era.[2] That might appear to be an exaggerated claim given the fact that histories were written centuries before the Common Era and many more since then. Yet what Szondi is referring to, and what I call historical thinking in an emphatic sense, is not just a matter of stories and histories; it implies an all-pervasive subjection of human affairs to the signifying power of history. History in this sense is the horizon of significance and therefore the horizon of understanding. To view things "ahistorically" means, in this framework, to miss their true significance.

In Germany, particularly since the late sixties, history has been valorized in opposition to "text-immanent" criticism. To be historical meant, and still means for many critics, to be aware of the social and material conditions of texts and of interpretation as opposed to a sinful ideological existence in the ivory tower. In the United States, the opposition generally takes a different shape. The strong dominance of New Criticism did not allow for much thought about historical problems beyond an occasional vague reference to "historical background." Only recently, under the pressure of a strong surge of theoretical reformulations and rethinking, history seems to emerge as an oppositional term to theory.

To classify the complex and sometimes confusing contemporary critical scene in such a way is obviously somewhat reductive. But it is precisely on the level of such reductions that the rhetorical effects of key terms take place, over the heads and behind the backs of the individual critics. In the opposition of history versus theory, specific significant assumptions play an effective role: pragmatism against speculation; natural and common language against jargon and artificial metalanguage; concrete narrative story against abstract systematic construction. In short—the human world of true humanists is pitted against the dehumanizing, bloodless abstractions of cold intellectuals.[3] The rhetorical shrillness of the latter formulation generally appears in more subdued forms, and the oppositions sometimes find more subtle and refined expression. They nevertheless remain charged by a powerful conviction, which, when threatened, causes some anxiety: it is the deeply rooted conviction that history is the natural shape of the human world and that the linear narrative is the movement of human experience.

Such assumptions have long been the subject of serious questioning in the historical disciplines themselves. The often-passionate confrontation between narrative historiography and structural or econometric systematization is only the most general and visible sign of more subtle and complex shifts in historical thought. One of the most dynamic scenes of such a shift was created by the French journal *Annales d'histoire économique et sociale*, founded in 1929. There is a tendency to move away from person-oriented political and dynastic historiography toward the history of social structures and relations. Fernand Braudel's major oeuvre *La Méditerranée* stages an expansive historical drama in which fluctuating agencies of cities, islands, and regions assume the role of historical subjects.[4] Even more important is Braudel's layering of historical time in the simultaneity and discontinuity of three temporal dimensions: the long duration of natural history, the middle duration of social history, and the short time of the events on the surface. These three layers cannot necessarily be integrated into a homogeneous structure. His critics seem to find this non-synthetic aspect of Braudel's work particularly disturbing.[5]

If the heterogeneity of the historical subject-agents and of historical time layers are the shaping forces or, rather, the "unshaping" forces, of Braudel's *Méditerranée*, Lucien Fèbvre's *Rabelais* points toward another kind of heterogeneity, that between different "mentalities."[6] The question of whether Rabelais was an atheist is treated in a way that opens up a fundamental problem of historical hermeneutics. Fèbvre's answer is not so much that Rabelais was not an atheist, but that atheism was epistemologically impossible for him, because there were no modes of thought and discourse that allowed the thinking of atheism.

The hermeneutical problem of understanding another, possibly heterogeneous, "mentality" also implies the problem of language in history and history in language. This latter problem has shaped some of the most influential recent developments in American intellectual history, as in the work of Hayden White and Dominick LaCapra.

While Hayden White's investigation of the tropes of history unsettles the neat division between the world "out there" and its reproduction in language, LaCapra, following Bakhtin, pursues the "interaction between language and the world" to the point where the carnival of heterogeneity undercuts all attempts of "unmasking" in order to find the naked face of one homogeneous historical object.[7]

Our historical survey has led us to a paradoxical result: the creation of a scene of historical thought where rather different names are gathered under the unifying name of heterogeneity.[8] Such is the nature of historical surveys. We cannot escape the laws and tropes that govern this kind of narrative, nor is it our intent to do so: we will have to work through it.

If psychoanalysis is primarily a scene of "working through," it might yet seem a rather far-fetched place for rethinking historical problems. Historians sometimes tend to discard "psychoanalytic approaches" as ahistorical and overly concerned with individual pathologies instead of social relations. What presents itself as "psychohistory" can only confirm such notions and perpetuate a specific misreading of Freud and psychoanalysis as individual psychology rather than as the dissolving of the "individual" on a scene of fluctuating agencies which produce the subject functions and participate in the structuring of social relations. Most of these psychohistories are informed by a *specific* misreading or even *determinate* non-reading. An anthology of essays collected under the title *Geschichte und Psychoanalyse* (History and Psychoanalysis) symptomatically does not mention Freud in its extensive bibliography (except as coauthor of W. C. Bullitt's *W. Wilson!*).[9] Only one of the contributors refers to Freud's *Basic Writings*. To perfect the farce, the German translation and introduction consistently retranslate Freud's *Verdrängung* from the English into the supposedly scientific German "Repression." The introduction speaks equally consistently of the subconscious (*Unterbewußtsein*) as if Freud had never, and with good reason, argued against this term. It is no wonder, then, that the editor explicitly cancels any discussion of fundamental analytic terms since this is not a scene to think through or even to remember the terms of Freud, but the very scene where they are acted out.

It would hardly be worthwhile bothering with such texts at all, were it not for their symptomatic character. As symptoms, however, they can be illuminating. What they reveal is something they want to forget, sometimes in the form of a denegation. In an unpublished manuscript recently sent to me for evaluation, I read the astounding assertion that both Freud and Heidegger are atemporal thinkers. To deny the thought of time to two thinkers who gave it a very special place in their works indicates a problem with temporality at the very core of the rhetoric of historicism. Paradoxical as it may sound, one thing historicism cannot think of is *time*. But, of course, time is not a thing, as Heidegger and Freud and, centuries earlier, Saint Augustine discovered. Historicism, even in its more modern forms, even sometimes under the claim of "dialectics," can only think of things, of facts, but not of that which transforms *facere* into *factum*.

"Quid est enim tempus?" With this question, Augustine starts his investigation of time in the eleventh book of the *Confessions* (14, 17). The *quid* in the question presupposes an *id* in the answer. But time is neither id nor it, rather that which is already forming the movement of the question and the answer: "Quis hoc facile breviterque explicaverit?" Even if there were someone who could explain it *briefly*, it would be an explanation *in* time and not of time. Augustine's thinking of time is not brief but long in its vertiginous moves through vanishing point after vanishing point. If I recall Augustine at this threshold, before entering into Freud's text, it is not only because of the analytic form of these confessions as a discourse before the Other, but also because I want to point out two remarkable and, in Freud's text, re-marked phenomena in time and in thought of time. The first is the seemingly banal observation that thought is always already marked by time (Freud specifically calls it a *Zeitmarke*).[10] This means, however, that thought has to move through what I called vanishing points which, for the subject, cause that vertigo which historicism cannot bear and which is nevertheless the *conditio sine qua non* for philosophical or poetic thought.[11]

By moving through the vanishing points, each tense of time disappears: the past *is* no more; the future *is* not yet; and when Augustine

wants to hold on to that which seems to be, the present, it dissolves
under the analytical gaze into points without extension in time. It is
a non-time. And yet Augustine, like Hegel and Freud after him, insists
that what is said is true, that language does not lie. We do say that
the past was, the present is, and the future will be. The question is,
how and where *are* they: what is the being of time? Here Augustine
makes the decisive move from presence to representation which articulates the correct form of the tenses as *praesens de praesentibus, praesens de praeteritis, praesens de futuris* (20, 26): the presence of
something which *itself is not*, and which is yet the foundation of
presence. This formulation already contains in a condensed and precise form the structure of that which Freud calls *Nachträglichkeit*,
translated in the Standard Edition as "deferred action," and in my
terminology as "belatedness."

  Nachträglichkeit and *Verspätung* (belatedness) are guiding terms
of Freud's thought.[12] Although the precise working of *Nachträglichkeit*
can only emerge from a minute tracing of its effects and movement
in the analytic process and in Freud's text, it might be helpful to
delineate some of the major characteristics of this phenomenon at
this—somewhat belated—beginning.[13] *Nachträglichkeit* touches upon
the fundamental relationship between event and history, between *Ge-
schehen* and *Geschichte*, between *facere/fieri* and *factum*. It designates
the transformation and rewriting of experiences, impressions, and
memory traces on the basis of later experiences and in the context of
a new phase of development. Already in his letter to Fließ on
December 6, 1896, Freud describes this process as *Umordnung* (reordering) and *Umschrift* (reinscription). Let us keep in mind at this
point, following Laplanche and Pontalis, three elements in this phenomenon: 1) the object of the reordering is not the totality of the past,
but fragments which, at the time of the event, could not be integrated
into a context of significance; 2) specific experiences and—often critical—situations determine the time and mode of the reordering; 3) all
phenomena of *Nachträglichkeit* are marked by a period of *latency*, of
forgetting.
  Freud did not discover the phenomenon as such, but he recog-

nized its essential and constitutive function in the formation of histories. Psychoanalytic praxis and theory after Freud generally have not given the phenomenon of *Nachträglichkeit* much thought, and in most cases seem to have forgotten it completely as the recent discussions of Masson's polemics have indicated.

It was Lacan who emphatically insisted here as elsewhere on a "return to Freud" and revalorized the constitutive function of *Nachträglichkeit*. Lacan gave one of his most condensed articulations of the function of *Nachträglichkeit* in his decisive lecture in Rome in 1953: "Fonction et champ de la parole et du langage en psychoanalyse."[14] In this talk, where Lacan sketches the fundaments of his reading of Freud in the name of the word and of language, the phenomenon of *Nachträglichkeit* appears in a network of specific relations that are essential to its understanding. A brief sketch of these relations will map the complexity of the field we are about to enter, before we pursue its topography in detail through two major texts of Freud.

At the very outset of his lecture, Lacan declares what he calls the "ahistoricism" of American ego psychology as the antipode of the analytic experience (*Ecrits*, 245). What is the mode of historicity that Lacan locates in the center of the analytic experience? This experience speaks in two modes: the *parole vide* and the *parole pleine*, the empty and the full word. History is located in regard to these two registers on the axis of the full word in the form of "anamnesis" (opposed to the analysis of the *hic et nunc*), of "hysterical intersubjectivity" (as opposed to obsessional intrasubjectivity), and as "symbolic interpretation" (as opposed to resistance interpretation). History and the realization of the *parole pleine* are thus intimately linked in the realm of intersubjectivity and in the symbolic order. In an explicit reference to Heidegger, Lacan formulates the constitution of the subject in this order as "having been" (*ayant été–gewesend*). But the temporal structure of this *ayant été*–"having been" is decisively marked by the situation of the *étant*, of that which is now. The being now marks the having been as a convergence of past events under the aspect of a now and its projection toward a future (*Ecrits*, 255).

Such a marcation of the order of the past under the aspect of the now raises of course the question of historical truth and reality. Here Lacan follows Freud's "non liquet" (which I will discuss in more detail

later) and locates the hysterical-historical story both in the imaginary
and the real, but—as *parole pleine*—in the form of truth: "la naissance
de la vérité dans la parole" (the birth of truth in the word). The truth
is the present word, and the present word gives testimony of the past,
but not so much of that which has been but of that which has been
rejected: "la parole témoigne de cette part des puissances du passé qui
a été écartée à chaque carrefour où l'événement a choisi" (it is the
Word which bears witness to that portion of the powers of the past
which has been thrust aside at each crossroads where the event has
made its choice) (*Ecrits*, 256). History here takes the specific form of
re-memorization as a reordering of the past in view of a future sense
or meaning.

At this point, a first objection might be raised: all this is perhaps
well and good for the individual on the couch who tries to reconstruct
his personal history, but History is quite another matter; here we are
dealing with collective subjects and constellations that cannot be made
dependent on individual whims. Yet it is precisely Freud's and Lacan's
point that the specific field of psychoanalysis, that what Freud called
the unconscious, is by its very nature located in an intersubjective
sphere. I will pursue this question again in more detail on the basis
of Freud's text. At this point, I will just refer to Lacan's condensed
formula: "L'inconscient est cette partie du discours concret en tant
que transindividuel, qui fait défaut à la disposition du sujet pour ré-
tablir la continuité de son discours conscient" (The unconscious is
that part of the concrete discourse in so far as it is transindividual,
which is not at the disposition of the subject to reestablish the continuity of his conscious discourse) (*Ecrits*, 258). The word that gives
testimony of the past and tells our histories does not belong to the
individual, it runs "from mouth to mouth"—*von Zunge zu Zunge* in
Hölderlin's *Brod und Wein*—and the subject receives his history and
the sense of his history from this sphere "in between."

We may follow the movement of this phenomenon in two of
Freud's texts, one concerning the reconstruction of an individual history, the other the reconstruction of a historical event: the history of
the Wolfman and the history of the man Moses.[15]

The neat division between an individual and a collective history is, however, already imprecise and is put into question by Freud's titles: the "individual" story of the Wolfman is called *Aus der Geschichte einer infantilen Neurose* (*From the History of an Infantile Neurosis*), and the history of the origin of monotheistic religion appears as the story of *Der Mann Moses* (The Man Moses).

Both titles are shaped by the urgency of a specific situation, a kind of crisis, and a certain polemical purpose. *From the History of an Infantile Neurosis* is intimately connected with the painful split between Freud and Jung. The title, with its emphasis on the *infantile* neurosis, marks the divisive line and radical difference of Freud's *Nachträglichkeit* from that of Jung. At first glance, it might seem that Jung's notion of *Zurückphantasieren* (fantasizing back into the past) would be a perfect example of *Nachträglichkeit*: an apparent memory from childhood turns out to be a fantasy of the adult, projected back into the past. The parallel in historiography would be a relativistic theory of history with all emphasis on the ideological and phantasmic determinations of the presence in the reconstruction of history, which is indeed only the simple inversion and thus the repetition of a naive objective historicism. Freud's *Nachträglichkeit* is never a simple projection into the past. Contrary to recently widely publicized legends, he insists on the *real* as a precondition for memory traces, although, as we will see, the real and reality assume a complex and evasive form.[16] The fact that there was an *infantile* neurosis in the Wolfman case is Freud's major argument against Jung's assertion of a simple projection from a later time back into infancy.

At the end of a long footnote in the latter part of the chapter on "The Dream and the Primal Scene," Freud unfolds the complex structure of *Nachträglichkeit*. The analysis of the wolf dream uncovers a primal scene in which the little child, waking up one afternoon, observes his parents engaged in *coitus a tergo*. The event is located at the age of one and a half years, the dream at the age of four; the analysis began at the age of twenty-three. Freud summarizes the temporal layering in the following way: "At the age of one and a half years, the child receives an impression to which he cannot sufficiently react; only at the age of four years he understands it, is grasped by it [*von ihm ergriffen*] through a reactivation of the impression [*bei der*

Wiederbelebung des Eindrucks], and only two decades later he can grasp with conscious thought the events that took place in him" (*S* 8:163, *S.E.* 17:44).

My schema includes three major elements: the impression of the real event (A), a moment of seizure and understanding (B), and, finally, the conscious grasping in the analysis (C):

A	B	C
impression (*Eindruck*)	being seized/understanding	grasping consciously
	(dream)	(analysis)
1½	4	23–27

A chronological, linear story would have to move from A to B to C. The analytical story, however, has a different movement: A appears at the end, as a result; the direct object of the analysis is B, the belated reactivation of the event, not the event; it is the moment when the subject is seized (*ergriffen*) by the event and understands it, although in a dream rather than in conscious thought. There seems to be a relation here between being seized and understanding: the subject understands because he is seized, or is he seized because he understands? Perhaps we must leave the relationship suspended in the form of a mutual interdependence: we understand only that by which we are seized, and we are seized only by that which we somehow understand. Or, to put it in other terms: only that which has entered into a structure of significance can become an object for us.[17] But what about the supposed real event? It is essentially exactly that: supposed, i.e., a necessary supposition or presupposition. Its mode is that of *necessity, Ananke* as the later Freud likes to call it, *Notwendigkeiten* in the language of Freud's contemporary Bertolt Brecht. It is not only an epistemological presupposition, but also a *real* limit, and it appears only in the form of a limit, a threshold, a resistance which forbids trespassing under the penalty of death. It cannot be represented, because it is the foundation and limit of representation. It is that which is necessarily excluded from the symbolic chain of signification, both its *a priori* and belated effect.[18]

What about Freud's description of the "primal scene"? To the degree it is articulated in a specific form, it is no longer the real, but an element of reality, questionable in its particular form and constantly questioned by Freud. Reality is not identical to the real, just as history is not the simple accumulation of "facts," but a specifically assembled coherence of pertinent facts. Reality is an effect of the real within an imaginary and symbolic constellation. To speak in terms of our schema: A becomes part of reality only under the condition that it has passed through B, only then it takes place in what the German language calls *Wirklichkeit*.

Inadvertently, we have been seized by a problem and perhaps by the dawning of an understanding that seems to lead us into a very different direction from our initial topic of *Nachträglichkeit*. Yet, if *Nachträglichkeit* indeed has anything to do with history, it also has to do with that central question historians are supposed to ask: what *really* happened? The answer, for the historian, is not only a question of the material from the past, but also a question of form: how to convince others of what really happened. Three problems are thus intimately linked: history, reality, and the forms taken by conviction and consensus.

Temporality is not just a question of the ordering of the analyzed material, it is also a problem of the structure of analysis. The analyst moves between two extreme poles of time: his position has to approach the "timelessness" of the unconscious (*S*. 8:132; *S.E.* 17:11), yet one of the most effective means is the introduction of a time mark, which in the Wolfman case takes the form of a threatened termination of the analysis at a certain point. In a dramatic way, the timing of and in the analysis shapes the time under analysis.

The position of both the analyst and historian between an attitude of timelessness and critical timeliness is paralleled by other limits and conditions of the analytical and historical involvement. Freud points out the limitations of a single case for generalizations: "Of course a single case cannot teach us everything we would like to know. To be more precise: it could teach us everything if we were only able to grasp everything, and if we were not forced by our untrained perception to be satisfied with less" (*S* 8:131; *S.E.* 17:10). It seems that it would be merely a matter of training our faculty of perception in order to reach a limitless attention capable of grasping everything. Yet, as Freud makes clear elsewhere, the very nature of perception is selection, because an unlimited perception would be deadly for the organism. And there is an additional limit on the other side of perception and attention: the unconscious, which determines, delimits, and distracts free-floating, infinitely open attention. If free-floating attention is the ideal of the analyst and the historian, there would seem to be a critical threshold against reaching this ideal. Absolutely free attention would have as a prerequisite the absence of the unconscious. Yet the most important dynamic in the analytic process takes place between the analyst's unconscious and that of the analysand. Reaching the ideal, even if it were possible, would thus make the analysis impossible. The patient would talk with more therapeutic effect to a plant than to an analyst without an unconscious.[19]

The next impossible limit Freud evokes will be more familiar to the historian. At the end of the first chapter, Freud explicitly enters into the problem of "conviction" and the unlikeliness of convincing others of the strange, "unbelievable" things with which he will confront us. He concluded with a reference to *Hamlet*: "There are more things in heaven and earth than are dreamt of in our philosophy. Whoever would be able to shut out even more fundamentally his prejudices [*mitgebrachte Überzeugungen*] could certainly discover more such things" (S. 8:133; S.E. 17:11). Prejudices, the convictions we carry with us, are, as we all know, the great detractors and blockages in our intellectual undertakings. As historians or literary critics we agree, at least theoretically, to suspend them. Yet, as any serious hermeneutical reflection will point out, not only can we never enter into a state of complete ideological suspension, but even if it were possible, we would be unable to understand anything, since every act of understanding presupposes a horizon of significant constellations.

Freud thus delineates his and our position between two necessary and impossible conditions of understanding. At the same time he introduces in the characterization of his patient a figure who, in a strange way, seems to embody one of the ideals: "The patient remained for a long time unassailably entrenched behind an attitude of docile indifference. He listened, understood, and let nothing come close. It seemed as if his unblemished intelligence was cut off from the libidinal forces, which dominated his behavior in the few other relationships left in his life" (S 8:132; S.E. 17:10). An unblemished intelligence listens, understands *sine ira et studio*. Is this not the ideal of a scholar?

But in the case of Freud and his patient, the result is a total blockage of the analysis. At this point, the scholar might want to insist on the incomparable difference between an analysis, where emotional problems are to be solved, and scholarly work, where objective understanding is at stake. Yet where does the studiousness of the scholarly enterprise come from if not from a *studium* cathected by that which the Latin word designates: eager desire? Are we opening up the floodgates of passion? Are we advocating scholarship ruled by emotions? Thus I hear the rhetoric of anxiety speak, the anxiety of the scholar, which also speaks in me. That there is such an anxiety, specifically where the fortifications against the invasion of libidinal forces into the country of rational debate have been firmly erected, indicates that something went wrong. Freud puts his finger right on the spot, which could be described as a slightly perverted *divide et impera*. (Latin seems to be a kind of primal scene for this scenario.) Intellect and emotions have been radically cut off from each other; each is kept in isolation, and it is precisely the act of isolating which allows the rule and domination of the "libidinal forces." The opposite, however, is not the rule of intellect and reason, but a kind of traffic and intercourse which would liquify and perhaps even liquidate the principle of domination.

Like many historians, Freud starts his story with a "Survey of the Milieu" and the general history of the case. Yet the first sentence makes clear that he will not be able to tell a simple story: "I can write the history of my patient neither purely historically [*rein historisch*] nor purely pragmatically [*rein pragmatisch*], I can give neither a history of the treatment nor a history of the illness, but will be forced to combine the two modes of presentation" (S 8:134; S.E. 17:13). Two modes of presentation, two histories, are entangled with each other. It is not immediately clear how precisely Freud differentiates the historical from the pragmatic history. If we read the second part of the quotation as a parallelism, "historical" would be aligned with "history of treatment" and "pragmatic" with "history of the illness." Later passages confirm such a parallel. In the third chapter ("The Seduction and Its Immediate Consequences"), Freud, after an excursion into the life of the sister, returns to the boy's story: "I now return to the (hi-) story of the brother, which I have to present, however, from here on for a while in a pragmatic manner [*pragmatisch darstellen muß*]" (S.

8:143; *S.E.* 17:23). As the mode of the following narrative demonstrates, Freud uses "pragmatic" to indicate a linear, chronological story as it emerges from the analytical process. He interrupts the presentation of the analytic unfolding in the fourth chapter ("The Dream and the Primal Scene") in a similar way: "Here comes the point where I can no longer follow the movement of the analysis. I am afraid it will also be the point where the faith of the reader will leave me" (*S.* 8:156; *S.E.* 17:36).[20] He then tells the story of the reconstructed primal scene. Under the pressure of narrative laws, the pragmatic history is thus separated from the "historical" account of the process of the reconstruction. But Freud also makes it clear that this pragmatic history cannot stand alone without the support of the history of the reconstruction, which is the "historical history." History in the full sense embraces both the past and the process of its discovery.

Freud starts with the immediately available material, which is both fragmentary and obstinately opaque. The story made up of this material offers us what is called "background" in history books. Three remarkably parallel paragraphs tell this story (*S.* 8:134–35; *S.E.* 17:13–14, second, third, and fourth paragraphs). I will refer to them as a, b, and c.

Paragraph a sketches the parental scene: "Young married parents, still living in a happy marriage on which soon their illnesses will cast the first shadows. . . ." As in a classic novelistic exposition, the general situation is already marked by three time dimensions of past, present, and the foreshadowing of the future. In an equally classic narrative gesture, the general situation is ruptured by a singular event: "One day" (*Eines Tages*) the boy overhears a phrase of his mother spoken to the doctor. This presently insignificant phrase will later enter into a significant constellation. The end of the paragraph leads back to the general situation, introducing a significant new character: the sister.

Paragraph b repeats the movement. The general situation is now marked by a parental substitute, the old nurse who cares for the boy as a substitute for her dead son. Again a singular event affects the situation by creating incision, *ein Abschnitt*, as Freud calls it. The child is cut off from his early environment by a move from the country to the city. At the end a new significant character is introduced: the

English governess, who will occupy a position parallel to the sister in the figural constellation around the Wolfman. A new element is added: a screen memory of the little boy watching the departure of his parents and sister while holding his nurse's hand and then return-ing peacefully into the house. The structure of the screen memory is an inversion of the singular event in paragraph a, where the boy is led, at the hand of the mother, away from the house.

In paragraph c we enter a new sphere, that of narrative represen-tation: "In later years he was told many stories of his childhood." The general situation is thus one of many stories and many disorganized memories. The singular event also enters in the form of a singular story ("Eine dieser Überlieferungen"). But since it has taken the form of a representation, it is also repeatable and "countless times repeated." Once again, the content of this story involves a specific form of pres-ence and absence, incision and cutting off: he used to be a very quiet boy and was therefore supposed to be the girl, while the much more active sister should have been the boy. This quietness of the boy/girl is suddenly interrupted one summer when the parents *return home* (again the inversion of the scene of the previous paragraph). A final inversion of the preceding two paragraphs concludes the third with the departure of a significant person (the governess) and the return of the parents.

In chapter 3 ("The Seduction and Its Immediate Consequences") the actual (re-)construction begins. Contiguity forms the first tentative links: the recurring word, already spelled out in the title, is *nächste* (nearer, next, proximate): *ihre nächsten Folgen; Die nächste Vermu-tung* (the first or next assumption); *Als nächste Wirkung* (the next or first effect). The problem of translation here points to an interesting ambivalence in this word *nächste*: not only does it belong to a spatial as well as temporal order, it also seems to indicate both a first and second position. More precisely, it designates a first position as the effect of something: it is the point of a *Nachträglichkeit*.

As a first effect in the analysis, certain dreams appear, from which a scene of seduction emerges. At the same time an inversion has occurred: what was *next* (*nächste*) at the beginning, the governess, is now far away (*entlegen*) and the sister has taken her place.

The effects are supposed to point to the real, which now asserts itself in Freud's text with a certain emphasis: "In reality the governess could have only a distant part in the seduction"; "The seduction by the sister was certainly not a fantasy" (S. 8:140; S.E. 17:20). We have already noted that the question of the real and Freud's insistence on the postulate of the real are central to the presentation of the Wolfman case and to the problem of *Nachträglichkeit*. Yet, while Freud insists that a reality has to be presupposed, he is at the same time extremely doubtful about establishing a specific form of that reality. All the more curious is Freud's emphatic certainty about what was *real* in this seduction scene, as well as the story which supports the certainty that the seduction by the sister was not a fantasy. It is the story told to and reported by the Wolfman by an older male cousin of how the sister, "a pert, sensual thing" (*ein vorwitzig, sinnliches Ding*), once sat down on his lap and opened his pants to grasp his penis. What is strange is not the story itself, which might be true or might well be a typical male fantasy, but that it should serve as a support for certainty. One might wonder whether this insistence on reality is not, like the particularly strong sense of reality in screen memories, precisely the symptom of a fantasy.

What remains certain, however, is the function of the real attributed to her in the drama of the Wolfman's story and biography. In that function she interrupts the (hi-)story, she interrupts and disturbs the imaginary and symbolic order: being boyish, active, and intelligent, she challenges the smooth transformation of the active-passive opposition to the masculine-feminine polarity. In the function of the real, she has to be excluded, ultimately, from the signifying chain, the movement of which will nevertheless be shaped by her. Not even mourning can acknowledge her. Lermontov will take her place, while she points with the finger of the real at the picture of the wolf, which will become the name of the boy with the initials eSPe, the decapitated (W)ESPE.

The wolf dream, representing a primal scene, constitutes itself as a primal scene of belatedness. If fairy tales are the first associations, the first connecting point for Freud is the strong feeling of reality in the dream. Such feelings and convictions of reality guarantee reality. This might seem to contradict my former reference to the function of the intense reality feeling in screen memories. Like the *vox populi*, which is God's voice, the voice of such strong feelings is the voice of the real. Yet, like God, the real speaks in riddles, and what it says is not what the speakers believe they say. Thus the reality feeling has a "determinate meaning": something is real, but it is "the reality of something unknown" (S. 8:153; S.E. 17:33).

The story that emerges seems incredible, as Freud emphasizes. Yet it is not incredible or improbable that it happened—after all, a *coitus a tergo* is certainly not an improbable event. It is only incredible as a remembered event, shaping the story and history of the Wolfman. The lack of credibility has to do with a rupture: "Here comes the point," Freud writes, "where I can no longer follow the process of analysis [*die Anlehnung an den Verlauf der Analyse verlassen muß*]. I am afraid it is also the point where the faith of the reader will leave me" (S. 8:156; S.E. 17:36). The belatedness of the analysis in relation to the dream and of the dream to the event forces a rupture and a shift in the entangled interrelation between the two histories, designated by Freud as "historical" and "pragmatic." Despite or perhaps because of their radical interdependence they cannot be bridged in a smooth continuity from the one to the other.

Indeed, one may ask: where did "it" happen? The obvious answer, if the reconstruction is right, of course, would be: on that warm summer afternoon at five o'clock, when Sergeii, not yet the Wolfman, one and a half years old, woke up from a feverish slumber. Something happened. Yet did "it" happen? As we know, even Freud wavered at times about "it." What seems to be certain is that "it" grasped Sergeii at the age of four and put the stamp of the Wolfman on him. Freud calls this event, in an explicit differentiation from memory, an "activation" (S. 8:162; S.E. 17:43). The standard English translation of *Nachträglichkeit* as "deferred action" makes good sense. Indeed, one may say, "it" happened here, in what I earlier designated as position B: it is here, in the form of the belated activation, that an event becomes a historical experience.

If belatedness creates the event as experience and constitutes historical significance, it also has an effect on its representation of the historical account and its language:

We now become aware that at this point of our presentation [*Darstel-

lung], we must change our terminology. He [the boy] has reached a new phase of his sexual organization during the dream. The sexual oppositions so far had been for him *active* and *passive*. . . . Now, the activation of the primal scene in the dream led him back to the genital organization. He discovered the vagina and the biological significance of male and female. He now understood that active was equal to male, passive to female.

The analytic terminology assumes the vocabulary of the history it constitutes. But the language is not simply re-presentation, it has its own force and its own taboos. The translation of passive into the sexual term "female" leads to sentences that cannot be uttered by the boy: "His passive sexual goal would now have had to assume the expression [*den Ausdruck annehmen müssen*] 'to be coited by the father'" (*S.* 8:165; *S.E.* 17:47). "To assume the expression" has to be understood in this context first of all as a verbal expression, the formulation of a desire, a goal that is unreachable. And it seems that it is the verbal expression that forces the desire into repression.[22]

The taboo effects an interrupted discourse. "We must interrupt here the discussion of his sexual development" (*ibid.*). The next chapter is entitled "Some Discussions." In place of the interrupted discussion other discussions emerge.

Discussions belong to that sphere where consensus is formed about what is true and not true, real or not real. But while the Habermasian precondition for any meaningful discussion lies in the principle of universal consensus, Freud starts his discussions with two animals at odds with each other and with no hope for a consensus: "Polar bear and whale, it has been said, cannot fight a war against each other because, restricted as each one of them is to its element, they cannot get together" (*S.* 8:166; *S.E.* 17:48). Thus, Freud's discussions start with the possibility of radical otherness, which does not even allow for fighting. Yet the voice of the Other, the potential *vox populi* ("it has been said"), does not seem to have chosen the best example for such alterity. A wolf and a shark would have illustrated the point of complete difference of the spheres much better, since, after all, whale and polar bear do share at least part of their spheres. But perhaps that is the point of the voice Freud quotes, and it certainly fits his application, because Freud's dispute is with those who work "in the field of psychology and neurology," thus close to Freud's own concerns. Otherness seems less a matter of total difference, as it is one of the small differences.

The small difference is nevertheless a fundamental difference based on incompatible premises. But is it not the ideal of the scholarly, the intellectual, and ultimately of the whole democratic community to open up its premises for discussion? That might be the ideal, but the reality and praxis of politics and discourse are something different. No political or discursive community can afford a *real* suspension of its fundamental, constitutive elements. Theoretical discussions of fundamental issues are social carnivals; their function is to solidify the taboo they seem to question.

Freud does not give a very positive evaluation of theory and theoretical debates: "Theoretical contradiction is usually fruitless. As soon as one has started to get away from the material, by which one is supposed to be informed, one runs the risk of getting intoxicated by one's own assertions and ends up defending opinions which contradict all observation" (*ibid.*). Theory that is not produced by a working-through of the material is as delirious as positivism, which takes the fetishistic object it has created for the real. Freud's insistence on the material and on observation can give no comfort to the positivist, who might look as aghast at Freud's material as, to paraphrase Karl Kraus, the unhappy fetishist who wants to kiss his lady's shoe and is forced to embrace the whole woman.

The goal, in Freud's most condensed description of what a "history" implies, is a complex construction: "that the particularities of such a scene, experienced and understood under such circumstances, are brought to consciousness in a coherent and convincing way" (*ibid.*). Two pairs of elements constitute this kind of history: particular events experienced (*erlebt*) by a subject and understood (*verstanden*) in a horizon of significance combined to form an experience in the emphatic sense (*Erfahrung*). This experience is brought into a historical narrative characterized by the two qualities of "coherent" (*zusammenhängend*) and "convincing" (*überzeugend*).

Whether something is "convincing" again appears to be a matter of discussion. But Freud insists that it is a "purely factual" question. However, facticity is not a given, but an effect of a labor of working through: he who has worked through the material will convince himself (*wird sich überzeugen*). It is thus indicated that there is no direct conviction of another which is not based on a self-conviction *by* the other. One can only convince oneself, or to be more precise, one can only be convinced and convicted by one's working through the material.[23] This might sound harmless; yet taking it seriously takes away the ground of the most cherished opinions and praxes of pedagogy and public debates. With no apologies, Freud points out the alternative: he who has not worked through the full analytical process has no judgment in this matter. The rest is silence, which usually is covered over by the noise of opinion.

Are those of us who have not undergone psychoanalysis, then, disqualified to judge in Freudian matters? As far as specific contents are concerned, which are the result of analysis, we have indeed no judgment. What am I talking about then? Like the whale and the polar bear, Freud and I may at times go fishing in the same waters. To the degree that my own fishing, i.e., my own attempts of (re-) constructing stories and histories from the texts before and in me have convinced me, I find Freud convincing. And I am interested in learning more from the ways in which he proceeds.

If understanding presupposes self-conviction, it also presupposes an almost unlimited ability to suspend disbelief. Freud demands from his reader the same attitude with which he listens to the patient: let us assume that what you say is true. It is the opposite of an ideology critique with the cheerful goal of "unmasking" and the less cheerful result of hitting everything except the truth. The only way of finding the truth of the other is by following the other, no matter how mad the (dis-)course might seem: "Thus one can do nothing else but follow him [the analysand] on his path" (S. 8:167; S.E. 17:49). Only at the end can the difference be articulated.

If my reading of the Wolfman case has led me to the problem of consensus and the sphere of the public, collective consciousness, Freud's path of analysis, partly shaped by the polemic with Jung, led him to the problem of the collective unconscious. It is a field in which Freud gropes his way with utter caution and reserve. When he returns to the problem in *Moses and Monotheism*, he even questions the usefulness of the term: "I don't think we gain anything if we introduce the term of a 'collective' unconscious. The content of the unconscious is in principle [*überhaupt*] collective, general possession of humanity. Thus we help ourselves with analogies" (*S.* 9:577; *S.E.* 23:132). Freud's argument against the term is not a denial of the quality "collective." The point is that talking of the "collective" unconscious is a tautology covering up the real problem: how can we understand such a collectivity? Freud, somewhat reluctantly, looks for a solution in a phylogenetic heritage. The child grasps for this phylogenetic experience "where his individual experience is insufficient" (*wo sein eigenes Erleben nicht ausreicht*; *S.* 8:210; *S.E.* 17:97). What does it mean, that an individual experience is insufficient? It seems to be a lack of meaning, a lack of integration within the individual horizon of significance, and thus in need of a precedent of integration in order to become a full experience (*Erfahrung*). We are directed more toward a semiological than a biological sphere.

We have already noted a remarkable chiastic inversion in the emphasis of the two titles of the studies on the Wolfman and on Moses and monotheism in regard to their subject matter. The individual case is put under the title of impersonal forces, the grandiose historical event of the genesis of monotheism is headed emphatically by the *man Moses*. The scene of the individual S.P. is strongly shaped by such collective matters as fairy tales and phylogenetic experiences, while in the Moses essay, Freud seems to make an explicit conservative gesture against contemporary trends in historiography (contemporary already to Freud)[24] and toward sociological and collective considerations, by insisting on the importance of great individuals, particularly great men, in shaping history.

Such chiastic inversions and transcriptions indicate that what is at stake is not an alternative between individual and collective history, but the constitutive principle of collectivity and individuation. Thus the emphasis on the *man* Moses is not only a continuation of Freud's search for the real, for the "real person," but also, and more important, the condensed formulation of a central theme: "man" as the principle of "mono" in the name of Moses.

If it seems that I have lost track of my title promising "belatedness," Moses brings it back in full force. It is not only Freud, but the biblical Moses story that thematizes the effect, that marks *Nachträg-lichkeit*. The Moses story is the continuation of the Joseph story, but after a rupture: "There came a new king in Egypt who knew nothing of Joseph," the Bible tells us (Exod. 1:8). This new king, who has forgotten something, sees himself confronted with a group of foreigners whose presence in his territory he cannot explain. His first move is an attempt to get rid of the foreign, inexplicable, unintegrable element. He decrees that all male infants should be killed. This decree, based on a forgetting, becomes the basis for the rise of Moses. Forgetting and latency will be the elements that shape the Moses effect as well.

The legends and myths gathered under the signature of Moses were written many centuries after Moses. Moses himself was made to remember an earlier history under the names of Abraham, Isaac, and Jacob. (It is odd that when God identifies himself to Moses as the God of those three men, he never calls himself the God of Joseph, who is so crucial as a link to Moses. God too seems to have forgotten, and emerges as this God perhaps because of this forgetting.)

Freud incribes himself as a subject of writing on the threshold between individuation and collectivity: "To deny a man to a people, whom it considers the greatest among its sons, is not something one undertakes comfortably, or lightly, particularly if oneself belongs to this people" (S. 9:459; S.E. 23:7). *Man* and *man selbst* (oneself) are the first forms in which the writing subject appears: the impersonal pronoun designates both the individuating distancing from the community whose hero Freud is going to take away (although, as we will see, in order to give him back with all the more force and effect) and an acknowledgment of belonging to that group out of which the man Freud individuates himself.

As in the analysis of the wolf dream, Freud searches for the individual origin through collective narrative patterns: fairy tale motifs in the Wolfman case, the structures of mythic narratives in the case of Moses. Following Otto Rank's study *Der Mythos von der Geburt des Helden* (*The Myth of the Birth of the Hero*, 1909) Freud lists the constitutive structural elements of such narratives: noble parents, difficulties or threats that lead to the child's expulsion from the original family, the salvation of the child raised in a lower-class family until as a young man he finds his true origin, takes revenge, and is recognized. As Freud points out, the pattern perfectly fits the Oedipus myth as well. With the Moses story, however, peculiar deviations from the narrative pattern create some difficulties.

Let us first remark, however, the compelling force Freud ascribes to the narrative structure as a framing principle. For Freud, the kernel of the compelling structure in this case is the opposition in the narrative of a noble family and a lower-class family. Following the pattern of the family romance, the analytic interpretation identifies the two as one. This narrative operation, together with its inversion, will prove to be a major force and theme in the Moses essay, whose most obvious formal characteristic seems to be the lack of a well-rounded, unifying economy and whose theme is the effect of one man and the creation not only of one God, but of the very principle of oneness: monotheism.

The first of the three parts of the Moses study ends in a suspended conclusion. Freud's working through the material has convinced him that Moses was of Egyptian origin, but he knows that the evidence is far from convincing others, and that the possibility of creating a scholarly consensus is indeed slim.

As the two concluding paragraphs reflect upon this outcome, they become the scene of yet another problematic of individuation and plurality. The sequence of grammatical subjects in the two paragraphs forms an almost perfect chiastic symmetry. The first paragraph starts with two "we" subjects (*Wir haben . . . unternommen, Wir haben gehört*; S 9:466; S.E. 23:15). The familiar "we" of the scholarly and critical discourse is the indicator of an authoritative agency. Of course, the modesty of the modern scholar does not allow him or her to attribute this authority to his or her individual person, but only to the persona as a representative of the scholarly community and of the laws that form the conditions of consensus and rational argumentation in the public sphere. On this level, something has been undertaken, something has been heard. But now, another grammatical subject appears: the impersonal *man* (one), continued by equally impersonal "objections" (*Einwendungen*) which block the easy formation of consensus on the level of the "we." They block it so successfully that, at the end of the first paragraph, an isolated *Ich selbst* (I myself) separates itself explicitly from the community of the "we": "I myself do not share this rejecting attitude, but I am not able to refute it" (S. 9:467; S.E. 23:16).

The next and last paragraph begins with the lonely "I" as the subject (*Warum habe ich, ich bedaure*), twice repeated, as is the "we" in the first paragraph, and then leads into a series of impersonal *man* sentences. If the *man* in the preceding paragraph appeared on the scene of a force of resistance and blockage, it now appears on the scene of a dynamic, violent force, that carries one away (*Läßt man sich . . . fortreißen*) and creates effects such as believing (*man glaubt*), grasping and understanding (*erfaßt man*), and grand theories (*wird selbst zu bedeutsamen Ansichten angeregt*). After this inverted move, one could expect to return to the originally blocked "we." But the position of the "we" remains void: something is missing for the constitution of this common sphere.

The two paragraphs thus stage the problem of convincing and conviction, already thematized in the Wolfman essay. Freud's position introduces a differential mark into the simple opposition of a universal consensus theory and irrational unverifiable claims for truth. The sentence quoted above—"I myself do not share this rejecting attitude, but I am also not able to refute it"—formulates the double difference in its most condensed form. It recognizes the public sphere of consensus formation as a legitimate place for communicable claims for truth. Freud goes to great lengths to exhaust the possibilities within that sphere. It is the very act of probing that sphere which also delineates its boundaries and limits and acknowledges the possibility of another truth effect, created as the result not of an act of faith, but of a rigorous working-through. It cannot claim any public authority, it carries no conviction for anyone else; the only assertion it makes is that of the limit itself. The acknowledgment of this limit makes the small but essential difference between a public sphere as a legitimate ground for consensus and generalizable interests, and the public sphere as the terrorism of universal communication.

The difference is created by that scene of the *man* which mediates and sometimes ruptures the traffic between the "I" and the "we" through detours and blockages. It is the scene of a third agency that prevents any simple dual relationship between two subjects. Any demand to sit down and be reasonable, usually uttered by the one already in the position of power, is likely to exclude this scene and thus maximize its force and effects.

When Freud is compelled to pursue the quest for Moses again in a second essay, under the tentative title "If Moses Was an Egyptian . . . ," the question of the one and the many appears with full force on the thematic level. Freud starts the investigation with the sharp opposition of the monotheistic Mosaic religion and the polytheistic Egyptian tradition. However, the opposition of the one and the many is not symmetrical, because the many are not simply an accumulation of many individual ones, but an assembly of blurred entities, "not sharply differentiated among each other" (S. 9:470; S.E. 23:19). Thus, the Egyptian polytheism lacks the very principle of oneness and individuation, whereas the Mosaic religion not only creates one God, but the one as the only one and the principle of oneness.[25]

The emphasis has undergone a subtle shift: if the first essay focuses on the origin of the man Moses, the second, in continuing that theme, extends it to the search for the principle of individuation and its origins in the rise of monotheism.

Individuation is presented as a complicated process of explication and setting apart (Auseinandersetzung) of one and the other. The immediate problem for Freud is to reconcile his claim for an Egyptian origin of Moses and the obvious sharp contrast between the two religions. So sharp is this contrast that, as Freud says, "one gets the impression, the contradiction [Gegensatz] between the Mosaic and Egyptian religion might be an intentional one" (S. 9:470; S.E. 23:19). It seems, in other words, that it is not merely an opposition but a contradiction, where the one constitutes itself through determinate denials of elements of the other: the taboos and silences of the one are abundant and prevalent features of the other.

If opposition, contradiction, intentional "setting-apart," and exclusion are elements constitutive of individuation and identity, the following question remains: how, under these circumstances, could a claim be made for the Egyptian origin of Moses? It turns out that this claim plays a crucial role in the answering of another implicit question: how is the other chosen, the other against which one identity sets itself up? It is not just some other, but one that already contains the elements of the new identity. Monotheism existed already as an episode within Egyptian history under Amenhotep IV, later renamed Ikhnaton. It lasted only for the seventeen years of Ikhnaton's reign and was then radically erased.

Freud follows his historical sources[26] when he associates this brief emergence of monotheism with the establishing of Egypt as a major imperialist power. "This imperialism," Freud writes, "was mirrored in religion as universalism and monotheism" (S. 9:472; S.E. 23:21). A crucial series of terms sets up a relationship between imperialism, universalism, and monotheism as principles of individuation and identity linking universalism and the principle of individuation based on a praxis of imperial domination.[27]

Imperialism is first seen as an opening-up to other local cultures and thus as a defeat of Egyptian provincialism. The universal gesture embraces the others. But the universal embrace desires homogeneous oneness. Universality becomes the principle of exclusion and exclusiveness (Ausschließlichkeit). According to Freud, this is the new significant element introduced by Ikhnaton. Through this element, the doctrine of the universal God became monotheism (S. 9:473; S.E. 23:22).

The exclusions introduced and practiced by Ikhnaton as well as the principle of exclusion itself became the marks that identify the Mosaic religion, ranging from the explicit exclusion of magic and pictorial representation to the silence concerning the fate of the dead, which was the central concern of the Egyptian polytheistic folk religion.

In characterizing Egyptian polytheism as the "folk religion" (S. 9:475; S.E. 23:25), Freud adds a new opposition between the common popular faith and the monotheistic dream of the lonely and singular Ikhnaton, "the first individual in human history," as he is described by Breasted, Freud's major source. Freud calls him a "dreamer" (Der Träumer Ikhnaton; S. 9:476; S.E. 23:26), "alienated from his people." If the dream of the little boy Sergeii shaped the name, the life, and the story of a man, the dream of the man Ikhnaton (continued by the man Moses) created a lasting historical effect. But how is it possible that a lonely dreamer, alienated from his people, would have such an effect? It seems all the more improbable, since Ikhnaton's dream right after his death fell victim to the same kind of violent exclusions and erasures he had directed against the monuments and inscriptions of the popular religion. The next explanation for this phenomenon of a revolutionizing effect seems to be an even greater man and dreamer: the man Moses who was successful where Ikhnaton failed. But that would only defer the problem and still rely on the unexplained assumption that one man, perhaps by some kind of missionary persuasion, shaped the beliefs and history of a whole people and opened up a new era of history. While many historiographers indeed rely on such assumptions, and while even Freud himself, at one point, seems to subscribe to such a notion, his analysis dissolves the effect of the one into a series of delayed effects. Even in the biblical accounts, Moses is not presented as a popular man. In several cases, God must intervene to prevent the outright rebellion of the people against their leader. Moreover, in Freud's reconstruction, the man Moses splits at the end of chapter 4 of the second essay into the two figures of a gentle Midianite priest and the aristocratic, forceful Egyptian Moses. The thread, so carefully spun, is torn again.

At this point, the rupture becomes both theme and solution. Taking up a suggestion from the biblical scholar E. Sellin in his book *Moses und seine Bedeutung für die jüdische Religionsgeschichte* (*Moses and His Significance for the History of Jewish Religion,* 1922) and extrapolating from the frequent biblical references to popular hostility against Moses, Freud postulates the possibility of an assassination of the leader by his people. Sellin based his thesis mainly on hints and traces in the books of the prophets, particularly in Hosea, and established an immanent relationship between the murder of Moses and Messianic expectations.

The violent death of an individual emerges as the constitutive ground for the formation of an identity and for the very principle of individuation. It is precisely the point around which Hegel's early writings trace the formation of Christianity, not simply as a religion, but as a historical event of individuation.

Freud's attempt to trace the workings of the unifying, individuating forces is shaped by a constant conversion of two or many into one, and the splitting of one into two. There are two textual sources of the biblical Scripture unified into one; the one man Moses seems to emerge from two very different men; the one God is the combination of an Egyptian spiritualized monotheism and a local volcano god Yahweh; the one people includes the Egyptian exiles and various Semitic tribes. "And all these dualities," Freud writes, "are the necessary consequences of the first duality, the fact that one part of the people had had an experience of traumatic character from which the other part remained distant" (S. 9:501; S.E. 23:52).

Freud tells the story of the unification in the form of a compromise formation. As the story is told (in chapter 5 of the second essay; S. 9:490; S.E. 23:41), it seems to take the form of a council in which two conflicting parties sit together for negotiations. The one party wants to establish the greatness and power of the new god Yahweh to whose guidance they attribute the liberation from Egypt. But this is an injustice to the memory of the man Moses and to his people. As a compromise, he is carried over to Kadesh and given the place of the Midianite priest, who fades away under the name of the Egyptian man.

If a first reading of the passage sounds like the story of a conflict solved in negotiations and debates by two groups of people, that is primarily the effect of a narrative necessity which, however, is at the same time subverted by Freud's style of radical depersonalization. The agencies of these negotiations are not personal subjects, but certain dynamics, "tendencies," as Freud calls them. The people are the scene on which this conflict of two forceful tendencies is carried out. The result, however, of this impersonal battle is the name of a man and a person who stands for the principle of monotheism, who is the guarantor of the unity of one people, and whose name is the signature of the five books that constitute the first unit of the one Scripture.

The effect is thus the "great man," the historical personality which, in its turn, effects history. Freud is a materialist. He does not believe in an immanent force of ideas offered by great men to the people. According to Freud, the "enlightened despots" all find the same fate that Ikhnaton and Moses were subjected to in his story: the "Enlightenment" is swept away by those on whom it was imposed (S. 9:496; S.E. 23:47).

It seems all the more improbable that the name of a local volcano god became the name of a principle that shaped future world religions. Why did this rather violent god, competing with the more spiritualized god of Moses and Ikhnaton, not enter into Flaubert's procession of past gods? Indeed, in Freud's story, Moses is killed and his god forgotten. But that did not matter (*machte nichts aus*; *S.* 9:499; *S.E.* 23:50), Freud asserts. One could also say that it mattered a great deal, but in the opposite sense: the forgetting and the violent rejection were the very matter which materialized a despotic idea into a historical force. The force has the shape of a new subject, no longer an individual man, but a *tradition* (*ibid.*). In this tradition a strange transformation takes place: the god Yahweh had usurped the position of Moses and his spiritualized god. But "the shadow of the god whose place he had taken became stronger than he; at the end of this development, the forgotten Mosaic god appeared behind him [the Yahweh god]. No one doubts that only the idea of this other god made it possible that the people of Israel survived all misfortunes into our time" (*S.* 9:499–500; *S.E.* 23:50–51).

Can the historical effect be located only in an idea, then, and can Freud's text be reduced to that of an idealist historian? If one follows the detours Freud sketches, it is obviously not that simple. Perhaps the very terms "idealism" and "materialism" have to be restated. In Freud's story, the idea as such has no historical or material force whatsoever. It is a delirious phantom among others. Yet it is not the real as such that produces the force. There is no direct effective relationship between a basis and a superstructure; there is only a rupture, a deferral based on an act of annihilation and forgetting. The idea has the basis of its force in a reality, but in a reality that has been done away with. A vanishing point and a temporal delay form the link between the real and its effects; there is the source of the material historical force. The power, emanating from persons and things seen with the knowledge of the last glance, gives a glimpse of that force.

The act of erasure and forgetting is, however, only the negative side of the historical effect which materializes its force in that which Freud calls *tradition*. This familiar, cozy term "tradition" assumes strange dimensions in Freud's writing. It is not the comfortable possession invoked by festive speakers when they appeal to tradition and culture heritage, but a force, returning from the forgotten, that takes possession of those whom it seizes. Freud's style assumes an almost biblical tone when he approaches the decisive moment: "At that time, men rose up from the middle of the people, in an uninterrupted chain, not related to Moses through origin, but seized by a great and powerful tradition, which had been growing gradually in the dark; and it was these men, the prophets, who untiringly preached the old Mosaic teaching" (S 9:500; S.E. 23:51). Tradition is based on both discontinuity and continuity: it sets in after a rupture, mediated by men with no continuous relation to Moses, but once begun, it is an uninterrupted chain (*in einer nicht mehr abreißenden Reihe*). These men, in contrast to Moses and Ikhnaton, do not come from elsewhere or from above, but rise, in the biblical terminology, "from the middle of the people." Through them, the foreign and singular becomes proper and general. In this process, the Egyptian Moses becomes truly the Moses of his people, because it is not the origin that determines what is proper and property, but the process of appropriation. If Freud started his first essay on Moses as an Egyptian with the apprehensive gesture of taking away the great man from his people, he now returns him all the more powerfully, not as the man, but as the myth that shapes history and tradition.

When Freud summarizes his investigation at the end of the second essay with the apparently simple observation "How impossible it is to deny the personal influence of individual great men in world history, and what injustice one does to the grandiose diversity of human life, if one only acknowledges motives coming from material needs" (*ibid.*), we get an inkling of the deceptiveness of Freud's simplicity. One could easily see this phrase incorporated into the rhetoric of many a conservative humanist or politician. But they would not know what they were saying. Freud's reinscription of the great man and individual as a motor force in history appears after a radical dismantling of that person, and the gesture against material reductionism follows a firm rooting of the force of ideas in the vanishing points of the material world.

There still remains for Freud the question "What is the actual nature of a tradition, and on what is its special power based?" (S. 9:501; S.E. 23:52). The third and last of the Moses essays is dominated by this question. As long as we think of tradition as that which is written down as an accessible source of information, transmitted from one generation to the next, there is no major problem. But this is not the power of tradition. In a first step, Freud separates written and oral tradition. Much that is lost and rejected by the written tradition lives on in oral history, in popular legends which were not subjected to the censorship of the canonical Scriptures. Yet oral tradition is not an undisturbed medium either; its distortions are only of a different kind. It is fragmentary, vague, and hard to grasp. And yet it seems to be the place of the force. Despite its evanescent, unstable character, it does not grow weaker, but "it becomes ever more powerful in the course of the centuries" (S. 9:518; S.E. 23:69). The voice and the mouth of the people indeed seem to be the voice and mouth of God, just as Luther looked at the mouth of the people for the shape of his translation of the Scriptures.

The voice of the people is strange and uncanny,[28] as Freud's vocabulary emphasizes: it "is not a familiar notion to us (*keine uns vertraute Vorstellung*). "We find ourselves in an area of mass psychology, where we do not feel at home" (S. 9:519; S.E. 23:70). Freud searches for analogies on his familiar ground, in the individual neuroses. The analogies found here—latency and the return of the forgotten with compelling force—show traits of the phenomena on the unfamiliar ground, approaching identity.

But despite the striking parallels, the question remains of how one can go beyond analogy to an explanation of an actual translation and transmission from the one to the other. "In what form does the effective tradition exist in the life of the peoples?" (S. 9:541, section E; S.E. 23:93). To orient himself and us, Freud recapitulates the psychological topology of the unconscious/preconscious/consciousness. But while the topology, once we grow accustomed to the spatial metaphor, is not too difficult to comprehend, the "dynamic nature of the psychic processes" leaves us in the dark. And this dynamic begins to blur the spatial boundaries of the topology. At least, we have to put into question one of the most common assumptions: that *thinking* belongs to consciousness, that here, at least, we know what we do. But "here" is precisely not where we know. According to Freud, perceptions, sensual impressions, and pain are conscious, but "the

thought processes [*Denkvorgänge*], and that which might be analogous
to them in the id, are in themselves unconscious" (*S.* 9:544–545; *S.E.*
23:97–98). The translation of thinking, which is unconscious, to
thoughts that are conscious is dependent on perception "via the language function" (*auf dem Wege der Sprachfunktion*; *S.* 9:545; *S.E.*
23:98).

Like the biblical Moses, Freud seems to have arrived at a point
where the view opens out to the promised land—but he will not enter
it. Almost abruptly he shifts ground, to return to a discussion of the
trauma. Yet the function of language, tantalizingly invoked without
being explored, has left its traces and will reappear at various points.

First there is the general and common arsenal of language symbols (*die Allgemeinheit der Sprachsymbolik; ibid.*) which children and
dreamers seem to know. But we don't know how we know them.
When Freud tentatively assumes a kind of symbolic heritage with
which we are born, he ties it together with the development of language (*das Beispiel der sicherlich "mitgeborenen" Symbolik die aus der
Zeit der Sprachentwicklung stammt*; *S.* 9:577, section H; *S.E.*
23:132). The development of language and the transition from ma-
triarchy to patriarchy constitute for Freud the two incisive events in
the development of human culture, sublimation, and spiritualization.
And it seems that the two are related: while a matrilineal genealogy
can be based on the testimony of the senses—the child visibly comes
from the mother when it is born—the patrilineal genealogy has to rely
on deduction and the testimony of the word.[29] The temporal delay
between the conception (*Zeugung*) through the father and the birth
through the mother erases sensual certainty and testimony. The father
as the physical progenitor disappears in order to reappear all the more
forcefully at the time of the birth as the carrier of the logos, who,
based on the testimony (*Zeugnis*) of the word, gives the child his name
and the law.

Yet, as Freud points out, the question of the legitimating authority is not resolved with the father: the authority of the father is the
result of sublimation and not its cause. The cause, the force that
enforces the authority of the father, seems to lie elsewhere: in his
disappearance as the physical father and man; in castration; in the
replacement of the testicles by the testimony of the logos. "Ότ' ούϰέτ

εἰμί, τηνικαῦτ᾿ ἆρ εἴμ᾿ ἀνήρ"; this is the question asked in rhetorical wonder by Oedipus at Kolonos: "Only when I have become nobody, I am, then, a man?" (l. 393). Freud saw the stories of the two men, Oedipus and Moses, related in the patterns of their birth. These stories seem to merge here on another level, as the story of the mythical effect, operating in the function and field of language, and through which stories turn into history.

NOTES

Unless otherwise noted, references to Freud's writings are to both the German *Gesammelte Werke* and the English *Standard Edition*; however, English translations are generally my own. The following abbreviations are used, with the appropriate volume and page numbers following:

S.E.   *Standard Edition of the Complete Psychological Works of Sigmund Freud*, tr. and ed. by James Strachey. 24 vols. London: Hogarth Press, 1953–1974; New York: Macmillan, 1953–1974.

G.W.   Sigmund Freud, *Gesammelte Werke*. 18 vols., vols. 1–17 (London 1940–1952), vol. 18 (Frankfurt a.M. 1968). Now the whole edition Frankfurt a.M.: S. Fischer, 1960–.

INTRODUCTION

1. The connection of this phenomenon with a reemergence of allegorical forms in the twentieth century will be the subject of a forthcoming study on "Allegory and Modernism," dealing specifically with Kafka, Brecht, and Beckett.

2. In German studies of the eighteenth century, this process has been well documented. For a recent summary and bibliography, see: *Hansers Sozialgeschicht der deutschen Literatur*, vol. 3: *Deutsche Aufklärung bis zur Französischen Revolution, 1680–1789*, Rolf Grimminger, ed. (Munich: Hanser, 1980).

3. The dialectic of this relation is traced most subtly by Theodor W. Adorno, *Ästhetische Theorie* (Frankfurt a.M.: Suhrkamp, 1970).

4. Peter Szondi, *Das lyrische Drama des fin de siècle* (Frankfurt a.M.: Suhrkamp, 1975), p. 17.

5. P. Szondi, *Einführung in die literarische Hermeneutik* (Frankfurt a.M.: Suhrkamp, 1975), p. 129.

6. Siegfried Kracauer, *Das Ornament der Masse* (Frankfurt a.M.: Suhrkamp, 1973).

7. Paul de Man, *Allegories of Reading: Figural Language in Rousseau, Nietzsche, Rilke, and Proust* (New Haven: Yale University Press, 1979).

8. Aurelius Prudentius Clemens, *Psychomachia.* (405 CE), in *Prudentii Clementis Aurelii quae exstant carmina*, edited by A. Dressel (Leipzig, 1860). Heiner Müller, *Die Hamletmaschine*, in *Theater Heute* (1977), no. 12.

9. Walter Benjamin, *Ursprung des deutschen Trauerspiels*, in *Gesammelte Schriften*, 1:1 (Frankfurt a.M.: Suhrkamp, 1980), pp. 203–430; on allegory specifically, pp. 336ff.

10. Lukács comes particularly close to Benjamin in his diagnosis (if not in his evaluation) of allegorical tendencies in modernism at the end of his essay "Erzählen oder Beschreiben: Zur Diskussion über Naturalismus und Formalismus," in *Schicksalswende: Beiträge zu einer deutschen Ideologie* (Berlin: Aufbau, 1948 [Written in 1936]).

11. Kurt R. Eissler, *Goethe: A Psychoanalytical Study* (Detroit: Wayne State University Press, 1963). Page numbers from this work will be given in the text.

12. K. R. Eissler, *Goethe: Eine psychoanalytische Studie* (Frankfurt a.M.: Roter Stern, 1983).

13. "Wer Biograph wird, verpflichtet sich zur Lüge, zur Verheimlichung, Heuchelei, Schönfärberei und selbst zur Verhehlung seines Unverständnisses, denn die biographische Wahrheit ist nicht zu haben, und wenn man sie hätte, wäre sie nicht zu brauchen." S. Freud, *Briefe, 1873–1939* (Frankfurt a.M.: S. Fischer, 1968), p. 445.

14. Augustine, *Confessions*, XI, 2, 3. For a more detailed discussion of this passage, see Beryl Schlossman, "Lesen am Rande des Augustinischen Textes," in *Der Wunderblock* (1985), no. 13, pp. 57–62. Now also available in English: "On the Margins of Augustine," *MLN* (1985), 100:1086–1091.

15. Ernst Jandl, *Sprechblasen* (Stuttgart: Reclam, 1979), p. 90.

16. S. Freud, *Der Mann Moses und die monotheistische Religion*, in *G.W.*, 16:216 (my translation); *S.E.* 23:109.

17. Freud has pointed out the relationship in German between *Zeuge* (witness) and *zeugen* (to procreate)—in English the relationship can be seen in the words "testimony" and "testicle." See Freud, "Bemerkungen über einen Fall von Zwangsneurose," in *G.W.*, 7:449; *S.E.* 10:232.

18. Shoshana Felman, "On Reading Poetry: Reflections on the Limits and Possibilities of Psychoanalytic Approaches," in Joseph H. Smith, ed., *The Literary Freud: Mechanisms of Defense and the Poetic Will* (New Haven: Yale University Press, 1980), pp. 119–148.

19. S. Freud, *G.W.*, 11:10; *S.E.* 15:17.

20. S. Freud, *G.W.*, 7:120; *S.E.* 9:92.

21. J. Lacan, *Encore, Seminaire XX* (Paris: Editions du Seuil, 1975), p. 20.

22. Avital Ronell, "Goethezeit," *Taking Chances: Derrida, Psychoanalysis, and Literature* (Baltimore: Johns Hopkins University Press, 1984), pp. 146–182.

1. THE WEAVING OF THE VEIL: GOETHE AND THE SYMBOLIC ORDER

1. Erich Trunz, in the notes to *Goethes Werke, Hamburger Ausgabe* (Hamburg: Wegner, 1964), 1:442; hereafter cited as *H.A.*

2. Jürgen Habermas, *Erkenntnis und Interesse* (Frankfurt a.M.: Suhrkamp, 1973), p. 191 (my translation).

3. See, on this aspect of Schleiermacher's hermeneutics, Manfred Frank, *Das individuelle Allgemeine: Textstrukturierung und -interpretation nach Schleiermacher* (Frankfurt a.M.: Suhrkamp, 1977).

4. As an example among many, see Lessing's letter to his father on April 29, 1749. He tries to justify the frivolity of some of his poems: "One must know me little to believe that my feelings harmonize in the least bit with them [these poems]. . . . Indeed, the only reason for their existence is my inclination to practice all modes of poetry." G. E. Lessing, *Das dichterische Werk* (Munich: Deutscher Taschenbuch, 1979), 2:598.

5. Herbert Cysarz, *Deutsche Barockdichtung* (Leipzig: Reclam, 1924), pp. 273ff.; Heinz Kindermann, *Der Rokoko-Goethe*, Deutsche Literatur in Entwicklungsreihen: Irrationalismus (Leipzig: Reclam, 1932), p. 10.

6. Gottfried Benn's often-quoted dictum "Ein Gedicht entsteht überhaupt sehr selten— ein Gedicht wird gemacht" (A poem very rarely grows—a poem is made) is in direct opposition against an organicist concept of literature. G. Benn, *Gesammelte Werke*, vol. 4: *Reden und Vorträge* (Wiesbaden: Limes, 1968), p. 1059.

7. Goethe, *H.A.*, 1:442f.

8. *Goethes Briefe, Hamburger Ausgabe* (Hamburg: Wegra, 1962), 1:577f.

9. Johann Christoph Gottsched, *Versuch einer Critischen Dichtkunst*, 4th ed. (Leipzig: Bernhard Christoph Breitkopf, 1751), p. 102.

10. *Ibid.*, p. 103.

11. Goethe, *H.A.*, 2:165.

12. *Ibid.*, 12:368.

13. Jean Paul, *Werke*, vol. 5: *Vorschule der Ästhetik*, Norbert Miller, ed. (Munich: Hanser, 1963). Page numbers will be given in the text.

14. See, on this aspect of Freud's theory of jokes, Samuel Weber, *Freud-Legende* (Olten and Freiburg: Walter, 1979), pp. 126ff.

15. See Peter Szondi, *Versuch über das Tragische* (Frankfurt a.M.: Insel, 1964), pp. 13–16.

16. Sigmund Freud, *G.W.*, 6:174; *S.E.* 8:155.

17. Gottsched, *Versuch einer Critischen Dichtkunst*, p. 262.

18. *Ibid.*, p. 103.

19. See Norbert Haas, *Spätaufklärung: Johann Merck zwischen Sturm und Drang und Französischer Revolution* (Kronberg/Ts.: Scriptor, 1975), pp. 13ff.

20. Quoted from Jürgen Stenzel, ed., *Epochen der deutschen Lyrik*, vol. 5: *1700–1770* (Munich: Deutscher Taschenbuch, 1969), pp. 227f.

21. G. E. Lessing, *Werke* (Munich: Hanser, 1970), 1:80.

22. *Ibid.*, 1:91.

23. Goethe, *H.A.*, 2:25.

24. Goethe, *Der junge Goethe*, Hanna Fischer-Lamberg, ed. (Berlin: de Gruyter, 1963), 1:165. Gleim's version is quoted on p. 469.

25. *Ibid.*, p. 170.

26. *Ibid.*, p. 179.

27. Goethe, *H.A.*, 1:18, 20.

28. *Ibid.*, 1:143.

29. *Ibid.*, 1:294.

30. Jacques Lacan, "Subversion du sujet et dialectique du désir dans l'inconscient freudien," *Ecrits* (Paris: Editions du Seuil, 1966), pp. 793–827.

31. *Goethes Briefe*, 1:248.
32. Samuel Beckett, *The Unnamable*, in *Three Novels* (New York: Grove Press, 1965), p. 291.

2. THE DISCOURSE OF THE OTHER: HÖLDERLIN'S VOICE AND THE VOICE OF THE PEOPLE

1. Hölderlin's work is now available in two critical editions: the *Stuttgarter Ausgabe*: Hölderlin, *Sämtliche Werke*, Friedrich Beißner, ed., 8 vols. (Stuttgart: Kohlhammer, 1946–); and *Frankfurter Ausgabe*: Friedrich Hölderlin, *Sämtliche Werke*, D. E. Sattler, ed., vols. 2–6, 9–14 (Frankfurt a.M.: Roter Stern Verlag, 1975–). Abbreviated *St.A.* and *F.A.* respectively.
2. For a detailed reconstruction of the genesis of the text from the earliest to the latest version, see *F.A.* 5:214–222; 290–293; 579–596.
3. Pierre Bertaux, *Hölderlin und die Französische Revolution* (Frankfurt a.M.: Suhrkamp, 1969).
4. See *F.A.* 5:292. At least it is assumed that the print is of Hölderlin's hand, although we presumably do not have a definitive fingerprint identification of him.
5. The letter is quoted by Beißner in his commentary to the Stuttgart edition: *St.A.* 2:495.
6. This and the following examples are mostly taken from the following anthology of political poetry in the late eighteenth century: *Deutsche Literatur in Entwicklungsreihen*, Reihe, *Politische Dichtung*, vol. 1: *Vor dem Untergang des alten Reichs 1756–1795* (Leipzig: 1930; hereafter cited as *P.D.*), Klopstock's poem, p. 129.
7. *P.D.* 1:143–146.
8. *P.D.* 1:152.
9. The same metaphors can be found in a poem by Huber, *P.D.*, 1:137.
10. William Blake, *The Complete Poetry and Prose*, David V. Erdman, ed. (Berkeley and Los Angeles: University of California Press, 1982), p. 286.
11. See Christoph Prignitz, *Friedrich Hölderlin: Die Entwicklung seines politischen Denkens unter dem Einfluß der Französischen Revolution* (Hamburg: 1976).
12. Quoted *ibid.*, p. 246.
13. J. W. L. Gleim, "Auch les Etats generaux: An Frankreichs Demokraten," in *Epochen der deutschen Lyrik*, 1770–1800 (Munich: Deutscher Taschenbuch, 1970), pp. 215ff.
14. See G. W. F. Hegel, *Phänomenologie des Geistes*, in *Werke in zwanzig Bänden* (Frankfurt a.M.: Suhrkamp, 1970), 3:36.
15. Freud's texts are quoted in my own translation with page references to both the German *Gesammelte Werke* (G.W.) and the English *Standard Edition*.
16. Jacques Lacan, *Le moi dans le théorie et dans la technique de la psychanalyse*, Le Seminaire, book 2 (Paris: Editions du Seuil, 1978).
17. J. Lacan, "Le stade du miroir comme formateur de la fonction de Je," *Ecrits* (Paris: Editions du Seuil, 1966), p. 99.
(Existentialism can be judged by the justifications it gives to the subjective dead-end streets that result from it: a freedom that affirms itself never more authentically than in the walls of a prison; an exigency of engagement where the impotence of pure consciousness to overcome any situation expresses itself; a voyeuristic-sadistic idealization of the sexual relation; a character who comes to realization only in suicide; a consciousness of the other that is satisfied only by the Hegelian murder.)

3. PUBLIC VOICE AND PRIVATE VOICE: FREUD, HABERMAS, AND THE DIALECTIC OF ENLIGHTENMENT

1. See Peter U. Hohendahl, "Habermas and His Critics," *New German Critique* (1979), 16:89–118; and Jack Mendelson, "The Habermas-Gadamer Debate," *New German Critique* (1979), 16:44–73.

2. Mendelson, "The Habermas-Gadamer Debate," p. 50.

3. Jürgen Habermas, *Erkenntnis und Interesse* (Frankfurt a.M.: Suhrkamp, 1973); this is the first paperback edition, from which I quote (E). The book was first published in 1968. The role of psychoanalysis and of Freud has not changed significantly since then. In his most recent *opus magnum*, *Theorie des kommunikativen Handelns* (Frankfurt a.M.: Suhrkamp, 1981), psychoanalysis appears still as basically a reflective act through which the subject gains control over his/her irrational motivations: "In such a process of *self-reflection* reasons play a role too. Freud has investigated this type of argumentation in the model of the therapeutic discourse between doctor and analysand" (p. 43). Translations of Habermas are my own.

4. J. Habermas, *Strukturwandel der Öffentlichkeit* (Frankfurt a.M.: Suhrkamp, 1971), quoted in the text as *S.W.*

5. See Hohendahl, "Habermas and His Critics"; Mendelson, "The Habermas-Gadamer Debate."

6. Hohendahl, "Habermas and His Critics," p. 92.

7. Oskar Negt and Alexander Kluge, *Öffentlichkeit und Erfahrung: Zur Organisations-Analyse von bürgerlicher und proletarischer Öffentlichkeit* (Frankfurt a.M.: Suhrkamp, 1977), p. 20.

8. I. Kant, *Kritik der praktischen Vernunft*, in *Werke* (Darmstadt: Wissenschaftliche Buchgesellschaft, 1968), 6:289.

9. Negt and Kluge, *Öffentlichkeit und Erfahrung*, p. 7.

10. "In relation to action, the ego has approximately the position of a constitutional monarch without whose sanction nothing can become law, but who will think twice before he enters his veto against the proposal of the parliament" (G.W. 13:286; S.E. 19:56). But just a little later in the text, Freud describes the ego as "not only the helper of the id, but also its submissive servant who begs for the love of his master."

11. See Klaus Theweleit, *Männerphantasien* (Frankfurt a.M.: Roter Stern, 1977).

12. Particularly the political rhetoric of the GDR of the early fifties liked to evoke the last monologue of Faust before his death, with its dream of building dikes and dams to create new land that has to be defended against the onrushing floods.

13. J. Laplanche and J. B. Pontalis, *Vocabulaire de la psychanalyse* (Paris: Presses Universitaire de France, 1967).

14. J. Habermas, *Zur Rekonstruktion des historischen Materialismus* (Frankfurt a.M.: Suhrkamp, 1976), quoted as *RHM*.

4. DRINKING THE WITCH'S BREW: NIETZSCHE AND THE (K)NOTS OF RESENTMENT

1. A rather extreme example of such an image emerging from a combination of sublime naïveté and disregard for the most basic hermeneutical and philological principles is Hermann Böschenstein's attempt to present us with a nice humanistic Nietzsche, compared with which Lukács's opposite Nietzsche image must at least be credited with an acute degree of perceptiveness and hermeneutical skill. H. Böschenstein, "Nietzsche und das Problem der Humanität," *Modern Language Notes* (1982), 97:636–655.

2. The Nietzsche colloquium of Cérisy-la-Salle in 1972 was seminal for a new semiol-ogical and rhetorical reading of Nietzsche. It was, however, preceded in 1971 by an important Nietzsche issue of *Poétique* 5 with essays by Jacques Derrida, "La mythologie blanche"; Philippe Lacoue-Labarthe, "Le détour"; Sarah Kofman, "Nietzsche et la métaphore"; and texts by Nietzsche on rhetoric and language. For a general and judicious survey of recent French Nietzsche reception, see Rudolf E. Künzli, "Nietzsche und die Semiologie: Neue Ansätze in der französischen Nietzsche-Interpretation," *Nietzsche-Studien* (1976), 5:263–288.

3. J. Derrida, *Eperons: Les styles de Nietzsche* (Paris: Flammarion, 1979), also available in a bilingual French-English version published in 1979 by the University of Chicago Press; Paul de Man, *Allegories of Reading: Figural Language in Rousseau, Nietzsche, Rilke, and Proust* (New Haven and London: Yale University Press, 1979).

4. Such institutional dichotomies are not always carried out in open conflict, but fre-quently rather by a mutual ignoring. A glaring example is a recent book on resentment: Amandus Altmann, *Friedrich Nietzsche: Das Ressentiment und seine Überwindung—verdeutlicht am Beis-piel christlicher Moral* (Bonn: Bouvier, 1977). Not only is there no reference made to any Nietzsche discussion outside of Germany, but even the excellent essay on resentment by the Hamburg philosopher Reiner Wiehl with its subtle unfolding of the problem of metaphor and genealogy is completely disregarded. R. Wiehl, "Ressentiment und Reflexion," *Nietzsche - Studien* (1973), 2:61–90. The same, of course, could be said of some of the French contribu-tions, but some of them at least are legitimized by the authority of their rigorous readings.

5. All references to Nietzsche's texts are to the German paperback edition of the complete works, by volume and page. Translations, if not indicated otherwise, are my own. F. Nietzsche, *Sämtliche Werke: Kritische Studienausgabe* (Munich: Deutscher Taschenbuch, 1980).

6. Paul de Man, "Genesis and Genealogy (Nietzsche)," in *Allegories of Reading*, pp. 79–102.

7. For a reading of this relationship between remedy and poison in Plato, see J. Derrida, "La pharmacie de Platon," in *La dissemination* (Paris: Editions du Seuil, 1972), pp. 69–108.

8. Sigmund Freud, "Die Verneinung," in *Psychologie des Unbewußten*, S., 3:371–377; S.E. 19:233–239.

9. There is a lot of material for the study of resentment in the name of "science" in a "Dossier" article by the journalist Dieter Zimmer in the German weekly newspaper *Die Zeit* (fall 1982), particularly in regard to its method of substituting a rigorous reading of relevant texts with the refutation of phantasmatically construed "concepts."

10. Gottlob Frege, *Logische Untersuchungen*, 2d ed. (Göttingen: Vandenhoeck and Ru-precht, 1976), particularly the chapter "Die Verneinung," pp. 54–71.

11. It might be interesting to note in this context that Nietzsche, from a rather early time on throughout his life, was very concerned about questions of diet. His biographer Curt Paul Janz points out that Nietzsche already in the early sixties tended to ascribe periods of nervous tensions and headaches to a faulty diet: Janz, *Friedrich Nietzsche: Biographie* (Munich: Deutscher Taschenbuch, 1981), 1:161. In a letter from Feb. 1–3, 1868, to his friend Erwin Rohde, Nietzsche calls the military training an antidote (ἀντίδυτον) against the paralyzing skepticism. F. Nietzsche, *Werke in drei Bänden*, Karl Schlechta, ed. (Munich: Hanser, 1966), 3:985.

12. For a brilliant discussion of Freud's complex arguments and reversals concerning this problem, see Jean Laplanche, *Life and Death in Psychoanalysis* (Baltimore: Johns Hopkins University Press, 1976), particularly ch. 5.

13. *Ibid.*, pp. 89ff.

14. The mixture of strangeness and familiarity also constitutes the uncanny—*das Unheim-*

liche—according to Freud. Nietzsche characterizes his *Genealogy of Morals* in *Ecce Homo* as "das Unheimlichste, was bisher geschrieben worden ist" (6:352).

15. For a subtle analysis of this game, see Norbert Haas, "Fort/da als Modell," in *Zeta 02: Mit Lacan* (Berlin: Rotation, 1982), pp. 29–46.

16. See, for example, 5:205, 259, 371; 12:12, 13.

17. For a detailed discussion of *Trieb* in Freud's text, see Laplanche, *Life and Death in Psychoanalysis*, particularly ch. 1. Nietzsche uses both terms *Instinkt* and *Trieb* quite frequently and, as it seems, not clearly distinct from each other. Perhaps a more detailed study might bring out subtle differences in their respective use.

18. Peter Szondi, "Das Naive ist das Sentimentalische: Zur Begriffsdialektik in Schillers Abhandlung," in *Schriften II* (Frankfurt a.M.: Suhrkamp, 1978), pp. 59–105.

19. Joel Fineman, "The Structure of Allegorical Desire," in *Allegory and Representation*, Stephen J. Greenblatt, ed. (Baltimore: Johns Hopkins University Press, 1981), pp. 26–60.

20. *Ibid.*, p. 45.

21. *Ibid.*, pp. 41–43. For a detailed discussion of this system, see R. Jakobson, *Kindersprache und Aphasie* (Frankfurt a.M.: Suhrkamp, 1969).

22. Fineman, "The Structure of Allegorical Desire," p. 42.

23. Ulrich von Wilamowitz-Möllendorff, *Zukunftsphilologie! Eine Erwiderung auf Friedrich Nietzsches "Geburt der Tragödie"* (Berlin: Borntraeger, 1872), p. 32. Wilamowitz identifies himself on the title page as "Dr. phil." and Nietzsche as "ord. professors der classischen philologie zu Basel."

5. BRECHT'S THEATER OF CRUELTY

Translation of the epigraphs:

"People act according to their hunger and receive their teaching from death."

"Can the teaching destroy violence? May the violence not destroy the teaching!"

"To perish in this case means always: to get to the ground of things."

1. For a brief comparison, emphasizing the difference between Brecht and Artaud, see Reinhold Grimm, "Bertold Brecht and Antonin Artaud: Some Comparative Remarks," in Ralph Lay et al., eds., *Perspectives and Personalities: Studies in Modern German Literature* (Heidelberg: Winkler, 1978), pp. 118–124.

2. The opposition voice-body is at the center of Heinz Weinmann's essay "peter handke: la fin de la représentation," *Jeu* (1977), 6:80–88.

3. Peter Szondi, *Theorie des modernen Dramas* (Frankfurt a.M.: Suhrkamp, 1956).

4. For a survey of Brecht criticism, see Reiner Steinweg, *Das Lehrstück: Brechts Theorie einer ästhetischen Erziehung* (Stuttgart: Metzler, 1972), and Jan Knopf, *Bertold Brecht: Ein kritischer Forschungsbericht. Fragwürdiges in der Brechtforschung* (Frankfurt a.M.: Athenäum Taschenbuch, 1974). The following abbreviations are used for Brecht's texts and frequently quoted works: W.S. (volume, page); Bertold Brecht, *Gesammelte Werke: Werkausgabe edition surhkamp* (Frankfurt a.M.: Suhrkamp, 1967); M: Bertold Brecht, *Die Maßnahme: Kritische Ausgabe mit einer Spielanleitung*, Reiner Steinweg, ed. (Frankfurt a.M.: Suhrkamp, 1972); J.N.: Bertold Brecht, *Der Jasager und Der Neinsager: Vorlagen, Fassungen, und Materialien*, Peter Szondi, ed. (Frankfurt a.M.: Suhrkamp, 1966); St 2: Reiner Steinweg, ed. *Brechts Modell der Lehrstücke: Zeugnisse, Diskussionen, Erfahrungen* (Frankfurt a.M.: Suhrkamp, 1976).

5. Jan Knopf, *Brecht Handbuch: Theater, eine Ästhetik der Widersprüche* (Stuttgart: Metzler, 1980).

6. See Reiner Steinweg, *Das Lehrstück*.

7. One remarkable exception is the essay by Hans-Thies Lehmann and Helmut Lethen on Brecht's *Lehrstücke* in R. Steinweg, ed., *Auf Anregung Bertold Brechts: Lehrstücke mit Schülern, Arbeitern, Theaterleuten* (Frankfurt a.M.: Suhrkamp, 1978), pp. 302–318.

8. Examples and models are found in Steinweg's *Auf Anregung Brechts*.

9. For a more detailed discussion of the phenomenon of isolating, see the Preface of this book and chapter 3 on Habermas.

10. On the relationship between pleasure, pain, and cruelty, see chapter 4 on Nietzsche.

11. "Unrichtig handeln, die dem Lernenden das Geschlechtliche als natürlich hinstellen, als sauber, harmlos und verständlich. Recht haben, die es ihm als unnatürlich beweisen, also als schmutzig, gefährlich und unverständlich. . . . Aber nicht um den Lernenden von der Liebe abzuhalten, soll man ihm die Liebe schmutzig oder unnatürlich schildern, sondern allein um ihm die Wahrheit zu sagen. Nicht um ihm Abscheu zu erregen, sondern um ihm Schrecken zu lehren. Darum ist die beste Art ihm die geschlechtliche Liebe zu lehren, so wie es die Knaben unter sich machen: sie reden lachend und erhitzt vom Geschlechtlichen und zeichnen große und schmutzige Symbole auf die Wände der Häuser, die jenen gleichen, die von den Religionen der Weisesten aller Rassen benützt werden. Und auch dadurch ist diese Art der Belehrung gut, weil sie unter solchen vor sich geht, die sich nicht nur mit Worten sondern ebenso auch mit Händen berühren können." (*St* 2, 43)

12. "es gibt eine bestimmte freude am mechanischen, am rechtzeitigen einsatz, am klappen, am teilnehmen an einer mathematischen übung, eine art *stichwortgenuß* jeder von 4 Spielern unterwirft sich demselben zahlensystem und jeder bereitet seinen einsatz vor wie der kartenspieler seinen stich wie jeder teil einer maschine seinen bestimmten schlag ausübt usw." (*St* 2:62f.)

13. "Oft sehe ich, sagte der Denkende, habe ich meines Vaters Haltung. Aber meines Vaters Taten tue ich nicht. Warum tue ich andere Taten? Weil andere Notwendigkeiten sind. Aber ich sehe, die Haltung hält länger als die Handlungsweise: sie widersteht den Notwendigkeiten.

"Mancher kann nur eines tun, wenn er sein Gesicht nicht verlieren will. Da er den Notwendigkeiten nicht folgen kann, geht er leicht unter. Aber wer eine Haltung hat, der kann vieles tun und verliert sein Gesicht nicht." (*W.S.* 12:410)

14. was immer du denkst verschweig es
geh hinaus mit uns mechanisch!
geh wie einer grüßt: weils üblich
vollführ die bewegung die
nichts bedeutet. (*St* 2, 103.)

15. "Im Verfolg der Grundsätze: der Staat soll reich sein, der Mensch soll arm sein, der Staat soll verpflichtet sein vieles zu können, dem Menschen soll es erlaubt sein weniges zu können, soll der Staat, was die Musik betrifft, alles hervorbringen, was besondere Apparate und besondere Fähigkeiten verlangt, aber der einzelne soll eine Übung hervorbringen." (*St* 2, 64f.)

16. Das Gemeinwesen bittet euch: Wiederholt
Die erste Befliegung des Ozeans
Durch das gemeinsame
Absingen der Noten
Und das Ablesen des Textes. (*W.S.* 2:567)

17. "Selbst wenn man erwartete, daß der einzelne 'sich in irgendwas dabei einordnet' oder daß hier auf musikalischer Grundlage gewisse geistige formale Kongruenzen entstehen, wäre eine solche künstliche und seichte Harmonie doch niemals imstande, den die Menschen unserer

Zeit mit ganz anderer Gewalt auseinander zerrenden Kollektivbildungen auf breitester und vitalster Basis auch nur für Minuten ein Gegengewicht zu schaffen." (*St* 2, 59f.)

18. L(EHRE): Woran also erkennt man die herrschende Art?
M(ASSE): Daran erkennt man die herrschende Art, daß sie sagt, daß es ohne Gewalt geht. (*St* 2, 77)

19. "Wenn der Denkende den Sturm überwand, so überwand er ihn, weil er den Sturm kannte und einverstanden war mit dem Sturm. Also, wenn ihr das Sterben überwinden wollt, so überwindet ihr es, wenn ihr das Sterben kennt und einverstanden seid mit dem Sterben." (*W.S.* 2:602)

20. "Nicht das Leben, das sich vor dem Tode scheut und von der Verwüstung bewahrt sondern das ihn erträgt und in ihm sich erhält." Hegel, *Werke in zwanzig Bänden*, vol. 3: *Phänomenologie des Geistes* (Frankfurt a.M.: Suhrkamp, 1970), p. 36.

21. To the degree that a translation can transmit such qualities, Donald Keene's edition of No plays is very helpful: *Twenty Plays of the No Theatre* (New York: Columbia University Press, 1970).

22. A German translation from the Japanese is available in Szondi's edition of Brecht's plays: *J.N.*, 83–102.

23. In the first of his theses on the concept of history, Walter Benjamin interprets the famous chess automaton with its hidden dwarf as an allegory of historical materialism: the puppet is historical materialism, the hidden dwarf is theology. W. Benjamin, *Gesammelte Schriften* (Frankfurt a.M.: Suhrkamp, 1980), vol. I.2, p. 693.

24. See Neil Hertz, "The Notion of the Blockage in the Literature of the Sublime," in G. Hartman, ed., *Psychoanalysis and the Question of the Text* (Baltimore: Johns Hopkins University Press, 1978), pp. 62–85; reprinted in N. Hertz, *The End of the Line* (New York: Columbia University Press, 1985), pp. 40–60.

Sade, whose more than contemporaneous affinity with Kant and the sublime of the Enlightenment has been noticed by Adorno and Horkheimer (*Dialectic of Enlightenment*) as well as by Lacan ("Kant avec Sade"), knew the effectiveness of the well-timed caesura for true jouissance: whenever her pupils are eager and ready to give themselves over to the raptures of their bodies, Madame Delbene, the Mother Superior of the convent of Panthemont in *Histoire de Juliette*, interrupts with her "Un moment!" "Just a moment" is the necessary caesura that transforms pleasure into jouissance: "Un moment, dit-elle, tout en feu; un instant, mes bonnes amies, mettons un peu d'ordre à nos plaisirs, on n'en jouit qu'en les fixant."

One of the prime showpieces of the Japanese Kabuki theater is called *Shibaraku*: "Just a moment!" According to tradition, the title is based on an incident in the eighteenth century, when the actor Danjuro II (1688–1758) was not given the right cue by an envious rival actor and stormed onto the stage shouting "Shibaraku" ("Just a moment") over and over. Thus he created the title of one of the most bombastic Kabuki plays. It emerged, so to speak, from what Brecht calls *Stichwortgenuß* (cue-word pleasure).

25. Beautiful souls tend to be feminine in the eighteenth century.

26. Roman Jakobson, "Der grammatische Bau des Gedichts von Bertold Brecht *Wir sind sie*," in *Hölderlin, Klee, Brecht: Zur Wortkunst dreier Gedichte* (Frankfurt a.M.: Suhrkamp, 1976), pp. 107–128.

27. "Mein Herz schlägt für die Revolution. Der Anblick des Unrechts trieb mich in die Reihen der Kämpfer. Ich bin für Freiheit. Ich glaube an die Menschheit. Aber ich weiß, daß die klassenlose Gesellschaft nur durch die Diktatur des Proletariats verwirklicht werden kann, und deshalb bin ich für die radikale Durchführung unserer Parolen." (*M*, 8)

28. See documents in *M*, 354, 371, 384.

29. Betrachtet genau das Verhalten dieser Leute:
    Findet es befremdend, wenn auch nicht fremd
    Unerklärlich, wenn auch gewöhnlich
    Unverständlich, wenn auch die Regel. (*W.S.* 2:793)
30. Hegel, *Phänomenologie des Geistes*, p. 36.
31. An attempt toward a classification of various modes of reception is made by H. R. Jauß, *Ästhetische Erfahrung und literarische Hermeneutik* (Munich: Hanser, 1977).
32. Roland Barthes, "Mère Courage aveugle" and "Sur la Mère de Brecht," in *Essais critiques* (Paris: Editions du Seuil, 1964), pp. 48–50 and 143–146, respectively.
33. Antonin Artaud, *Ouevres complètes*, vol. 4: *Le Théatre et son double* (Paris: Gallimard, 1978), p. 88.

6. PAUL CELAN: CONFIGURATIONS OF FREUD

1. All Celan quotations are from *Gesammelte Werke in fünf Bänden* (Frankfurt a.M.: Suhrkamp, 1983). All translations of poems are my own. They are, however, mere reading aids because of the extreme difficulty and often untranslatability of Celan's poems.
2. Georg Büchner, *Sämtliche Werke*, W. R. Lehmann, ed. (Hamburg: Wegner, 1967), 1:9. In Henry Schmidt's translation, the passage reads:

JULIE: You know me, Danton.

DANTON: Yes, whatever "knowing" means. You have dark eyes and curly hair and a nice complexion and you always say to me: dear Georges. But (*he points to her forehead and eyes*) there—there: what's behind that? No, our senses are coarse. Know each other? We'd have to break open our skulls and pull each other's thoughts out of the brain fibers.

G. Büchner, *The Complete Collected Works* (New York: Avon Books, 1977), p. 17.
3. Franz Kafka, *Hochzeitsvorbereitungen auf dem Lande und andere Prosa aus dem Nachlaß* (Frankfurt a.M.: Fischer, 1953), p. 51.
4. "Eisbär und Walfisch, hat man gesagt, können nicht miteinander Krieg führen, weil sie, ein jeder auf sein Element beschränkt, nicht zueinander kommen. Ebenso unmöglich wird es mir, mit Arbeitern auf dem Gebiet der Psychologie oder der Neurotik zu diskutieren." S. Freud, *Aus der Geschichte einer infantilen Neurose*, in *S*, 8:166. "It has been said that polar bear and whale cannot carry out a war against each other, because, restricted as each one of them is to its element, they cannot get together. In the same way, it is impossible for me to enter into a discussion with workers in the field of psychology or neurology." *G.W.* 12:76; *S.E.* 17:48. See also chapter 7 on this passage.
5. F. Kafka, *Tagebücher* (Frankfurt a.M.: Fischer, 1967), p. 210.
6. S. Freud, *Die Traumdeutung*, in *S*, 2:291ff. I am very thankful to Peter Henninger, who recalled this passage to me.
7. The prefix *ver-* seems to be itself the product of a condensation according to the Duden grammar: "In ver- sind (schon im Althochdeutschen mehrere Partikeln zusammengefallen, die 'vorbei,' 'weg,' 'heraus' bedeuten." *Der große Duden* (Mannheim: Bibliographisches Institut, 1966), vol. 4, no. 4585.
8. For a concise and illuminating discussion of this uneasy relationship, see the chapter "Dichtung und Wahrheit" in Peter Henninger, *Der Buchstabe und der Geist: Unbewußte Determinierung im Schreiben Robert Musils* (Frankfurt a.M. and Bern: Lang, 1980), pp. 161–192.
9. I am thankful to Beryl Schlossman, who suggested this connection.
10. Franz Kafka referred to himself as *Dohle* to Gustav Janouch: G. Janouch, *Gespräche mit Kafka: Aufzeichnungen und Erinnerungen* (Frankfurt a.M.: Fischer, 1968), p. 36. In his

diary he remarks that his Hebrew name is Amschel (*Amsel*, blackbird, is closely related to the *Dohle*), and finally the name Gracchus in the story "Der Jäger Gracchus" can be related to the Italian *graccio*, jackdaw. See Hartmut Binder, "Leben und Persönlichkeit Franz Kafkas," in *Kafka-Handbuch I* (Stuttgart: Kröner, 1979), pp. 110f.

11. Binder, "Leben und Persönlichkeit Kafkas," pp. 110–111.

12. See Roman Jakobson, *Kindersprache und Aphasie* (Frankfurt a.M.: Suhrkamp, 1969); and my essay "Die Arbeit des Textes: Notizen zur experimentellen Literatur," in P. M. Lützeler and E. Schwarz, eds., *Deutsche Literatur in der Bundesrepublik seit 1965* (Königstein: Athenäum, 1980), pp. 30–45.

13. Winfried Menninghaus, *Paul Celan: Magie der Form* (Frankfurt a.M.: Suhrkamp, 1980).

14. Such configurations, where characteristics of several figures merge into one, or where the characteristics of one figure are distributed among many, are typical for what Freud calls *Verdichtungsarbeit* (work of condensation).

15. Freud, *Die Traumdeutung*, p. 130; see also p. 503. "Each dream has at least one spot where it is inexplicable [or ungroundable], something like a navel that connects it with the unknown."

16. *Ibid.*, p. 503. For a detailed discussion of the implications of this "navel" in Freud's thought, see Samuel Weber, *Freud-Legende* (Olten and Freiburg: Walter, 1979); particularly the chapters "Die Bedeutung des Thallus," pp. 91ff., and "Der Aufsitzer," pp. 126ff. The book has now been published in English by the University of Minnesota Press, 1983.

17. "Edgar Jene und der Traum vom Traume" was first published in 1948 with pictures by Jene. The text is now reprinted in Celan, *Gesammelte Werke*, 3:155–161.

18. We might remember, using the metaphor of the coin, Lacan's warning against a facile discarding of the value of the worn-out coin: "Quelque vide en effet qu'apparaisse ce discours, il n'en est ainsi qu'à le prendre à sa valeur faciale: celle qui justifie la phrase de Mallarmé quand il compare l'usage commun du langage à l'échange d'une monnaie dont l'avers comme l'envers ne montrent plus que des figures effacées et que l'on se passe de main en main 'en silence.' Cette métaphore suffit à nous rappeler que la parole, même à l'éxtreme de son usure, garde sa valeur de tessere." "Fonction et champ de la parole et du langage en psychanalyse," in *Ecrits* (Paris: Editions du Seuil, 1966), p. 251.
(Indeed, however empty this discourse may appear, it is only so if taken at its face value: that which justifies the remark of Mallarmé's, in which he compares the common use of Language to the exchange of a coin whose obverse and reverse no longer bear any but worn effigies, and which people pass from hand to hand "in silence." This metaphor is sufficient to remind us that the Word, even when almost completely worn out, retains its value as a *tessara*.) Translation by Anthony Wilden.

19. Jean Paul, one of Celan's favorite authors, is among the few who have given some serious thought to puns and have pursued their ambivalence. See chapter 52 on "Wortspiel," in *Vorschule der Ästhetik*, *Werke* (Munich: Hanser, 1967), 5:191–196. See also chapter 1.

20. The topological model describing most accurately this surface would be the Moebius strip, which is indeed also the paradigmatic topological model for Lacan. See, for example, Lacan's essay "La science et la vérité," in *Ecrits*, pp. 855–877.

21. "Wer auf dem Kopf geht, meine Damen und Herren,—wer auf dem Kopf geht, der hat den Himmel als Abgrund unter sich" (3:195). "He who walks on his head, ladies and gentlemen, he who walks on his head has the sky/heaven as abyss below him." This inversion parallels and counters at the same time Pindar's perspective of the gods for whom the earth is the sky and the island Delos a star in that sky. Pindar, Fragm. #17 Tusculum, #33c Snell.

22. At least on one level, Celan's earliest known poetological text is intimately connected with one of Kafka's earliest narratives, *Beschreibung eines Kampfes*, where the fat man talks to the supplicant about the sea sickness: "Deren Wesen ist so, daß ihr den wahrhaftigen Namen der Dinge vergessen habt und über sie jetzt in einer Eile zufällige Namen schüttet." F. Kafka, *Beschreibung eines Kampfes: Die zwei Fassungen* (Frankfurt a.M.: Fischer, 1969), p. 88.
(Their essence is such that you have forgotten the true name of things, and now you pour in a hurry accidental names over them.)

23. For a more detailed discussion of Habermas's Freud interpretation, see chapter 3.

24. Freud, *Die Traumdeutung*, p. 577. Freud's *via regia* seems to echo in a late poem of Celan, *Der Königsweg hinter der Scheintür* (3:106), merging with the biblical landscape of these late poems, but also with the pharaonic tombs of Egypt.

25. H. v. Hofmannsthal, *Ausgewählte Werke*, Rudolf Hirsch, ed. (Frankfurt a.M.: Fischer, 1966), p. 19.

26. R. Musil, *Gesammelte Werke* (Hamburg: Rowohlt, 1978), 6:7. The passage in the original text of Maeterlinck reads as follows: "Des que nous exprimons quelque chose, nous le diminuons étrangement. Nous croyons avoir plongé jusqu'au fond des abîmes et quand nous remontons à la surface, la goutte d'eau qui scintille au bout de nos doigts pales ne ressemble plus à la mer d'ou elle sort. Nous croyons avoir découvert une grotte aux trésors merveilleux; et quand nous revenons au jour, nous n'avons emporté que des pierreries fausses et des morceaux de verre; et cependant le trésor brille invariablement dans les ténèbres."
(As soon as we pronounce something, we strangely devalue it. We believe to have dived into the depth of the abysses, and when we come back to the surface the drop of water on our fingertips no longer resembles the sea from which it stems. We fancy to have discovered a treasure mine of wonderful treasures, and when we come back into daylight we have brought with us only false stones and broken pieces of glass; and yet the treasure gleams unchanged in the darkness.)

27. Celan's text is a clear and succinct diagnosis of all "honest" confessional literature and the now-popular *Verständigungstexte* in Germany.

28. Lacan, *Ecrits*, pp. 247ff.

29. The opposition appears also as *Gespräch* vs. Gesagtes in the poem *Ein Blatt, baumlos* (3:385). See also Menninghaus, *Paul Celan*, pp. 38f.

30. Kafka, letter to Kurt Wolff, October 11, 1916, *Briefe 1902–1924* (Frankfurt a.M.: Fischer, 1966), p. 150.

31. For a particularly interesting discussion of this motif, see Norbert Haas, *Spätaufklärung* (Kronberg: Scriptor, 1975).

32. See especially chapter 6, C, of Freud, *Die Traumdeutung*.

33. "Die Unbestimmtheit all unserer Erörterungen, die wir metapsychologische heißen, rührt natürlich daher, daß wir nichts über die Natur des Erregungsvorganges in den Elementen der psychischen Systeme wissen und uns zu keiner Annahme darüber berechtigt fühlen. So operieren wir also stets mit einem großen X, welches wir in jede neue Formel mit hinübernehmen." Freud, *Jenseits des Lustprinzips, in S*, 3:240. "The vagueness of all our investigations, which we call metapsychological, comes of course from the fact that we know nothing about the nature of the process of excitation in the elements of the psychic systems and that we feel not justified in making any assumptions about it. Thus, we always are operating with a great X, which we take over into each new formula." *G.W.* 13:30; *S.E.* 18:30.

34. Freud, *Jenseits des Lustprinzips, S*, 3:237.

35. *Goethes Werke, Hamburger Ausgabe* (Hamburg: Wegner, 1964), 1:142.

36. While the Freud echo is the most evident, it might have been filtered also through

reminiscences of Benjamin's essay "Über einige Motive bei Baudelaire." See, on this relationship, Menninghaus, *Paul Celan*, pp. 96ff.

37. Freud, *S*, 2:127; *G.W.* 2/3:112; *S.E.* 4:107. Again, I have to thank Peter Henninger who, in a letter, pointed this connection out to me.

38. Wilhelm v. Humboldt, *Werke in fünf Bänden*, Andreas Flitner and Klaus Giel, eds. (Darmstadt: Wissenschaftliches Buchgesellschaft, 1979), 3:368–756.

39. For a more detailed discussion of this relationship between seeing and not seeing, see chapter 1.

40. I use the term "notion" for the German *Vorstellung*, for which there is no precise equivalent in English: it describes a kind of mental "image" that is neither purely iconic nor purely conceptual.

41. The significance of the silent *h* was a matter of deep concern to many language philosophers and mystics; above all, in the eighteenth century, to Johann Georg Hamann.

7. BELATEDNESS: HISTORY AFTER FREUD AND LACAN

1. Yosef Hajim Yerushalmi, *Zakhor: Jewish History and Jewish Memory* (Seattle and London: University of Washington Pres, 1982), p. 6.

2. Peter Szondi, *Poetik und Geschichtsphilosophie I* (Frankfurt a.M.: Suhrkamp, 1974), p. 15.

3. The opposition appears in the normative and descriptive categories of Lukács's *Aesthetics* when he differentiates the "anthropomorphizing" modes of representation in everyday language and in art from the de-anthropomorphizing modes in the sciences.

4. Fernand Braudel, *La Méditerranée et le monde méditerranéen à l'époque de Philippe II* (Paris: Colin, 1949).

5. It is not by chance that these two factors, the heterogeneity of different subject agents and the heterogeneity of simultaneous temporal movements, have met particularly strong criticism in Germany, where the concept of history is firmly based on a homogeneous, totalizing subject and homogeneous time. Even a German anthology devoted to the *Annalistes* school and with the purpose of presenting models for rethinking history follows the same line of criticism in the introduction: *Schrift und Materie der Geschichte: Vorschläge zur systematischen Aneignung historischer Prozesse*, Claudia Honegger, ed. (Frankfurt a.M.: Suhrkamp, 1977); cf. particularly pp. 22 and 23.

6. Lucien Fèbvre, *Le problème de l'incroyance au XVIe siècle: La religion de Rabelais* (Paris: A. Michel, 1942).

7. Dominick LaCapra, *Rethinking Intellectual History: Texts, Contexts, Language* (Ithaca and London: Cornell University Press, 1983), p. 26. Bakhtin's concept of carnivalization has become a major category of LaCapra's thought, not, of course, as a unifying subject, but as a scene where oppositions play and battle each other.

8. One can and must add to the heterogeneity of this scene by at least pointing at a remarkable German tradition of a critique of linear and homogeneous history: Walter Benjamin, of course, confronting us with Klee's Angelus Novus as the angel of history; Adorno's insistence on the "other" and a negative dialectic that does not overlook and sublate the losses; Kracauer, who deserves to be remembered and read for more than his *Caligari to Hitler*, particularly his book *Geschichte: Vor den letzten Dingen*; in more recent times, Peter Szondi's rethinking of the relation between history and text. In a remarkable essay, Jürgen Söring has recently taken up some of this tradition: "Zur poetischen Erfahrung von Geschichtlichkeit," in W. Haubrich, ed., *Probleme der Literaturgeschichtsschreibung* (Göttingen: Vandenhoeck, 1979), pp. 31–64.

9. Hans-Ulrich Wehler, *Geschichte und Psychoanalyse* (Berlin: Ullstein, 1972). Contributors include H. Stuart Hughes, Cushing Strout, Alexander and Juliette George, and one French author, Alain Besancon.

10. The term *Zeitmarke* is particularly crucial in *Der Dichter und das Phantasieren*.

11. Lacan has given this phenomenon a specific place and term, "aphanisis," most explicitly in the *Seminaire XI: Les quatres concepts fondamentaux de la psychanalyse* (Paris: Editions du Seuil, 1973), particularly in chs. 16 and 17 on *aliénation*, pp. 185–208. See also Regis Durand, "On Aphanisis: A Note on the Dramaturgy of the Subject in Narrative Analysis," *Modern Language Notes* (1983), 98:860–870.

12. The importance of *Nachträglichkeit* is also underlined by Derrida in his essay on "Freud and the Scene of Writing" in *L'Ecriture et la difference* (Paris: Editions du Seuil, 1967), p. 303.

13. For a concise mapping of this and of other major Freudian terms, see J. Laplanche and J. B. Pontalis, *Vocabulaire de la psychanalyse* (Paris: Presses Universitaire de France), 1967.

14. The lecture is now part of the *Ecrits*: Jacques Lacan, *Ecrits* (Paris: Editions du Seuil, 1966), pp. 237–322.

15. Since my discussion involves a close reading of Freud's text, I follow the German text with my own, sometimes literal and inelegant, translation. In the text I will give as much as possible chapters and sections for easier location of the passages in various editions. The two texts discussed here can be found in the following places: *Aus der Geschichte einer infantilen Neurose*: S 8:125–231; G.W. 12:29–157; S.E. 17:7–122. Der Mann Moses und die monotheistische Religion; S 9:455–581; G.W. 16:101–246; S.E. 23:1–137.

16. The American media have given much publicity to Jeffrey M. Masson's supposed new discoveries about Freud's seduction theory: *The Assault on Truth: Freud's Suppression of the Seduction Theory* (New York: Farrar, Straus and Giroux, 1984; a brief, condensed version appeared earlier in the *Atlantic Monthly*). While Masson's complaint about the Freud heirs and the Freud archives might well be justified, his own handling of the material can only be called irresponsible. The "new" material he presents has been extensively discussed in two books which both appeared in 1979: Marie Balmary, *L'homme aux statues: Freud et la faute cachée du père* (Paris: Editions Grasset et Fasquelle, 1979), now also available in English: *Psychoanalyzing Psychoanalysis: Freud and the Hidden Fault of the Father* (Baltimore: Johns Hopkins University Press, 1982); Marianne Krüll, *Freud und sein Vater: Die Entstehung der Psychoanalyse und Freuds ungelöste Vaterbindung* (Munich: Beck, 1979). Furthermore, Masson's basic presupposition that Freud renounced the seduction theory is simply false. Freud insisted throughout his life and as late as in the *New Lectures on Psychoanalysis* on the reality of many of these stories. What Masson in his simplistic reductionism completely leaves out is precisely the crucial structure of *Nachträglichkeit* in the function of reality effects.

17. The historical analogy is what LaCapra calls the "pertinent fact": "A fact is a pertinent fact only with respect to a frame, a reference involving questions that we pose to the past." *Rethinking Intellectual History*, p. 31.

18. At this point it is, of course, tempting to parallel our temporal structure derived from Freud to the Lacanian categories of the real (A), the imaginary (B), and the symbolic (C). But this might be possible only if we translate the temporal categories into logical terms.

19. See, for a similar argument concerning the role of transference in analysis, François Roustang, *Psychoanalysis Never Lets Go* (Baltimore: Johns Hopkins University Press, 1983).

20. The German wording here is "Anlehnung an den Verlauf der Analyse." Freud thus uses a central analytical term, *Anlehnung* (anaclisis), for the narrative movement which is not strictly identical with the movement of the analysis, but "leans on it."

21. For an extensive discussion of the phenomenon of screen memory, see Freud's early essay of 1899 "Über Deckerinnerung," G.W., 1:531–554; S.E. 3:303–322.

22. It is a rather common experience in sexuality, as in politics, that it is often easier to *do* things than to *say* them.

23. In order to avoid confusion with the edifying sentimental pathos of a certain existentialist vocabulary, it might be useful to point out that Freud's self-conviction is essentially a materialist one, based on that stuff that dreams are made of: the wishes, desires, interests, and needs of the subject, as an individual, or a class, or whatever interest group forms a subject.

24. At least to the later Freud. The *Annales*, mentioned at the beginning of this chapter, started publication in 1929.

25. Freud is very aware of this principle, as his later formulation of a "progress from Henotheism to Monotheism" (S 9:573) demonstrates. Henotheism would be the veneration of one God among others; monotheism is the assertion of the one as the singular and only one.

26. Mainly J. H. Breasted, *History of Egypt* (1906) and *The Dawn of Conscience* (1934).

27. Theodor W. Adorno posits a similar relation between the principle of individuation and domination in the *Negative Dialectic*.

28. Hölderlin traced this strangeness in his poem *The Voice of the People*. (For an extensive discussion of this poem, see chapter 2.) Any revolution, any political movement, even the gentle bourgeois emancipation, appeals to the voice of the people, were it only by singing its songs.

29. According to some anthropological reports, there still seem to be tribes who do not see any causal connection between the act of conception and birth.

INDEX